Making Tales

The Poetics of

Making Tales

Wordsworth's Narrative Experiments

Don H. Bialostosky

The University of Chicago Press
Chicago and London

Don H. Bialostosky is associate professor of English at
the State University of New York at Stony Brook.

The University of Chicago Press, Chicago 60637
The University of Chicago Press, Ltd., London

© 1984 by The University of Chicago.
All rights reserved. Published 1984
Printed in the United States of America
91 90 89 88 87 86 85 84   1 2 3 4 5

Library of Congress Cataloging in Publication Data

Bialostosky, Don H.
  Making Tales.

  Includes bibliographical references and index.
  1. Wordsworth, William, 1770–1850—Technique.
2. Wordsworth, William, 1770–1850—Style.   3. Narrative
poetry, English—History and criticism.   I. Title.
PR5891.B52   1984   821'.7   83-5069
ISBN 0-226-04575-7
ISBN 0-226-04576-5 (pbk.)

To My Father and Mother

It is no tale; but should you think,
Perhaps a tale you'll make it.

Wordsworth, "Simon Lee"

The function of critical discourse need not be to substitute the enjoyments of thought for the satisfactions of perceiving and the joys of imagining; it may rather simply enable us to take up deliberately the position in and from which these goods may be stabilized and enlarged.

Charles Wegener, *Liberal Education and the Modern University*

Contents

Acknowledgments

This book culminates an engagement with *Lyrical Ballads* begun at the University of Chicago in Norman Maclean's seminar on Wordsworth, pursued through a dissertation on the Preface to *Lyrical Ballads* supervised by Wayne Booth and Stuart Tave, and followed into the richly settled country of Wordsworthian criticism on my own postgraduate authority.

At the University of Washington I have benefited from conversations with many colleagues and students and from readings of all or part of my manuscript by colleagues Raimonda Modiano, Alan Fisher, Leroy Searle, Charles Hartman, David McCracken, Charles Schuster, Charles Altieri, Hazard Adams, and Donald Reiman, who was on a visit from the Carl H. Pforzheimer Library. Four graduate students in a special study group on *Lyrical Ballads* also read parts of the manuscript—Jeanne Moskal, Margaret Garner, Ron Starr, and Robert McNamara. The university's support has extended beyond readings and discussions to a grant for completion of the manuscript from the Graduate School Research Fund and the provision of Marilyn Gray's excellent typing from the Department of English. Marilyn herself provided patience, good cheer, and intelligence.

I must add special thanks to Gene W. Ruoff of the University of Illinois, Chicago Circle, who, when I thought the book was finished, compelled an additional chapter and a tighter argument from me.

I am also grateful for permission to reprint in Chapters 1 and 3 versions of articles first published in *Comparative Literature* 34, no. 4 (1982): 305–29; *JEGP* 82 (1982): 227–43; and *The Wordsworth Circle* 11 (1980): 207–11.

My wife Sue has eased my labor pains, as I have tried to ease hers. To make a home would have been help enough, but she proofread and edited with professional skill and domestic tact. I hope my children Sophia and Ivan will some day read this and remember my pleasure when they learned to knock at the study door.

Abbreviations

BL   Coleridge, *Biographia Literaria,* ed. J. Shawcross, 2 vols. (Oxford: Oxford University Press, 1907).

LB   Wordsworth and Coleridge, *Lyrical Ballads,* ed. R. L. Brett and A. R. Jones (London: Methuen, 1971). I do not follow the editors in italicizing the 1802 variants of the Preface.

Prelude   *The Prelude, 1799, 1805, 1850,* ed. Jonathan Wordsworth, M. H. Abrams, and Stephen Gill (New York: W. W. Norton, 1979). All references will be specified by year, book, and line.

Prose   *The Prose Works of William Wordsworth,* ed. W. J. B. Owen and Jane Worthington Smyser, 3 vols. (Oxford: Clarendon Press, 1974).

Introduction

Good taste follows and is developed by the study of literature; its precision results from knowledge, but does not produce knowledge.

Northrop Frye, *Anatomy of Criticism*

The Fate of Taste and the Spirit of Human Knowledge

The primary purpose of this book is to guide our understanding of Wordsworth's experimental narratives in *Lyrical Ballads* toward a position from which they will give us a greater and a better pleasure than most of his readers have previously received. This purpose, and the language in which I announce it, echo Wordsworth's stated aims, and in repeating them and making them my own I imply that I do not believe they have yet been satisfactorily achieved.

The judgment that Wordsworth's experiment had failed gained the authority with which it has persisted into the present from Coleridge's arguments in *Biographia Literaria*. The defects he identified in Wordsworth's poetry—inconstancy of style, matter-of-factness, and undue predilection for the dramatic form—all find their chief illustration in the experimental ballads (*BL*, 1, chap. 17). Coleridge treats these defects as a consequence of Wordsworth's mistaken poetic principles and establishes his own judgments on other principles that draw on a strong critical tradition and have defined one ever since. Even Wordsworth's admirers, among whom Coleridge enlisted himself, have generally been compelled by this tradition to sacrifice his misguided experiments and establish his claim to attention on the basis of his elevated lyric poems. "Tintern Abbey" for this tradition is the only survivor of the 1798 *Lyrical Ballads* besides "The Ancient Mariner."

The experimental poems have never been without their own admirers, however, and in the late 1950s several critics made important gains in appreciating them. John Danby, Robert Langbaum, and Stephen Maxfield Parrish reclaimed several previously neglected poems and opened the way for other critics to extend their insights. They did not convince Geoffrey Hartman, however. In his *Wordsworth's Poetry*, a work that since 1964 has been the book on Wordsworth assigned immediately after *Biographia Literaria*, he could still declare after reading Danby, Langbaum, and Parrish that "though we can explain some of the difficulties in appreciating the more experimental of Wordsworth's ballads, this does not mean that the experiments are not failures. The reaction of Wordsworth's critics is essentially correct."[1] Though he was able to find the poems interesting for their illustration of psychological syndromes and their relation to traditional genres, he did not claim to enjoy them or to imagine that many others have done so. "Wordsworth was fated," he declared, "to displease both the gentle reader of his day and ours: the former because he committed a solecism (a breach of decorum or social contract) by elevating to poetic dignity words, matters, and attitudes permitted only on the pedestrian or comic level of prose; and the latter, because the tide (though turning) has run, in poetry and fiction, against the intrusive author." Hartman shared the fated (though changing) preference of his age in finding that "the poet's obvious pleasure while narrating 'The Idiot Boy' . . . draws too much attention to Wordsworth's own 'burring.' " The poet's intrusive narration is both an expense of spirit so "wastefully apparent" that it led Hartman to "suspect deeper causes for his [the poet's] delight than he is willing to acknowledge" and an "overloading" of a "rhetorical device" which "in purely artistic terms" reveals that "he has not found his best medium." Sophisticated psychological and formal grounds converge here to justify dissatisfaction with the author's intrusions. Hartman saw but was not swept away by a turning tide on this question; he accepted his fated position and bolstered it with reasons.

Hartman's metaphors of "fated" tastes and turning critical tides tempt me to describe my own enterprise as a product of the new wave he saw but did not go along with, for the year after his book was published I was introduced to college-level reading of fiction and poetry by Wayne Booth, whose *Rhetoric of Fiction*, then four years old, had to be a part of the tide Hartman noticed. Booth's defense of the authorial "intrusion," his interest in the "rhetorical device" Hartman suspects, and his challenge to the critical consensus of our day were all, it appears, part of my fated orientation to literature. I was included in a new consensus before I knew that there had been an old one, became interested in Wordsworth's poems for their use of the very devices Hartman questioned, and was surprised and irritated by my discovery that the poems that pleased me were considered failures by respected critics. It would not be difficult to imagine myself as swept away by the rising waters Hartman saw.

I might even appeal to Wordsworth to corroborate this vision, for in his 1800 Preface he recognized that his readers' judgment of his poetic experiments depended upon established literary norms which changed unaccountably from age to age. He feared that he had violated the current norms, and he acknowledged the almost fateful power of his readers' existing "habits of association" by holding back from the "hope of *reasoning* him [his reader] into an approbation of these particular Poems" and allowing himself only to show that he *had* reasons for writing them as he did (*LB*, p. 242). The speaker of the 1800 Preface, impressed as he is by the strength of the habitual responses his project would have to overcome before his poems could give pleasure to many of his readers, might have found it tempting to admit that his tendency to displease some readers and even his ability to please others were equally fated.

This was not Wordsworth's first or his final view of the possibilities of creating the taste by which his poetry was to be enjoyed, however, nor is it my view. Wordsworth concerned himself with this problem from the first publication of the poems in 1798 and never published them without pronouncements, directions, and defenses designed to explain or to solve it. His most thorough and thoughtful attempt to address the problem and his most sustained argument on the "fortunes and fate of poetical Works" recapitulates his early efforts, criticizes their terms, and builds upon their incomplete accounts of the problem. In the "Essay, Supplementary to the Preface" (1815) he goes to great length to show that "neglect, perhaps long continued, or attention wholly inadequate to their merits—must have been [and must continue to be] the fate of most works in the higher departments of poetry," but he concludes not that this fate must be acquiesced in by poets and their readers alike but that "every author, as far as he is great and at the same time *original*, has had the task of *creating* the taste by which he is to be enjoyed." This task is not an impossible one (though in carrying it out he is "ever doomed to meet with opposition, . . . still triumphing over it"), but it *is* difficult, and Wordsworth reviews his previous and present efforts to carry it out in answering the question, "Where [in creating taste] lies the real difficulty?" (*Prose*, 3:62–84).

He first proposes, in the form of amplifications of his original question, three answers, each of which formulates a position he has taken in attempting to solve the problem of creating taste. Does the "real difficulty" lie, he asks, "in breaking the bonds of custom, in overcoming the prejudices of false refinement, and displacing the aversions of inexperience?" Wordsworth had thought so in the Advertisement of 1798, where he divided his resistant readers into the inexperienced and the falsely refined, and in the 1800 Preface, where he acknowledged the power of the bonds of custom, the habits of enjoyment which his readers had already formed. "Or," he goes on, "if he labour for an object which here and elsewhere I have proposed to myself, does it consist in divesting the reader of the pride that induces him to dwell upon those points wherein men differ from each other, to the exclusion of those in which all men are alike, or the same; and in making him ashamed of the vanity that renders him insensible of the appropriate excellence which civil arrangements, less unjust than might appear, and Nature illimitable in her bounty, have conferred on men who may stand below him in the scale of society?" (*Prose*, 3:80). "Elsewhere" must be the Preface to *Lyrical Ballads* as a whole, which in 1800 raises the issue of representing human nature in men from low and rustic life and in 1802 tries to divest the reader of the pride which makes him distinguish himself from such men. The chief burden of the 1802 addition to the Preface is to identify the poet, the reader, and the rustic subjects of the poems in a common principle of pleasure that grounds their "native and naked dignity" as men and weakens the claim of social and professional distinctions.

"Finally," he asks, "does it lie in establishing that dominion over the spirits of readers by which they are to be humbled and humanised, in order that they may be purified and exalted?" This interpretation of the "real difficulty" reflects the posture of the Essay Supplementary itself in which the poet sets aside his appeal to the reader on the basis of a common humanity and asserts his own claims to greatness. He is not here a "man speaking to men" who emphasizes that he differs from other men only in degree but not in kind (though he still does claim to exercise the capacities of human nature); he is a genius preferring his claim to be considered in the company of Spenser and Shakespeare and Milton, all of whom suffer from "the too common propensity of human nature to exult over a supposed fall into the mire of a genius."[2] The writer of this essay repeatedly compares himself to poetic geniuses and great conquerers (Alexander, Hannibal). He claims to have widened "the sphere of human sensibility, for the delight, honour, and benefit of human nature," and he asks, "What is all this but an advance, or a conquest, made by the soul of the poet?" One who has made such a conquest may in the name of the humanity whose sphere he has widened assert a dominion over the spirit of his readers to move them to enter his domain, but he may find, as Wordsworth does, that it seems inadequate to call what he is doing "creating taste."

The idea that "taste" was the proper name of his problem had gone unchallenged in Wordsworth's earlier pronouncements. In the Advertisement of 1798 and the Preface of 1800 he repeated the admonition from Reynolds that an "accurate taste in poetry" is "an acquired talent, which can only be produced by severe thought, and a long continued intercourse with the best models of composition" (*LB*, pp. 8, 271). In 1802 he attacked those "who will converse with us as gravely about a *taste* for Poetry, as they express it, as if it were a thing as indifferent as a taste for Rope-dancing, or Frontiniac or Sherry" (*LB*, p. 257n). The first passage insists that *forming* a taste in poetry is serious business, the second that a taste for *poetry* is more serious than a taste for "amusement and idle pleasure," but neither doubts that "taste" in some sense is what is needed. The argument of the "Essay," however, insists that the idea of "taste" itself as it is ordinarily understood imports a false supposition into the question of "creating" taste. As a "metaphor, taken from a *passive* sense of the human body," the idea of "taste" brings into the problem of poetic enjoyment the supposition that "the mere communication of *knowledge*" of the objects in question is sufficient to arouse enjoyment. In certain instances Wordsworth allows that this may be true. He notes that "proportion and congruity, the requisite knowledge being supposed, are subjects upon which taste may be trusted; it is competent to this office;—for in its intercourse with these the mind is *passive*, and is affected painfully or pleasurably as by an instinct" (*Prose*, 3:81). Similarly in some kinds of pathetic compositions: "As the pathetic participates of an *animal* sensation, it might seem—that, if the springs of this emotion were genuine, all men, possessed of competent knowledge of the facts and circumstances, would be instantaneously affected. And, doubtless, in the works of every true poet will be found passages of that species of excellence, which is proved by effects immediate and universal" (*Prose*, 3:82). Indeed in the Preface of 1802 he had *aimed* at giving such "immediate pleasure to a human Being possessed of that information which may be expected from him . . . as a Man." But such immediate universal and passive response to available knowledge in a poem cannot itself provide the knowledge necessary to the appreciation of an original work of genius whose essential character is "the introduction of a new element into the intellectual universe: or, if that be not allowed, it is the application of powers to objects on which they had not before been exercised, or the employment of them in such a manner as to produce effects hitherto unknown" (*Prose*, 3:82). With works such as these, knowledge is not the solution but the problem. The question is not, "Given knowledge, how does it affect the reader?" but "How does one get the reader to *know* it so that he can *have* a response to it?" The advice Wordsworth repeated from Reynolds here comes up against its limits, for at best it will do for the enjoyment of an original genius only what his predecessors can have done for him—"smoothed the way for all he has in common with them . . . but, for what is peculiarly his own, he will be called upon to clear and often to shape his own road" (*Prose*, 3:80). Neither will the untutored knowledge of "human passions, human characters, and human incidents" (*LB*, p. 7) to which he also appealed in 1798 and 1802 be sufficient to provide the basis for enjoyment of an original poetic work, for "there are emotions of the pathetic that are simple and direct, and others—that are complex and revolutionary; some—to which the heart yields with gentleness; others—against which it struggles with pride." The original poet will not be able to depend for the appreciation of his works only on knowledge of natural sensations and established poetic conventions. Having exercised his own powers in the production of original works, he will be compelled "to call forth and bestow power, of which knowledge is the effect; and *there* lies the true difficulty" (*Prose*, 3:82).

The reader, then, cannot expect to enjoy the work of an original poet passively "like an Indian prince or general—stretched on his palanquin, and borne by his slaves. . . . No; he is invigorated and inspirited by his leader, in order that he may exert himself; for he cannot proceed in quiescence, he cannot be carried like a dead weight." What he must exert upon the poem is "a co-operating *power*," "a corresponding energy" to those powers the poet has exercised in the production of it. If genius is "the application of powers to objects on which they had not before been exercised, or the employment of them in such a manner as to produce effects hitherto unknown," the enjoyment of the works of genius issues from the application of corresponding powers to his poems. But once it becomes clear that the reading as well as the writing of original poetry is an active exercise of the powers of the mind which produces knowledge and not a passive response to given knowledge, another question arises. What guides the reader's exertion of his powers to assure that it is indeed a *co*-operating or *co*-responding exertion to those of the poet? If he cannot rely simply on conventional expectations or natural human responses, what prevents his making up his own poem or his taking what the poet *says* about what he has made for an actual accomplishment?

Wordsworth sees only one way out of this difficulty and provides only one portrait of a reader who may reliably learn to enjoy and judge the works of genius without arbitrary invention of his own poem or servile submission to the poet's declarations of intent. At the end of his list of the classes of readers unable to exercise a sound judgment of poetry, he writes,

> Whither then shall we turn for that union of qualifications which must necessarily exist before the decisions of a critic can be of absolute value? For a mind at once poetical and philosophical; for a critic whose affections are as free and kindly as the spirit of society, and whose understanding is severe as that of dispassionate government? Where are we to look for that initiatory composure of mind which no selfishness can disturb? For a natural sensibility that has been tutored into correctness without losing anything of its quickness; and for active faculties, capable of answering the demands which an Author of original imagination shall make upon them, associated with a judgment that cannot be duped into admiration by aught that is unworthy of it?—among those and those only, who,

never having suffered their youthful love of poetry to remit much of its force, have applied to the consideration of the laws of this art the best power of their understandings. (*Prose*, 3:66)

Wordsworth places his confidence here in the exercise of two powers—love and the understanding—applied to the art of poetry conceived as a systematic or lawful discipline, and he believes that the exercise of these powers on the art conceived in this way will issue in a knowledge from which true taste can follow. It is to the knowledge thus generated that he returns at the conclusion of his essay when he declares his faith in the intellect and wisdom of "the People" and " 'the great Spirit of human knowledge' " which issues from them. That spirit, "faithfully supported by its two wings, the past and the future," is not a standing body of principles or passively received lore but an active and progressive enterprise, grounded in the work of the understanding (*Prose*, 3:84). It resembles the enterprise of criticism Northrop Frye imagines in the polemical introduction to his *Anatomy of Criticism*. Frye believes that "there is a totally intelligible structure of knowledge attainable about poetry" and is confident, like Wordsworth, in the hope that "the systematic progress of scholarship flows into a systematic progress of taste."[3] Wordsworth bases his faith in the ultimate triumph of his work not in the fateful tides of taste or even in the enduring powers of love or the human heart alone but in the disciplined activities of the human mind in the enterprise of literary study.

Few critics of Wordsworth's poetry have fully recognized the implications of this faith for their approach to his experimental ballads. Even those who have not fallen back upon the fated taste of their age or Wordsworth's and have acknowledged the "immense demands" which Wordsworth's poetry makes upon its readers rarely see that Wordsworth's most important demand is for the active study of poetry as a systematic discipline. Paul Sheats, for example, locates the demands in the reliance of Wordsworth's poetry "to perhaps an impossible degree, on implication and indirection, and thus on the reader's heart." John Danby identifies the pressure Wordsworth's poems place on the reader's judgment and his attitudes toward common human reality. Stephen Parrish clearly recognizes the centrality of the art of poetry for Wordsworth but he stops short of systematically elaborating its "laws."[4]

Only Coleridge has put himself forward as Wordsworth's critic on the basis of the long-standing love of poetry informed by systematic study of the art which Wordsworth calls for, presenting his praise and blame of Wordsworth's poetry in *Biographia Literaria* in terms of "the principles, which he holds for the foundation of poetry in general" (*BL*, 2:85). The authority which his judgments (including his judgment of the ballad experiment's failure and his dispraise of some of its chief instances) have enjoyed in subsequent criticism derives in part from the power of this approach, which has led Thomas M. Raysor to say of "the Wordsworth essay in chapters fourteen to twenty-two of *Biographia Literaria* . . . [that] I know of nothing in all modern European criticism which seems to me to represent so fully and deeply the possibilities of literary criticism as an intellectual discipline."[5]

My own judgment of the success of the experiment compels me to argue in Chapter 1 that Coleridge errs, albeit systematically, in his judgment of those poems and the theory that defends them. His essay, published two years after Wordsworth's Essay Supplementary, demonstrates the prescience (or perhaps the basis) of Wordsworth's anticipation that, as the class of systematically informed lovers of poetry "comprehends the only judgments which are trust-worthy, so does it include the most erroneous and perverse. For to be mistaught is worse than to be untaught; and no perverseness equals that which is supported by system, no errors are so difficult to root out as those which the understanding has pledged its credit to uphold" (*Prose*, 3:66). Coleridge, of course, made similar claims about the perverse effects of Wordsworth's system, and he held that much of the controversy in which the poems were embroiled resulted less from the poems themselves than from Wordsworth's theoretical defense of them.

The critic who would understand and appreciate Wordsworth's experimental poems and share the basis of his enjoyment cannot circumvent these systematic claims and rely on his unassisted human heart or on the unexamined resources of taste which his age or school provides. Such an undertaking calls for a critical examination of the poetic systems of Coleridge and Wordsworth as those systems guide the reading of Wordsworth's experimental poems; it also calls for a systematization of the recent work on *Lyrical Ballads* that has begun to find new interest in them. This work has reached a stage at which the grounds of its successes with some poems can be clarified and from which those successes may be extended to other poems long held in derision or contempt. If it is to do more than win our admiration for isolated poems or secure our conviction on isolated critical topics, this work needs to be grounded in a coherent alternative to those systems which have left our understanding and enjoyment of Wordsworth's poems incomplete. I shall argue in what follows that the alternative system that will permit us to account for what we already enjoy and extend our appreciation to Wordsworth's still neglected narrative experiments is a poetics of speech.

Chapter One

Long have I wished to see a fair and philosophical inquisition into the character of Wordsworth, as a poet,
on the evidence of his published works; and a positive, not a comparative, appreciation of their *characteristic* excellencies, deficiencies, and defects. . . . I
should call that investigation fair and philosophical, in
which the critic announces and endeavours to establish the principles, which he holds for the foundation
of poetry in general, with the specification of these in
their application to the different *classes* of poetry. Having thus prepared his canons of criticism for praise
and condemnation, he would proceed to particularize
the most striking passages to which he deems them
applicable, faithfully noticing the frequent or infre-
quent recurrence of similar merits or defects, and as
faithfully distinguishing what is characteristic from
what is accidental, or a mere flagging of the wing.
Then if his premises be rational, his deductions legitimate, and his conclusions justly applied, the reader,
and possibly the poet himself, may adopt his judgement in the light of judgement and in the independence of free-agency. If he has erred, he presents his
errors in a definite place and tangible form, and holds
the torch and guides the way to their detection.

Coleridge, *Biographia Literaria*

Narrative Diction and the Poetics of Speech

The term "narrative" almost always appears in discussions of Wordsworth's experimental ballads, but never simply or alone. Always its use is complicated by its relations to the other terms in the set to which it belongs, "dramatic" and "lyric," used both in their substantive and their adjectival forms. Thus Karl Kroeber uses the phrase "narrative lyricism" to characterize Wordsworth's poems which, "at the same time narrative and lyrical . . . express 'the primary laws of our nature' in a concrete, particularized, and (relatively) dramatic fashion." Stephen Parrish sees the ballads as "experiments in dramatic and narrative technique" whose distinctive feature is found in "what we might in one sense consider the 'lyrical,' in another the 'dramatic' qualities of the ballads—the feeling revealed by the speaker or narrator." John Danby speaks of "the mixed mode of the dramatic-narrative poem" which merges the methods of "straightforward narrative" and "dramatic monologue." The terminological difficulties such formulations reveal may tempt us to follow Robert Langbaum in wondering whether the kind of poetry he credits Wordsworth with inventing "is not itself a new genre which abolishes the distinction between subjective and objective poetry and between the lyrical and dramatic or narrative genres," but they may also invite us to examine the ground of these distinctions and the range of their application to Wordsworth's poems and poetics.[1] In taking the latter course, we shall find that "narrative" is a troublesome but not a dispensable term. Much of its difficulty can be traced to an ambiguity in its use that stems from the deepest roots of Western poetics. It has been used from the beginning in the context of two different poetics, Platonic and Aristotelian, which subsequent criticism has not usually distinguished. Once we see the differences between them and recognize Wordsworth's affinities with Plato's poetics of speech, we will see more clearly what Wordsworth was doing in his narrative experiments, why Coleridge objected to them, and how we may learn to understand and appreciate them.

Wordsworth provides his only connected explication of the terms "narrative," "dramatic" and "lyric" in his Preface of 1815, where he uses them to distinguish three "moulds" by means of which the materials of poetry may be cast into "divers forms." In the narrative mold, in which he includes the forms of "the Epopoeia, the Historic Poem, the Tale, the Romance, the Mock-heroic, and . . . the metrical Novel . . . the distinguishing mark is, that the Narrator, however liberally his speaking agents be introduced, is himself the source from which every thing primarily flows." A secondary distinction is that, though some epic poets "represent themselves as *singing*," narrative poems "neither require nor reject the accompaniment of music." In the dramatic mold, where he places the forms of "Tragedy, Historic Drama, Comedy, and Masque, . . . and [sometimes] Opera . . . and impassioned Epistle," "the Poet does not appear at all in his own person, and . . . the whole action is carried on by speech and dialogue of the agents; music being admitted only incidentally and rarely." The lyrical mold, "containing the Hymn, the Ode, the Elegy, the Song, and the Ballad," includes those forms "which, for the production of their *full* effect," require a musical accompaniment.[2]

Wordsworth distinguishes these categories as part of an unsystematic or perhaps deliberately multisystematic analysis, following several lines, only one of which he pursues exhaustively. He determines the relation of each kind to musical accompaniment but distinguishes only the narrative and dramatic kinds in terms of whether the "speaking agents" are introduced directly or mediated through the voice of a narrator. He says that the "Poet does not appear at all in his own person" in the dramatic kind and that a "narrator" must appear in narrative, but he does not say, though we expect him to, that the poet appears in lyric. In distributing "forms" under "moulds," he places the ballad, which some systems identify as a primary narrative form,[3] under the lyrical heading, and he distinguishes "narrative" in a way that does not necessarily interfere with this odd classification. Though we may be accustomed to a definition of narrative that would make the ballad one of its obvious forms, as in the assertion of one recent critic who defines narrative discourse as "the oral or written discourse that undertakes to tell of an event or a series of events,"[4] Wordsworth distinguishes "narrative" without reference to storytelling. For him the mark of narrative is not the narrator's telling of events but his speaking himself and repeating the speech of his characters. The system of distinctions he outlines and especially his way of defining narrative link Wordsworth's position to Plato's classic formulation (in the *Republic*) of what has become the lyric-narrative-dramatic distinction, not to the more familiar distinction of narrative and dramatic manners of imitation in Aristotle's *Poetics*. Though Aristotle's terms have strongly influenced both translation and inter- pretation of Plato's, the two positions, as I shall show, divide different domains and belong to different systems of distinctions with importantly different consequences for understanding Wordsworth's ideas.[5]

The Platonic context that permits this comparison is the third book of the *Republic*, where Socrates and his friends are deciding how to regulate the musical education of their ideal city's guardians (392c–403e). There they divide music into three categories, tales (λόγων), diction (λεξεως), and musical accompaniment (τρόπου καὶ μελῶν), including modes and rhythms (ἁρμονιὰς καὶ ῥυθμοῦ)—a division which, we may note, bears striking resemblance to Wordsworth's division of his Preface to *Lyrical Ballads* under the heads of subjects, language or diction, and meter. In Plato as in Wordsworth the distinction of lyric, narrative, and dramatic is one of "diction," that is, of who is represented as speaking. The poet may be considered as speaking solely in his own person (ἁπλῇ διηγήσει, often translated "simple narration") or as imitating the speech of others (μιμήσεως) or as speaking in a combination of the two modes (ἀμφο- τέρων, 392d). The last corresponds closely to Wordsworth's "narrative" category, for in it the poet himself is sometimes "the speaker and does not even attempt to suggest to us that anyone but himself is speaking" (393b), but at other times, "when he delivers a speech as if he were someone else, . . . he then assimilates thereby his own diction [τὴν αὐτοῦ λέξιν] as far as possible to that of the person whom he announces as about to speak" (393c). In the mixed mode we are presented with "a man speaking," to use Wordsworth's phrases of 1802, who in some parts "speaks to us in his own person and character" and in other parts "speaks through the mouths of his characters" (*LB*, pp. 255–61).

Although Aristotle adopts a similar distinction in his *Poetics*, his treat- ment of narrative as a manner of imitating action differs significantly from the idea of narrative diction in Plato and Wordsworth. In Aristotle's distinction, the poet either narrates the action (ἀπαγγέλλω, 1448a21) or he presents the agents dramatically "as acting and functioning" before us.[6] Plato—and Wordsworth—on the other hand, distinguish the nar- rative mode, in which the poet speaks himself and impersonates the voices of others, from the dramatic mode, in which "one removes the words of the poet between and leaves the alternation of speeches" (394b). Aristotle does preserve the distinction between the poet's telling a story "by becoming someone else as Homer makes his poems, or by being himself and not changing" (1448a20), but for him these are just two varieties of narration, two ways of telling the story instead of presenting it. For Plato and Wordsworth, however, the categories of pure speech in the poet's own person and mixed speech in his own person and that of his characters are correlative with the dramatic presentation of the speech of the characters alone, and none of these kinds has a necessary connection to the representation of an action. The first kind is simply that which "employs the recital [ἀπαγγελίας] of the poet himself, best exemplified . . . in the dithyramb" (394c)—a lyric genre which some-times tells stories but need not do so, and uses, as Shorey notes, "little if any dialogue" (p. 231n). The second category, exemplified by Homer, holds what Wordsworth means by narrative, and the last category, which includes tragedy and comedy, is the dramatic. The coordinate distinction of these three poetic kinds is thus originally and exclusively Platonic. Lyric poetry for Aristotle is not coordinate with narrative and dramatic or even a subordinate branch of narrative but, I suspect, a pre-imitative or proto-imitative kind associated with the "hymns and encomia" (1448b27) that developed into the more truly imitative epic and finally into the purely imitative tragic drama. The definition of narrative within the lyric-narrative-dramatic distinction is thus a mark of a Platonic and Wordsworthian poetics of speech, not of an Aristotelian poetics of im-itated actions.

The distinction between a poetics of speech and a poetics of imitated actions is not a widely recognized one, for critics have long been ac-customed to take Aristotle's outline of poetics as defining poetics itself, while they have thought of Plato not as the founder of a poetics but as the archenemy of poetry. Without an authoritative source like Aristotle's *Poetics,* the poetics of speech has appeared either as a revolutionary movement within orthodox Aristotelian poetics or as an attempt to bring theories of discourse from outside poetics proper to bear on poetry and poems. Thus efforts like Wordsworth's to defend and work in terms of a poetics of speech have generally been understood as revolts against the art of poetry and violations of its canons, not as articulations of an art of poetry on a different basis. Efforts to apply to poetry terms and questions from the art of rhetoric and, more recently, from philosophical inquiries into speech-acts and linguistic inquiries into pragmatics also have not given us a recognized poetics of speech, though they have kept the issues proper to such a poetics alive. Self-conscious elaborations of what I call a poetics of speech have become available in the last decade, however, making it possible now to recognize earlier attempts to artic-ulate such a poetics and to clear up misunderstandings surrounding them. Most of the issues raised by Wordsworth's poetics and his ex-perimental poems, especially his narrative experiments, can be clarified in the context of a poetics of speech.[7]

The first issue to which this perspective permits us to bring new light is one which has dogged Wordsworth's poetry and poetics since he broached it in his Preface to *Lyrical Ballads*. "Poetic diction" becomes a special problem when poetry is thought of as "the representation of speech" (Smith, *Margins*, p. 24), for if poetry represents something other than speech, its language may be considered as a medium for the representation of that thing, but if poetry represents speech, its language is the object of representation itself and no distinct medium of representation is apparent. The differences between these views appear already in Aristotle's and Plato's analyses of poetry. "Diction" is one of Plato's three major categories of subject, diction, and music or meter; in Aristotle's division of object, manner, and medium of imitation, "diction" is only one possible medium for which rhythm or melody or paint or bodily movement might be substituted to imitate the same action. Plato treats all poetry as representation of someone's words, which may vary according to what is said or according to the speaker from whom they are supposed to issue or according to the rhythm and intonation with which they are spoken or sung but which cannot vary from being someone's words without losing their defining character. In Aristotle all artificial making imitates actions which may be represented in various materials, including language, and, if in language, then through the more or less immediate manners of showing or telling what happens. In the poetics of speech there is only the representation of telling or talking, which in narrative diction may imitate other talking—the speech of other speakers whose characteristic speech or diction is distinct from that of the primary speaker. In the poetics of imitated action, speech is one material through which action may be figured, and even when it is the sole medium it is still only a means of portraying something else.

A more radical way to describe the difference between these two poetics is to say that in the poetics of speech there is no medium and no criterion of artistic excellence specific to mastery of a medium (see Smith, *Margins*, pp. 25–27). The poem's words are not that material in which an action is artificially and skillfully embodied but the artfully represented body of someone's thought. While a critic who thinks in terms of medium looks to the diction of the poem for evidence of the poet's skill and genius as a synthesizer of language, one without that category considers the poet's capacity to represent speech expressive of a speaker's attitudes toward himself, his subjects, and his auditors. The style for the one bespeaks the artist, for the other the represented speaker, whether he is a lyric representation of the poet, a represented narrator, or a dramatic character.

Aristotle's account of diction in the *Poetics* shows clearly what it means to think of words as the elemental language material out of which a poet composes his poem. Words in that context are the poet's palette; his choice and arrangement of their sounds, rhythms, and meanings are his distinctive mark as an artist. Thus Aristotle defines diction in the *Poetics* as "the synthesis of the meters" (1449b35) and analyzes it first as a sequence of parts from the most elemental and indivisible unit of potentially intelligible sound through various higher or more complex syntheses (the syllable, conjunction, "joint," noun, verb, and case) to the highest synthesis, speech (λόγος). The poet making things of words must attend to characteristics of language beneath this highest level of meaningful utterance because he is controlling not just meaning but all the effects which his material is capable of producing. Language perceived as the material of composition appears broken down into elements for ready assembly, like packaged Tinker-Toys, or assembled into various subunits, like wheels already on axles, or constructed into various recognizable forms—a wagon or a tower. The maker of things in language may have use for its properties at all these stages or may disassemble more complex units into their more elemental forms for reassembly into some new composition.

The maker in language, however, is probably most accustomed to thinking of language as coming in words, the building blocks of speech, and Aristotle accordingly provides a classification of words into "authoritative, foreign, metaphorical, ornamental, made-up, extended, contracted, or altered" (1457b1–3), but the salient distinction here is between the first of these and all the rest, i.e., between the authoritative or literal or proper (κύριος) word and all the other departures from this usage, the varieties of strange (ξενικός) words (relative to any given community) achieved through foreign words, metaphorical transfers of words from their proper use to some other one, made-up or poetized words, and various extensions, contractions, or alterations of the material form of words themselves. The distinction between proper and strange words is the important one, Aristotle goes on to imply, because the diction desirable in poetry is not merely the proper or literal—that usage in itself is "abject" or humble or low—but a combination or blending of proper and strange usage which attains the desired condition of clarity which is not abject, avoiding the obscurity of purely strange usage and the lowness of the proper or literal taken by itself. Though Aristotle does not say it explicitly, I think that as we come to recognize the close parallel between his position and Coleridge's we shall see that he prefers this blended style because it at once communicates its meaning and carries the signs of its own making, the marks of art which are evident not just in the object made of language but even in the language of which it is made. The modifications of words, changes in word order, and metaphorical usages which Aristotle here defends and praises as proper to the poet though not strictly proper in common use are the modifications

which reveal the genius of the poet at work on his medium and give
the peculiar dignity of poetic mediation to the objects he presents.

These ways of analyzing language into its material elements and classifying it according to its artificial modifications are out of place in a
poetics of speech, which lacks the category of medium. In this context
poetry is concerned only with the highest synthesis of speech (λόγος),
which it represents not as a synthesis of elements but as the utterance
of speakers, who are thought to be not making something out of words
but saying something in them. The poet who represents these speakers'
utterances does not call attention to himself through modification of the
words and order of words they speak but by other signs—titles, versification, prefaces, and the like—that indicate the fictiveness of the utterances he presents (see Smith, *Margins*, pp. 14–40). His poem is not an
imitation of something nonverbal in the medium of words but a fictive
thing whose existence is literally verbal, a made-up speech which presents the possible declarations, questions, appeals, affirmations, denials,
emphases, and ellipses of "a man speaking." I do not add the familiar
Wordsworthian "to men" because, though the poet himself must be
thought of as presenting his poem to a human audience, the voices he
represents may pray to God or talk to daisies, complain to the vacant
air or confide in an oblivious infant. Praying or praising, complaining
or confiding, singing in the present moment or recounting a past event,
these voices are to be understood first *as* possible voices speaking the
way natural human voices do. Their presence in an artificial object may
lead us to expect them to be more interesting and revealing than natural
voices encountered in real-life situations, but it should not lead us to
expect their language to be modified by any "foreign splendour" of the
poet's own (*LB*, p. 255).

Aristotle recognizes and rejects this interpretation of "diction" at the
beginning of his account. "Of things concerning diction," he writes,
"one form of theory is of the [inflectional] modes of diction, the knowledge of which belongs to the art of declamation and the man who
possesses such an architectonic art. It says, for example, what an in-
junction is, a prayer, a description, a threat, a question, an answer, or
anything else of this sort. For the knowledge or ignorance of these brings
to poetic science no censure deserving of the effort" (1456b9–15). From
his perspective the distinction between the maker of imitated actions
and the performer or oral interpreter is fundamental, and the two arts
have their own distinctions and sources of credit and censure, but from
the perspective of a poetics of speech both the poet who inscribes and
the reader who recites the poem are primarily concerned with voices.
Without control of these voices' inflections and the other signs of their

tone which have not been grammatically systematized, the poet does not fully control the poem, and without the realization of these same features the reciter does not properly interpret it. The catching of these nuances and the communication of them have the place in this poetics which the mastery of the material properties of words—their rhythmic, alliterative, and assonantal qualities—has in the Aristotelian system. It is in each case the kind of grasp of "diction" that properly belongs to a poet—the control in the one case of the linguistic signs of passion and thought and in the other of the material qualities of language itself.

Coleridge, who shares Aristotle's preference for a distinctive poetic diction, is even more vehement than Aristotle in rejecting "diction" as it operates in a poetics of speech, because his theory of poetry focuses even more exclusively than does Aristotle's on the "synthesis of the meters" and its corresponding artful diction. He has defined a poem not as an imitation of action in language or as a representation of speech but as a "species of composition," a way of putting words together, which differs from scientific composition in aiming immediately at pleasure rather than truth and from all other literary composition in "proposing to itself such delight from the *whole,* as is compatible with a distinct gratification from each component *part*" (*BL*, 2:10). Since the "parts" here are the meter, the diction ("words and the order of words") and the "poetry," the diction must satisfy the attention raised by the use of artificial meter, in order that both should remain in keeping with the "poetry"—the part which directly expresses the modifying and unifying power of the poetic genius. Coleridge's poet is a maker not of plots, like Aristotle's, or of fictive utterances, like Wordsworth's, but of metrical compositions aimed at giving sustained and overall pleasure, and his use of metaphor, which for Aristotle marks "the naturally well-endowed poet" (1459a7) with respect to the category of diction, becomes for Coleridge, without qualification, the mark of the poet. Coleridge makes the category of medium, which distinguishes Aristotelian poetics from the poetics of speech but remains a subordinate category in Aristotle's analysis, the primary category of his poetics. The poet's modifications of ordinary language become the signs of the faculty that makes the poet, and the deliberate attempt to avoid those modifications appears as a perversion of the deliberate cultivation of them that is the poet's art.

This, of course, is the perversion of which Coleridge accuses Wordsworth's theory of poetic diction, but it is a perversion only in light of the definition of poems and poetry from which Coleridge starts. If a poet is thought of as a representer of speech who sets speeches to meter rather than as a genius who composes in metrical language, other considerations govern the relation between meter and diction. Whereas genial composition in meter requires that the parts of the poem which are not poetry be composed *"in keeping* with the poetry" and that the adoption of meter be accompanied by a diction "supporting the purpose and known influences of metrical arrangement" (*BL*, 2:10–11), the metrical presentation of an utterance keeps the functions of meter and diction separate. Poems conceived as represented utterances use meter to call attention to their being fabricated by the poet for the purpose of giving pleasure, without requiring the *speakers* in the poem, whether stand-ins for the poet or imitated others, to adopt a diction peculiar to poetry. The maker in the poetics of speech is not at pains to conceal that his works are works rather than natural utterances but to confine the evidences of his making to those aspects of the work, like meter, that do not distort the speech which he is interested in representing. Since his speakers' use of metaphors and figures is one of the chief ways in which their passions and thoughts can be made manifest, one of the principal indices of their tone, he cannot permit himself to use the same sort of language as a sign of his compositional art. Meter will have to serve him as the primary indication of that art while diction—available as a sign of poetic art to poets who represent something other than speech or who do not represent at all—will express the speakers he represents.[8]

If we can thus distinguish the constraints that govern diction in a poetics of speech from those that determine it in a poetics of imitated action or a poetics of metrical composition, we can set aside judgments of Wordsworth's diction that are inappropriate to the poetics in which he is working, but we are left with a problem that has sometimes made it difficult to see a poetics of speech as a poetics at all. When the poet is seen not as a maker in the medium of language but a maker of poems representing speaking persons, it becomes difficult to distinguish between the poet as representer of speakers, the poet as represented speaker, and the poet as speaking person. In Wordsworthian criticism, where this difficulty has been particularly troublesome, Wordsworth's declaration that a poet is "a man speaking to men" has contributed to the confusion by presenting the poet as a natural person speaking to other persons in a specific speaking situation. Though Wordsworth shows an awareness of the poet's engagement in producing a composition that includes parts "where the Poet speaks through the mouths of his characters" and parts "where the Poet speaks to us in his own person and character," he describes the poet in these phrases as "speaking," not as representing or composing fictive speech-acts.

So strong has been the corresponding tendency in Wordsworthian criticism to ignore the poet as representer of speech and to conflate the poet as represented speaker and as speaking person that even New Criticism and Aristotelian criticism have tended to exempt Wordsworth from the formal distinctions they otherwise observe and to treat him as an expressionist whose poems ultimately obey other laws than those of objective poetry or dramatic form. Thus his poetry has been viewed as a foil to the poetry which invites "objective" analysis, as the expression of "personality" rather than the embodiment of impersonal combinations of elements, as a "poetry of sincerity" rather than a poetry of masks. In his case the "intentional fallacy" has rarely been considered a fallacy; more frequently it has been a fundamental principle for interpreting his work. The authoritative account of Wordsworth's critical position has made the expression of the poet's own feelings the "ground idea" of his poetics,[9] and the common view of his poetic production has perpetuated Coleridge's judgment that his most important and characteristic work appears in those lyric poems and passages "where the poet interposes the music of his own thoughts" (*BL*, 2:53).

The first critics to make important contributions to understanding Wordsworth's ballad experiments, however, departed from this accepted view of Wordsworth as a speaking person or speaking poet and chose to treat him as an artful maker of poems representing speaking persons. Insisting upon the distinction between the poet and his represented speakers that had previously been thought inappropriate to Wordsworth's poetry, both John Danby and Robert Langbaum discover new interest in his narrative and dramatic experiments. The different ways they draw this distinction, however, direct their attention to different sets of poems and raise different critical problems for our present attempt to formulate a comprehensive poetics of speech adequate to the full range of Wordsworth's experiments.

Danby considers both the status of the represented voices in the poem and the way in which we imagine the poet in relation to them in terms of a concept of "tone" that postulates a single underlying voice of the poet manifesting itself through the personae of his narrators and characters. For him "the poet can take up and lay down his masks. And with each assumption or discard a new, sometimes excitingly dramatic, shift of standpoint is possible" (p. 38). Of "The Idiot Boy" he remarks that "we are aware of the distinctive narrating voice, and of the narrator's power to merge his own voice in that of the actors in the story, as well as of his capacity to re-emerge when necessary and regain his commenting distinctness" and that "it is Wordsworth himself, of course, who is the narrator, and he makes us aware of his masks" (pp. 48–50). His comments on "The Thorn" are particularly revealing, for though he recognizes that "at the lowest level the poem does dramatize a particular speaker," he insists repeatedly that this speaker "is merely a device whereby the varying flow of our experience is controlled," (pp. 61–62) and he argues emphatically against Wordsworth's elaborate attention to the psychology of the speaker. For Danby, "Wordsworth's use here of the narrator, both in his direct statement and in his evasions—Wordsworth's own disappearance behind the speaker and the speaker's indirectness—is cunningly calculated" (p. 67). Danby, in short, is conscious at all times of the sophisticated poet "up to something" (p. 39) behind and through the voices of the poems.

Danby's focus on the "poet manipulator" behind the masks of the poem is most successful, however, in reading those poems where the speaker is represented as a poet manipulator, i.e., where the speaker is presented as a poet telling a story and working for effects on the reader. His readings of "Simon Lee" and "The Idiot Boy" follow the narrators' control of their readers' attitudes and expectations, their deliberate offerings of possibilities for response which they deliberately undercut, their shifting responses to the characters in their "tales" and to their readers' sense of what a "tale" is like. Where the represented poet is missing, Danby is quick either to declare the poem a "straight narrative with a neutral narrator" (as in "The Last of the Flock" and "Anecdote for Fathers") or to doubt the integrity of the represented narrator (as in "The Thorn"). Despite his recognition of the individuality of some of Wordsworth's narrators, he selects his best instances from among the poems in which the poet has represented speakers in his own character, if not his own person, instances for which it is not necessary to infer a "poet manipulator" but to watch one in action.

While Danby tries to read the voices in a poem as masks or devices of the ever-present poet, Langbaum reads them as the voices of dramatized characters who have been "endowed by the poet with the qualities necessary to make the poem happen to [them]" and with qualities that permit the reader to identify or sympathize with them, i.e., make them what Langbaum calls a "pole for sympathy" (p. 52). Instead of referring their every move directly to the poet who manipulates them to his purpose, the reader is invited, in Langbaum's terms, "to consider the motives for which the speakers undertake to speak" (p. 182) and represent things as they do in light of their peculiar situations, perspectives, and psychological makeups. At the extreme of the lyrical dramatic monologue, indeed, Langbaum permits just the subjectivizing of a poem which Danby argued against for "The Thorn"; in such poems, Langbaum says, "we look to the speaker for the rationale of the poem, while regarding the situation as in every way problematical and therefore a projection of the speaker, the agency of his self-revelation."

Stephen Parrish reads "The Thorn" in this light and finds, in the one poem for which Wordsworth was careful to specify the distinct mind

and character of a dramatized speaker, that we must consider the source
of everything we are told and regard all of the details of Martha Ray's
history and of the narrator's account of his meeting with her as what
Langbaum would call "problematic," as possible projections of the
speaker's excited mind rather than as actual happenings. He finds the
poem's center of interest not in Martha Ray's suffering but in "the manner in which the narrator associates ideas" (*Art*, p. 100), a manner whose
order and repetitiveness Wordsworth has represented with "dramatic
propriety" (*Art*, p. 111).

Though Danby and Langbaum introduce terms that improve on the
unsophisticated view of Wordsworth as a speaking person and open
previously neglected poems for appreciation, neither provides an adequate general account of the relation between representing poet and
represented speakers (whether in the person and character of the poet
or in some other person or character). Danby's vocabulary, native to the
criticism of lyric utterance, tends to identify the representing poet as a
speaking person who does not speak directly but is nevertheless ap-
prehensible as a "voice" behind the voices he represents or adopts. The
utterances of represented speakers are read as indirect expressions of
his motives and values. His "tone," or expressed attitude toward his
subjects and readers, is that to which all the represented voices in the
poem must ultimately be referred. Wordsworth's poems, however, represent *him* speaking in his own person and character and in the person
and character of others, and *others* speaking without the mediation of
his voice. In all three instances he functions as a writer who inscribes
the signs from which those speakers may be reconstructed, revises their
lines, rearranges verses, entitles and versifies for the purpose of providing an object provocative of pleasurable contemplation. Though in
the process of composition he may "bring his feelings near to those of
the persons whose feelings he describes, nay, for short spaces of time
perhaps . . . let himself slip into an entire delusion, and even confound
and identify his own feelings with theirs" (*LB*, p. 256), he does not remain in this "delusion" or make a poem designed to perpetuate it. His
identification with the impassioned speakers he represents is meant in
any case, to permit him to realize and reproduce a language appropriate
to *their* passions, not to permit him to express *his* feelings through their
voices. This same relation holds even in his representation of his own
speech, for though in the process of composition he may revive his
former passion in his mind and for the moment be caught up in it and
the language it provokes him to utter, he does this for the sake of giving
life to the former passion he represents, not for the sake of dissembling
his present passion through the mask of a lyric persona. As representer
of his own impassioned utterance he contemplates his former passion

and composes under the impression of it; he does not invent devices through which a present feeling may find expression.

Langbaum's focus on the speaker of the poem as a dramatized person and Parrish's related emphasis on Wordsworth as a dramatic poet correct the tendency of Danby's lyric terminology to reduce represented speakers to expressions of the motives and attitudes of a poet speaking through his representations. By giving the represented speaker independent motives for speaking and describing things as he does, this perspective makes it possible to interpret his speech as we would a natural utterance, in terms of what Barbara Herrnstein Smith calls "the situation and motives that produced it, the set of conditions 'external' and 'internal,' physical and psychological, that caused the speaker to utter that statement at that time in that form" (*Margins*, p. 22).

This conception of the represented speaker is a useful correction to Danby's, but in Langbaum's dialectic it is transformed into its opposite and much of its usefulness is lost. Though Langbaum starts by considering the represented speaker of the "dramatic lyric" situated in relation to "experience," specific time, place, and circumstance that motivate and authenticate his utterance, he shifts his focus to the represented speaker of the "lyrical drama" or dramatic monologue whose utterance cannot be accounted for by the specified dramatic situation. In the "dramatic lyric" the poet represents the speaker with an awareness of the speaker's overall situation that the speaker does not share until the end of his "experience," if he comes to share it at all: the representing poet and the audience that recognizes the distinction between him and his speaker thus have a perspective from which to judge the speaker's understanding of his own meaning. But in the "lyrical drama" the "shift of attention from the situation to the speaker . . . [makes] it impossible to judge the situation; so that we look to the speaker for the rationale of the poem" (*Experience*, p. 196). Langbaum seems to suppose that the authoritative perspective of the representing poet is lost in this poetic mode, and any practical difference between reading a poet's direct self-expressive utterance and reading a represented speaker's utterance is sacrificed. Though Langbaum calls the source of direct expression the "speaker" rather than the "poet," he loses the potential vantage ground which we should have for every represented speaker—lyric, narrative, or dramatic—by virtue of his being represented in a poem.

We recognize this vantage ground most clearly in the dramatic mode of presentation in which it is physically or imaginatively manifest to us in our *seeing* the speakers acting and speaking before us on the stage, and we have some reason therefore to identify our discovery of a similar vantage in lyric or narrative representation by speaking of "dramatic" lyric or "dramatic" narrative. It is confusing, however, to designate a property common to the poetic representation of any speech with a name drawn from only one of the modes in which that representation is possible. Represented talking (lyric) and represented telling (narrative), though neither requires us to construct a visible objectified speaker like a dramatic character on a stage, are nonetheless represented utterances that imply a perspective from which they have been "heard" and inscribed distinct from the perspective from which they are spoken. Even when the poet sets down speeches which he owns (or does not expressly disown), his setting them down differs from his saying them and opens a space in which these different perspectives can be explored. No matter how much he specifies the context of his represented talking, however, it will remain a lyric representation unless it compels us to visualize not just the scene that provokes it but the speaker who utters it on the scene. Even if the represented speaker is distinguished from the poet, there will be no need to call the poem "dramatic" unless it compels us to objectify the speaker as if his speaking were part of a visible enactment. We can recognize lyric representations in which someone other than the poet is represented as speaking as easily as we can imagine a drama in which the poet represents "himself" as a character. We can still tell the lyric from the dramatic poem, as we should be able in both cases to distinguish the perspective of the representing poet from those of the speaker or the character he represents.

There is no doubt, however, that these critical distinctions are easier to make and sustain in dramatic representations than they are in lyric and narrative ones, for in drama a third party, the actor, brings the words of the represented character to life before the eyes of the spectator, while in lyric and narrative the reader himself must enter into and bring to life the words of the represented talker or teller. Like the poet who in the process of composition may lose himself in the speaker he is representing, the reader in the act of sympathetic interpretation may lose himself in the speaker he is interpreting. Though this self-loss does not in either case nullify the distinction between the speaker's perspective and the perspective from which his speech is represented, it may well obscure it. Since the reader of lyric and narrative poetry must put himself in the place of the represented speaker in order to realize the tones that animate his words, the speaker's position becomes palpable, like that of another person into whose motives and situation he has entered. But the poet's position as representer of the utterance is not available in the same way, and the reader may lose sight of it the way an actor caught up in the character he is playing may lose sight of the overall design of the poet. In the staging of a play, the responsibility for keeping the poet's perspective in mind is delegated to the director, but in the interpretation of literary narrative and lyric, the reader either divides and integrates the functions in his own mind or gives himself uncritically to the speaker's perspective.

Such uncritical participation in the speaker's perspective is what Socrates and his friends expect from the young people of guardian nature whose education they discuss in the conversation Plato represents in the *Republic*, Book III. Their attempt to discriminate the kinds of diction in which we have already discovered the origins of a poetics of speech was for them, as I have said, part of an attempt to determine the proper "musical" education of the future guardians of the ideal city. In their inquiry, the fables or tales told, the diction of recitation, and the rhythm and mode of singing are all found to have educationally relevant aspects, characteristics which are likely to effect the transformation of the youth of guardian nature into a properly educated guardian of his fellow citizens. Diction is educationally significant because Socrates imagines the impressionable and uncritical young people he wishes to train not just as spectators of actions performed by others or as hearers of tales related by others but as reciters of the speeches the poets have written. He thinks of them as taking on the voices which the poems embody and considers whether his single-minded guardians should be allowed to imitate poets and the myriad characters whose voices they assume.

I say "single-minded" because the criterion Socrates applies here and throughout his construction of this city is the premise agreed upon in Book II, and reiterated after the distinction of kinds of diction has been clarified in Book III, "that each one could practise well only one pursuit and not many, but if he attempted the latter, dabbling in many things, he would fail of distinction in all" (394e). Agreeing that the same rule applies in the case of imitation of other voices or sounds, Socrates and Adeimantus find that the same man cannot imitate more than one thing well, one man not being able to imitate both tragedies and comedies or even smaller differences. Socrates adds, in a formulation with striking resonances for our discussion of Wordsworth, that "to still smaller coinage . . . proceeds the fractioning of human faculty [Rouse translates ανθρώπου φύσις here as "human nature"] so as to be incapable of imitating many things or of doing the things themselves of which the imitations are likenesses" (395b).

Socrates' application of this principle leads not (at this point in the *Republic* at least) to the banning of all imitation from the education of the guardians but to the restriction of what they may imitate to "what is appropriate to them—men, that is, who are brave, sober, pious, free and all things of that kind; but things unbecoming the free man they should neither do nor be clever at imitating, nor yet any other shameful thing, lest from the imitation they imbibe the reality" (395c). The reason for restricting instead of completely abolishing imitation becomes apparent in the power Socrates attributes to imitated activities, which "if continued from youth far into life, settle down into habits and (second) nature in the body, the speech, and the thought" (395d, "speech" here being φωνὰς, which might also be translated "voice"). To imitate the speech (or action or thought) of a man with the characteristics proper to us is to acquire those characteristics ourselves; to imitate unbefitting characteristics corrupts us by violating our proper identity and the function in the city for which we are exclusively suited. We are what we habitually and consistently imitate, and we ought to imitate only what we are supposed to be.

The list of objects of imitation Socrates proscribes for his gentleman-guardian reads almost like a gallery of speakers from the 1798 *Lyrical Ballads*. He is not to imitate women, including those "involved in misfortune and possessed by grief and lamentation," or "smiths and other craftsmen or the rowers of triremes," a group which could easily include shepherds and sea captains, or "madmen," or even the good man himself "when he is upset by sickness or love or drunkenness or any other mishap" (395–96). Though Socrates does not think to exclude imitation of children or the "burr burr burr" of an idiot or the vagaries of a good man under the influence of "the first mild day of March," he makes it clear enough that the imitation of such things would not be permitted his guardians, who usually speak *in propria persona* and imitate no one but the good man at his best. Only the no-account person would imitate all such things "seriously and in the presence of many" (397a).

Wordsworth chooses to imitate the speech of such characters in full knowledge of such strictures, whether it comes to him from Plato or from commonplaces of moral and literary decorum for which Plato provides the clearest model. If, as Robert Mayo argues, the representation of such persons was fashionable in the literature of Wordsworth's time,[10] Wordsworth imitates them not in easy conformity with that fashion but in steadfast denial of Platonic decorum and the principle upon which it is based. He claims that a good man ought to imitate such speakers for the sake of his goodness, that imitating them will put him in sympathy with them, and that such sympathy will affect him and be good for him. Wordsworth imitates them "seriously and in the presence of many" and claims that he ought not to be taken for an unworthy man or poet. He himself recognizes that some of his contemporaries have been criticized for allowing "triviality and meanness both of thought and language" into their poems, but he distinguishes himself from them by asserting his deliberateness. Whether or not the poems in which he presents low subjects in low language were all written with a "distinct purpose formally conceived" (*LB*, p. 246), they were all written on principle and for the sake of teaching, elevating, and improving his reader.

Neoclassicists, many of whom survived the Romantic period in good health, have sensed Wordsworth's reversal of this classical decorum, and the more intelligent among them, Coleridge especially, recognized with dismay its basis in principle. But their account of the fundamental principle involved has usually been distorted by their assumption that something obviously foolish must underlie a position so clearly wrongheaded. Coleridge's objections to the position show a sensitivity to its basis worthy of his intellect, though his attack upon it does not dignify it with an accurate explication.[11] Others, however, who commonly identify the "ground-idea" of Wordsworth's position as the declaration that "all good poetry is the spontaneous overflow of powerful feelings"[12] not only misread Wordsworth's text but, more important, mistake the ground-idea on which their own position is based. Ordinarily they base their position on the belief that reason properly rules over emotion—a belief which makes Wordsworth appear as the irresponsible liberator of emotion from the power that ought to govern it. But in the present context we can see that this familiar opposition depends upon the prior assertion that the soul, like the city upon which Plato models it, is properly divided into distinct functions which correspond to the functional classes in the city and the natures which perform those functions. Thus the soul divides into reason, emotion, and desire, the city into philosopher-kings, guardians, and craftsmen, and human nature into the rational, emotional, and desiderative types governed by the three parts of the soul and suited to the three functions in the city. The normative arrangement, of course, is that reason should rule the other two parts of the soul as the rational members should rule the others in the city, and the presumption of the familiar attack on Wordsworth is that he sets out to overthrow this normative order. His position, however, is more radical: he stands not against the dominion of reason over emotion but against the division of the city, the soul, and the nature of man into the "small change" demanded by Socrates' premise that each man is suited by nature for a single function by virtue of which he gets his social identity, which constitutes the whole of his human identity. Wordsworth asserts not the uprising of emotion against reason but the essential interrelation of feeling and thought and the essential community of all men in their shared experience. He threatens those who pride themselves on the triumph of reason and who fear the emotions and their social representatives, the lower classes, not because he releases the emotional energies they have so diligently suppressed but because he denies the distinction by which they have defined themselves and their essential difference from what is alien to them, in their souls and in society.

Wordsworth reaches his most positive statement of a fundamental human identity in his attempt, in the addition to the Preface of 1802, to establish "upon general grounds" the reason for his use "of the language really spoken by men" (*LB,* pp. 254–55). In defense of his diction he inquires into the language to be expected of a poet "in those parts of composition where the Poet speaks through the mouths of his characters" as well as in those parts of poems "where the Poet speaks to us in his own person and character" (p. 260), i.e., in his narrative and lyric diction, and he finds that in both a common human language is required by the common nature and experience of all men. The argument in this famous though infrequently examined passage[13] rests squarely on a denial of essential difference between the *poet,* about whom there is "nothing differing in kind from other men, but only in degree" (*LB,* p. 261), his *reader,* who is imagined not in his professional capacities as "a lawyer, a physician, a mariner, an astronomer or a natural philosopher [or, he later adds, as a poet], but as a Man" (pp. 257–58), and his *subject,* whom he considers "in his own nature and in his ordinary life" reflecting upon his intercourse with "the objects that surround him" (*LB,* p. 258).

In this commonality there is a vision not of a single city of men divided according to their faculties and functions, some thinking and ruling, some acting from well-trained emotion, and some providing for the others without thinking or acting on their own, but of "the vast empire of human society, as it is spread over the whole earth, and over all time" bound together "by passion and knowledge," which the poet expresses as its spokesman (*LB,* p. 259). He "thinks and feels in the spirit of the passions of men" (*LB,* p. 261), representing the language which some of his fellows express under the pressure of "real and substantial action and suffering" (*LB,* p. 256) to the rest of his fellows, for whom his expression of that passion does "more nearly resemble the passions produced by real events, than anything which, from the motions of their own minds merely . . . [they] are accustomed to feel in themselves" (*LB,* p. 256). He thus binds himself together with his experiencing subjects and his readers, who stand for the moment outside immediate experience, in expressions of "thoughts and feelings" concerned with "our moral sentiments and animal sensations, and with the causes which excite these; with the operations of the elements and the appearances of the visible universe; with storm and sun-shine, with the revolutions of the seasons, with cold and heat, with loss of friends and kindred, with injuries and resentments, gratitude and hope, with fear and sorrow" (*LB,* p. 261).

The device through which this binding is accomplished is that sympathetic imitation of voices through which the poet in composing participates in the feelings and thoughts of the speakers whose speech he represents, while the reader similarly participates, in his impassioned recitation or silent imaginative interpretation, in the represented speakers' feelings and thoughts. The same device through which Socrates' guardians come to acquire their proper character is used here to form a

character of a radically different sort, that of a man who habitually finds
pleasure through the "voluntary exertion" of "the discriminating powers
of the mind" (*LB*, p. 249) upon all human beings' expressions of their
experience in the world. Wordsworth's reader is not only not restricted
to participating in the limited range of speeches "proper" to him in a
professional capacity like that of Plato's guardians; he is enjoined to
participate in the widest possible range of human utterances. But he is
also imagined not to take on uncritically the character of the voices in
which he participates but to acquire the character of one who is capable
of discriminating among them even as he participates in them. He is
then a critical participant, capable not just of sharing in the feelings of
the speakers the poet presents to him but of sharing with the poet a
perspective from which he recognizes the various motives and ideas
they express as part of an intelligible pattern, as illustrations of a general
law of human nature. The reader who practices sympathetic interpretation of the speeches the poet provides him discovers that they ex-
emplify and that he himself participates in "the grand elementary principle
of pleasure, by which he knows, and feels, and lives, and moves" and
without whose operation "we have no sympathy . . . [and] no knowledge" (*LB*, p. 258). He ultimately learns to expect all voluntary utterances
(and the utterances the poet spontaneously composes "in a state of
enjoyment" [*LB*, p. 266] will be voluntary in this sense) to be intelligible
as expressions of pleasure. His critical participation in the speeches the
poet represents leads him to share in and become conscious of the
community of pleasure which is "our natural and unalienable inheritance" (*LB*, p. 259).

As critical participants in this community, the poet and reader do not
differ essentially from the diverse represented speakers from low and
rustic life in whose utterances they participate. All subject to "the grand
elementary principle of pleasure," they all speak voluntarily only from
a perspective from which they find pleasure in what they relate, and
they understand each other by discovering such a perspective in the
features of the speech that reveal their governing emphases and ruling
ideas. It matters less what those ideas are than that they constitute that
"certain quantity of immediate knowledge, with certain convictions,
intuitions, and deductions which by habit become of the nature of intuitions" that characterize the speaker's interpretation of his experience.
What is constant is that whatever the content of those ideas, a speaker
uses them to resolve "the infinite complexity of pain and pleasure" in
the experience which he relates in the direction of an "overbalance of
pleasure" (p. 258).

The representing poet and his critical reader are *aware* of this tendency,
however, while the poet's uncritical represented speakers are not. The
poet indeed is characterized, distinguished professionally from his fel-

low men, not by any exemption from the operation of the principle of pleasure, but by his conscious commitment to the idea that his representations of human expressions of human experience ought always to please his readers (his readers are distinguished by their expecting to find this pleasure in reading the poet's representations). The poet consciously thinks, as the premise of his professional life, of "man and nature as essentially adapted to each other, and the mind of man as naturally the mirror of the fairest and most interesting qualities of nature" (*LB*, p. 259), and insofar as he represents speeches in his professional character he is marked by his application of this premise to his experience. In light of this conviction, which by habit becomes an intuition, *he* can be thought to find satisfaction and to give his readers pleasure both in the speeches he presents himself speaking and in the speeches of others which he represents. Though his represented speakers may be thought to rationalize their experience no matter what their habitual intuitions, his own intuition of the universality of their tendency to do so must be seen as the condition of his being a poet at all. For him the workings of any particular represented account of personal experience is most interesting for the pattern which it shares with all such accounts, for it is the consistency of the pattern that underlies the claims he makes for himself not merely as someone who recounts a given experience according to his pleasure but as someone whose business it is to represent such recountings as illustrations of the true pleasurable relation of the human mind to its experience in the world.

Were such a poet to find nothing but pain or self-deception in the accounts of human experience he represents, were his own experience to become "real and substantial action and suffering," were the natural relation between the human mind and the world not essentially "gratulant if rightly understood" (*Prelude*, 1850, XIV, 387), he would no longer take pleasure in human speech or be moved to share it in his poetic representations. If the pleasure he purported to share were not also truth, his representations would mock the misery of the human lot, declaring his obliviousness to it, his attempt to escape it, or even his corrupt pleasure in it. If he abandoned the premise that voluntary human utterances express man's ability to take pleasure in his experience, he could not imagine that the metrical representation of such utterances, of "the real language of men in a state of vivid sensation," might communicate "that sort of pleasure and that quantity of pleasure . . . which a Poet may rationally endeavour to impart" (*LB*, p. 241). A poetics of represented speech would not be possible if there were no basis for this premise, and a poet who no longer believed it but was still committed to giving pleasure would have to choose to remold the materials of a fallen world, including its language, into ideal forms or transform the fallen world itself with his unfallen word. Wordsworth sticks to his premise, however, and does not become the Coleridgean or Blakean poet such a fallen world calls for. Though he does not pretend to know whether the world in itself is fallen or unfallen, he does find confirmation for his claim that the mind of man reflecting on its experience in the world is capable of resolving the "infinite complexity of pain and plea-sure" of that experience into "an overbalance of enjoyment" (*LB*, p. 258). On the strength of this confirmation he pursues his vocation "sing-ing a song in which all human beings join with him, . . . [rejoicing] in the presence of truth as our visible friend and hourly companion" (*LB*, p. 259). Pleasure and truth, the real and the ideal may in themselves be categorically distinct, but in experience they are mixed and in the ac-counts of experience the poet of speech represents they are discovered to be manifestly and frequently one.

Coleridge, with whose position I have implicitly contrasted Words-worth's, saw clearly that this issue of the relation of real and ideal, truth and pleasure, in Wordsworth's imitation of his characters and their speech was the "point, to which all the lines of difference [between his views and Wordsworth's] converge as to their source and centre" (*BL*, 2:33). As he puts it in his first formulation of the issue in Chapter 17: "I adopt with full faith the principle of Aristotle, that poetry as poetry is essen-tially *ideal*, that it avoids and excludes all *accident*; that its apparent in-dividualities of rank, character, or occupation must be *representative* of a class; and that the *persons* of poetry must be clothed with *generic* attri-butes, with the *common* attributes of the class: not with such as one gifted individual might *possibly* possess, but such as from his situation it is most probable before-hand that he *would* possess" (*BL*, 2:33–34). Be-tween "essentially" and *"ideal"* he appends a footnote which, at the end, complicates the notion he sets forth in an especially revealing way:

> With the ancients, and not less with the elder dramatists of En-gland and France, both comedy and tragedy were considered as kinds of poetry. They neither sought in comedy to make us laugh merely; much less to make us laugh by wry faces, accidents of jar-gon, *slang* phrases for the day, or the clothing of common-place morals drawn from the shops or mechanic occupations of their characters. Nor did they condescend in tragedy to wheedle away the applause of the spectators, by representing before them facsimi-les of their own mean selves in all their existing meanness, or to work on the sluggish sympathies by a pathos not a whit more re-spectable than the maudlin tears of drunkenness. Their tragic scenes were meant to *affect* us indeed; but yet within the bounds of pleasure, and in union with the activity both of our understanding

and imagination. They wished to transport the mind to a sense of its possible greatness, and to implant the germs of that greatness, during the temporary oblivion of the worthless "thing we are," and of the peculiar state in which each man *happens* to be, suspending our individual recollections and lulling them to sleep amid the music of nobler thoughts. (*BL*, 2:33)

The poet, Coleridge says, is to make his subject ideal, but his text and his note show that he is taking *ideal* in two senses. In the text the ideal differs from the individual along Aristotelian lines in being generic or typical, while the individual contains accidental variations from the traits of the class to which it belongs. In the footnote the ideal reappears in Platonic guise as the highest conception, the perfected representation which lacks all of the meanness and transitoriness of the individual. It is not merely the typical; it is also the noble.[14]

Whichever way we take Coleridge's commitment to the ideal in poetry, it does not allow room for Wordsworth's poetic enterprise. If the ideal is the generic, in which characters are clothed "in the common attributes of the class," a poetry which attempts to move beyond classes to discover the workings of one law in all minds is unthinkable. When Coleridge says he thinks that poetic characters should be "*representative* of a class," he means social class, as the following application of his principle shows: "The characters of the vicar and the shepherd-mariner in the poem of 'THE BROTHERS,' that of the shepherd of Greenhead Ghyll in the 'MICHAEL,' have all the verisimilitude and representative quality, that the purposes of poetry can require. They are persons of a known and abiding class, and their manners and sentiments the natural product of circumstances common to the class" (*BL*, 2:34). He wants rustic characters to be represented *as rustics* and "clothed" in the attributes of rustics, but Wordsworth wants to represent them *as men*, clothed in as little as possible that does not appertain to them as men. What are for Coleridge the generic attributes of the class are for Wordsworth the accidents of class.

In this sense, Wordsworth would see his poetry as more universal and ideal than would Coleridge because it aims to discover in its characters a higher genus, one in which there is "no essential difference" between the classes Coleridge discriminates. Coleridge, however, when he takes up this same issue in his criticism of Wordsworth's poems, reveals that the preservation of "essential differences" is precisely what is endangered in Wordsworth's intention, under the conditions of a fallen world, "to attack and subdue that state of association, which leads us to place the chief value on those things in which man DIFFERS from man, and to forget or disregard the high dignities, which belong to HUMAN NATURE, the sense and the feeling, which *may* be, and *ought* to be, found in *all* ranks" (*BL*, 2:104). Coleridge's most fundamental objection to Wordsworth's intention, as he has clearly stated here, is that "the object in view, as an *immediate* object, belongs to the moral philosopher, and would be pursued, not only more appropriately . . . in sermons or moral essays, than in an elevated poem. It seems, indeed, to destroy the main fundamental distinction, not only between a poem and prose, but even between philosophy and works of fiction, inasmuch as it proposes *truth* for its immediate object, instead of *pleasure.*" Though Coleridge can look forward to "the blessed time . . . when truth itself shall be pleasure, and both shall be so united, as to be distinguishable in words only, not in feeling," he insists that under present conditions the poet is bound "to proceed upon that state of association, which actually exists as *general;* instead of attempting first to *make* it what it ought to be, and then to let the pleasure follow" (*BL,* 2:104–5). He must, that is, respect the distinctions between pleasure and truth, prose and poem, philosophy and fiction, and the higher and lower human faculties and social ranks which belong to the fallen world and limit the imperfect pleasures we can enjoy in that condition. Wordsworth, however, does not recognize the essentiality of the empirical classes which the Aristotelian ideal accurately represents, nor does he concede the generality of the fallen condition which makes it necessary to respect them.

Wordsworth's position, however, is no more compatible with the Platonic interpretation of "ideal" that Coleridge offers in counterpoint to his Aristotelian empiricism; for Coleridge defines this ideal in contradistinction to the spectators' "own mean selves in all their existing meanness" and to "the worthless 'thing we are,' " while Wordsworth insists that what is valuable in the poet, his represented speakers, and his readers is to be discovered in them as they are, in the natural operation of their human minds. Poetry for Wordsworth is not the lulling to sleep of individual recollections "amid the music of nobler thoughts" but a recognition of grandeur in the reawakening of individual recollections; not a "transport" to "possible greatness" but a discovery of actual greatness in things already known.

Poetry that is ideal in Coleridge's second sense is not the dramatic poetry of the Aristotelian "ideal" but the lyric poetry of the secondary imagination, which "dissolves, diffuses, dissipates, in order to recreate; or where this process is rendered impossible, yet still at all events it struggles to idealize and to unify" (*BL,* 1:202). It reflects not the generic attributes of the class to which the character belongs but the modifying, idealizing and unifying power of the poet's own mind. It is, in fact, the kind of poetry which Coleridge finds characteristic of Wordsworth's genius, the kind which animates, illuminates, and consecrates what Coleridge sees as an otherwise lifeless, dark, and profane world, the kind Coleridge prefers to the dramatic poetry which, he thinks, grows out of a misguided theory at odds with Wordsworth's characteristic gift. It is also, however, as Shawcross long ago recognized, not the kind of poetry which Wordsworth thought of himself as writing. Coleridge claims, quoting lines from Wordsworth's "Stanzas Suggested by a Picture of Peele Castle," that Wordsworth "does indeed to all thoughts and to all objects '—add the gleam, / The light that never was, on sea or land, / The consecration, and the poet's dream' " (*BL*, 2:124), but Shawcross notes:

> Coleridge is unfortunate in quoting as a description of the essence of imaginative power a passage in which Wordsworth wished to characterize the errors, or at least the limitations, of the imagination in youth. He has thereby originated and helped to perpetuate a misunderstanding of Wordsworth's conception of the faculty; for Wordsworth has been held, on the strength of this passage, to conceive of the charm of art as something adventitious, which the artist or poet puts into nature and does not find there. But this is exactly the opposite of Wordsworth's real meaning. (*BL*, 2:293n)

Shawcross goes on to explain what he sees as Coleridge's lapse from his usual understanding of Wordsworth's art, but in the present context we can see that this misunderstanding is systematic, the result of a commitment to principles at variance with Wordsworth's and to distinctions alien to the real classes of Wordsworth's endeavor.

Coleridge, as we have seen, distinguishes two classes of poetry, the dramatic and the lyric. The first kind, an Aristotelian dramatic poetry, is committed to representing the essential distinctions of a fallen world. Coleridge's idea of the poet who writes such poetry is best described in his account of how Shakespeare's aloofness from his characters in his narrative poems reveals "the great instinct, which impelled the poet to the drama": "it is throughout as if a superior spirit more intuitive, more intimately conscious, even than the characters themselves, not only of every outward look and act, but of the flux and reflux of the mind in all its subtlest thoughts and feelings, were placing the whole before our view; himself meanwhile unparticipating in the passions, and actuated only by that pleasurable excitement, which had resulted from the energetic fervor of his own spirit in so vividly exhibiting, what it had so accurately and profoundly contemplated" (*BL*, 2:15). The poet is thus not sullied by the low characters and impulses he accurately presents, and his audience is saved from the same corruption by artful devices which "preclude all sympathy with" them (*BL*, 2:16). One hardly need insist that this poetic kind leaves no legitimate place for the poet who in composing "describes and imitates passions" through a deliberate choice to "bring his feelings near to those of the persons whose feelings he describes, nay, for short spaces of time perhaps, to let himself slip into an entire delusion, and even confound and identify his own feelings with theirs" (*LB,* p. 256) or for one who insists that his readers too must participate in these feelings.

No more does Coleridge's other poetic category, the lyric poetry of the secondary imagination, accommodate Wordsworth's lyrics or his other poems which the first category excludes. We have already seen how Coleridge's emphasis in this category on the signs of the artist's transformation of reality and language violates the fundamental commitment of the poet working within a poetics of speech. Such a poet does not distinguish himself from others in his power to remake his language or the world but in his sensitivity to common experience and his heightened powers of communicating it. He, like other men, "upon fit occasion" will speak in a language "dignified and variegated, and alive with metaphors and figures" (*LB,* pp. 254–55), but this is not his distinguishing mark, even when, as sometimes in his lyrics, he represents himself speaking in "his own person and character." Even then he is "a man speaking to men."

Between the lyric and dramatic kinds Coleridge leaves no room for the special character and virtues of a mixed or narrative mode. Throughout the second volume of the *Biographia,* he consistently judges works in this kind along one of two lines. Either, like Aristotle praising Homer, he admires works in this mode as they approach the imitative ideal of the dramatic ("You seem to be told nothing but to see and hear everything" [*BL,* 2:15]), or he criticizes them as they juxtapose or confuse the lyric voice of the poet with the dramatic voices of his characters. Wordsworth's experimental narratives fail, he repeatedly claims, either because they subject the reader to an experience of sinking as they shift from the poet's elevated style to the character's low style or because, like a ventriloquist, they project language proper to the poet into the mouths of his characters. Such poems have no positive character in his scheme but stand as anomalies that should have been written either in prose, where the stylistic sinking would not occur, or entirely in the poet's own character, where the elevated diction could have been consistently and probably maintained.

In Coleridge's poetics we may contemplate characters from an aesthetic distance analogous to the distance from which the spectator of a play contemplates actors on the stage or we may recognize the working of the poet's genius in the harmonious reconciliation of meter, poetry, and elevated diction in his poem, but we cannot, as we must in Wordsworth's poetics, participate sympathetically in a represented speaker's utterance while maintaining ourselves and attributing to the poet a critical awareness of the motives that provoke it and the laws of mind it

illustrates. Neither can we make sense in Coleridge's terms, as again
we must in Wordsworth's, of the relation between the motives and tones
of a reported speaker's utterance in narrative diction and the motives
and tones in which a reporting speaker reports it. This diction is of
special interest to the poetics of speech because it represents not just
interesting utterances but utterances that take interest in other utterances.[15] It is not surprising that poems written in this diction should
have been central to Wordsworth's experiments in the poetics of speech
or that they should have been singled out as failures from Coleridge's
alien poetic perspective. What is surprising, however, is that Coleridge's
premises have persisted so long in Wordsworthian criticism and continued to sustain his judgments of Wordsworth's successes and failures
and that the premises of a poetics of speech have been so long in gaining
recognition and application to Wordsworth despite his effort to formulate
them. In the context of recent developments in the poetics of speech to
which I shall now turn, this situation need not persist much longer.

Chapter Two

The problem of a sociological poetics would be
resolved if each factor of form could be explained as
the active expression of evaluation in these two
directions—toward the listener and toward the object
of utterance, the hero.

M. M. Bakhtin, "Discourse in Life and Discourse in
Art"

Discourse in Life
as Discourse in Art

We are now in a position to recognize Wordsworth's "experiment . . . [in] fitting to metrical arrangement a selection of the real language of men in a state of vivid sensation" (*LB*, p. 241) as an experiment in the poetics of speech. We can now also distinguish such a poetics from a poetics of action or of metrical composition and distinguish poetically represented speech in general from direct natural speech as well as from the special case of represented dramatic speech. With the distinctions that define a *poetics* of speech thus established, we may proceed to examine the additional distinctions it entails by virtue of its being a poetics of *speech*. In other words, we may turn to the properties that poetically represented utterances in general and Wordsworth's experiments in particular have, not by virtue of being poetically represented but by virtue of being utterances.

Wordsworth and his recent critics have called attention to most of these properties in the course of various defenses and explications, but an examination of them within a developed framework for the poetics of speech will allow us to discover their interrelations and to pursue their implications more systematically. For this purpose I have chosen to build on the outline provided by M. M. Bakhtin's essay "Discourse in Life and Discourse in Art," an elaboration of a poetics of speech (he calls it a "sociological poetics") more comprehensive and fully articulated than any other I have discovered, one closely connected with Bakhtin's work elsewhere on narrative diction, and, finally, one that follows lines strikingly similar to Wordsworth's in the Preface to *Lyrical Ballads*. Taking discourse in life as a model for discourse in art, as Wordsworth takes the "real language of men" as a model for language in poetry, Bakhtin gives us a chance to see what "a systematic defence of the theory, upon which the poems [of *Lyrical Ballads*] were written" (*LB*, p. 353) might have been like.

For Bakhtin as for Wordsworth, the words of an utterance in life are to be taken as intelligible not in themselves or even in relation to their speaker alone but in relation to a situation in response to which the speaker speaks. The words of a speaker always assume and may be taken to imply a listener (even if only an inner listener) who knows what the speaker is talking about, understands the relation in which he stands to the speaker, recognizes the speaker's intentions, and shares (potentially at least) the speaker's evaluations. Wordsworth's interest in the language of men in low and rustic life makes sense in these terms as an interest in the language of speakers who can take the satisfaction of these conditions for granted. Speaking in a community where speaker and listener enjoy common objects of experience and regular intercourse with one another, Wordsworth's rustic speakers can safely assume that they will be understood by their fellows without needing to elaborate on what they are talking about or where they stand toward their listeners or what they are trying to do or what they take to be important in what they are saying.

A "simple and unelaborated" expression spoken under these conditions may carry evaluative weight in inverse proportion to its elaboration, for the less it is necessary to say, the more it is assumed a listener will be able to understand of the situation that provokes the utterance. A brief remark—"The key I must take, for my Ellen is dead' "—uttered (or in the case of "The Childless Father" "perhaps" uttered) by Old Timothy as he shuts his door is all that needs to be said to resolve for his companion the situation of Timothy's first return to the life of the village after six months of mourning for his daughter. Death and communal gaiety are familiar enough to both of them, their friendship is assumed, Timothy's reminding himself to take the key needs no explanation. The importance of the dead child, of the communal hunt for which he leaves her memory behind, and of the key with which he both locks the memory up in private and preserves his future access to it are evident to his companion without explanation or justification.

For Timothy or the speaker who recounts his possible utterance to have to explain or justify any of these values would mean, as Bakhtin puts it, that the value "has ceased to organize life and, consequently, has lost its connection with the existential conditions of a given group." A problematic value becomes part of the content of discourse, itself an object of concern and debate, but "a health[y] social value judgment remains within life and from that position organizes the very form of an utterance and its intonation" ("Discourse in Life," p. 101). One need only imagine a community for which the hunt is considered a life-denying institution rather than a life-affirming one, or another for which his concern with the key might appear to show shrewd attention to preserving private property even as he joins the communal festival, to imagine Timothy's gesture taking on possible meanings that require explanation or defense. For Old Timothy and his companion, no such problems arise.

We have perhaps become so accustomed to the ease with which assumed values like those which shape Timothy's utterance can be "problematized" that we see Wordsworth's or Bakhtin's interest in communities of speakers for whom such problems are rare as nostalgic or primitivistic. Such an interest in the assumed conditions that make shared meanings possible, however, is necessary to understanding and dealing with those situations in which such conditions have broken down, just as some shared sense of literal or proper usage is necessary to the recognition and appreciation of metaphorical departures from it. There is no sense of the figurative without a prior assumption about the literal, and there is no problematizing values unless someone has assumed an unproblematic relation to them. But there is also no special importance to the figurative and the explicitly problematic, for their own sakes. Both, for Wordsworth and Bakhtin, are not values in themselves but signs of active relations to values. Figurative language indicates its user's charged relation to his important subject, as explicit defenses or criticisms of values mark a speaker's active separation from the consensus of a community that holds other truths than he does to be self-evident. Such departures from the norm are functions of the same system as the norm itself, however, and they cannot be separated from a relationship to it and cultivated for their own sakes without becoming vitiated. Wordsworth sees the poetic language which cultivates figures of speech for their own sake as vitiated in just this way, as he also sees the sophistication which pretends to no commonality with the assumed values of rustic life as vitiated. As the one loses its meaning when it preserves figurative expressions without attention to their literal provenance, the other loses its humanity when it pretends that its sophisticated awareness of the contingency of all values exempts it from participation in the assumed values that ground the speech of men in low and rustic life.

Wordsworth's poetic project is intended to counteract such vitiation by cultivating his readers' capacity to recognize and participate in expressions that assume knowledge of the "great and permanent forms of nature" and the "general passions and thoughts and feelings of men." His problem is to compose represented utterances that activate this knowledge, or if, as he later feared, it is not latent but absent, bring it into being. His speakers' words, then, are supposed to be taken not as things of interest in themselves but as responses to a situation in which the permanent forms of nature and the general passions of men are implicated. The words are scripts into which the reader must read the tones that connect the words with the situations they resolve. To discover the tone is to realize and share without explicitly articulating the assumed values that shape the speaker's response. The difficulty readers have had in re-creating many of Wordsworth's experimental poems is directly connected, I believe, with the vague or incomplete concepts of tone that criticism has provided and with the unsystematic connection that it has made between these concepts and the observable features of poems. Without an adequate concept of tone and a sense of how to discover it in specific represented utterances, even the best-willed of Wordsworth's readers have sometimes been left unsure whether their own humanity or Wordsworth's poems were to blame for their dissatisfaction.

Here Bakhtin offers us help, for he shows us how to "read" the intonation that connects the words of an utterance to the speaker's unstated evaluations. Without a "reading" of these evaluations as well as of the words, the whole import of the utterance may be completely mistaken, as it is when we fail to register the signs of an ironic reversal. With a reading of them, we may learn to hear what Wordsworth hears in the words of his represented speakers as well as what they hear in each other's words.

We "read" the tone of an utterance and discover the evaluations it implies in light of some model of what the tone expresses or what the evaluations evaluate, and on this topic Bakhtin's model achieves a fullness and a clarity about what is at stake that most treatments of tone lack. In the literature on this question we can find accounts which refer the tone of the utterance to the speaker, whose subjective mood it expresses (or in the case of poetic works to the poem as a whole on an analogy with the mood of a speaker). More familiar and authoritative is I. A. Richards's definition of "tone" as the aspect of the utterance which reflects exclusively the speaker's "attitude to his listener." In addition we may find "an author's attitude or point of view toward his subject" stated as a separate and complete account of that to which tone is to be referred. Definitions as comprehensive as Bakhtin's are available in statements such as Hugh Kenner's that "tone is determined by the writer's or speaker's *sense of the situation,* [which] . . . includes both his sense of the gravity of his subject, and his relationship . . . with his audience," but none, so far as I know, gives this recognition of the "double orientation" of tone the force or focus Bakhtin does:

> Every instance of intonation is oriented *in two directions:* with re-
> spect to the listener as ally or witness and with respect to the object
> of the utterance as the third, living participant whom the intonation

scolds or caresses, denigrates or magnifies. *This double social orientation is what determines all aspects of intonation and makes it intelligible.*[1]

Two features of this claim are especially important for my present
purpose. First, to recognize the "object of the utterance as the third,
living participant" is to see more than a speaker's "attitude or point of
view toward his subject" or his sense of its "gravity." It is to find in the
speaker's intonation an active relation to the things he talks about which
makes them, even when they are "inanimate objects and phenomena,"
into animate participants and agents in life, i.e., to discover in the "live
intonation in emotionally charged behavioral speech . . . an inherent
tendency toward personification" (p. 103). This tendency, which leads Bakhtin suggestively to discuss the intonational and gestural metaphor as
well as the more commonly recognized semantic metaphor, makes it
reasonable to speak of the object of an utterance as its "hero" and to
recognize the relation between speaker and hero as potentially charged
with all the energies possible in personal relations. To recognize this
tendency in ordinary speech, as Wordsworth clearly does ("if the Poet's
subject be judiciously chosen, it will naturally, and upon fit occasion,
lead him to passions the language of which . . . must necessarily be
dignified and variegated, and alive with metaphors and figures" [*LB*,
pp. 254–55])—is to find a ground for the rejection of conventional per-
sonifications and the habit of reading them conventionally in poetry. It
is not unreasonable to expect a reader to find greater interest in metaphors which express the represented speaker's dynamic relations with
his hero than in those which merely indicate the poet's conformity to
his readers' "poetic" expectations.

The second aspect of importance in Bakhtin's account of tone is his
claim that the double orientation of intonation both gives it its form and
makes it intelligible. This is not to make tone just a topic among topics
(one, for example, in the trio of diction, tone, and image in which Kenner
places it) but a fundamental hypothesis for the reconstruction of any
utterance as intelligible. To do so is to recognize the words of the utterance not as the thing we are interested in but as "a 'scenario' of a
certain event." The evidences of tone and gesture accompanying the
'scenario' move us to *"reproduce"* the event itself as "the mutual relationship between speakers, . . . with the person wishing to understand
taking upon himself the role of listener. But in order to carry out that
role, he must distinctly understand the positions of the other two participants, as well" ("Discourse in Life," p. 106).

The implications of this claim for reading poetically represented discourse, to which I shall now turn attention, are fundamental. If, as
Bakhtin states earlier in his argument, *"what characterizes aesthetic* [or

poetic] *communication is the fact that it is wholly absorbed in the creation of a work of art, and in its continuous re-creations in the co-creation of contemplators"* ("Discourse in Life," p. 98), then our conception of the poem as a scenario of an event involving the mutual interrelations of speaker, hero, and listener tells us what sort of thing to "make" of it. It will not be for us just the words on the page or even the words understood in their grammatical relations to one another; nor will it be words reflective solely of the artistic work of a poetic maker or words expressive of an individual subject's moods and feelings; neither will it be words exhausted in their reflection of the rhetorical manipulations of a listener by a speaker or in the objective mimesis of an object by a self-effacing subject.[2] Though these limitations of what is to be reconstructed may be occasional determinations of the relations among speaker, listener, and hero, in which one or another of the participants is suppressed or effaced, they by no means exhaust the possible relations which we may discover in a given poem. None of them even allows for the possibility of free, creative interchange of equal or potentially equal participants, for the exchange of roles, or for the independence of mutually attentive judgment, which can make our participation as actively co-creative readers of a poem a fulfillment rather than a limitation of our humanity and the humanity of those whose words we recreate.

The differences, however, between a poetically represented utterance and a natural utterance make the activity of reconstructing these relations different in the two cases, for the contextual conditions that must be met if an utterance is to be intelligible in either case, are met in a poem in other ways than they are met in social communication. Most obviously, a "common spatial purview" is not evident to the reader who does not occupy the same scene as the poem's speaker, just as their common temporal reference cannot be assumed. Unless he wishes to exploit the effects of indeterminate temporal and spatial reference, or speak timeless truths, the poet will have to indicate in or outside the poem that for the purposes of understanding his speaker we must recognize that "It is the first mild day of March" and that he is out of doors, aware of the red-breast singing in the "tall larch / That stands before our door," or that the lines in which he refers to "these steep and lofty cliffs, . . . these hedge-rows" were *"written a few miles above Tintern Abbey,"* or that his encounter with the demoralized shepherd took place "on English ground, / And in the broad high-way." In the same way, the poet's presuppositions of "common knowledge and understanding" will pose a problem for him that they do not for a person speaking to another who shares his community and understands the world as he does. The poet who wishes the speeches he represents to be intelligible to a reader in this way (and not all do) will have to try to identify and rely on "that information which may be expected from him [a human being], not as a lawyer, a physician, a mariner, an astronomer or a natural philosopher, but as a Man," the knowledge that "cleaves to us as a necessary part of our existence, our natural and unalienable inheritance" (*LB*, pp. 257–59). He will, if he aims for relatively permanent intelligibility, recognize with Bakhtin that the purview of common knowledge is of varying scope from the family and clan to the nation, class, and common human experience, from the assumptions of the moment to enduring "constant, stable factors in life and substantive, fundamental social evaluations" ("Discourse in Life," p. 101), and he will opt for the widest purview which allows for the most constant suppositions. He will try to identify the "great and permanent forms of nature" and make the understanding of his utterance depend on them rather than on the temporary interests of small coteries and classes.

But in conveying his speakers' evaluations he will face the biggest difference between his communicative task and that of the speaker in ordinary life, for he will lack the resources of intonation that all speakers of natural utterances have. The link which those resources make in such utterances between the words and their extraverbal context of evaluation, that is, between the words and the dynamic evaluative relations of speaker, listener and hero they imply, must be otherwise made in the verbal artifact, for those resources, like the speaker, hero, and listener themselves, have become internal to the verbal work and have no existence simultaneous with and distinct from what it gives them. If we are still to reconstitute the work *in terms of* such constitutive entities, the question becomes how, without the evaluative signs provided by heard tone and seen gesture, we are to discover their relations. In answer Bakhtin directs attention to three aspects of the form of a work corresponding to the three divisions of a poetics of speech—diction, meter, and subject: the selection of epithets or metaphors, the "rhythm and other formal elements of verse," and the *"manner of the unfolding* of the depicted event"—each of which in its way is "permeated with value judgments" or "express[es] a certain active attitude" ("Discourse in Life," pp. 107–8).

Bakhtin does not treat any of these aspects of form in great detail, but his recognition of their common function in the re-creation of tone pulls together several topics that Wordsworth and his critics have treated separately. Without this recognition of function we might easily fail to see that the evaluative implications of choice of language are parallel in importance to the comparable implications of the "rhythm and other formal elements of the verse" and the "manner of unfolding of the depicted event," for in Wordsworth's theoretical statements and in studies of his poems, though all these factors have been appealed to on occasion, their common importance for discovering intonation is not made explicit. As Danby may be most closely associated with choice of language, Sheats is most explicit about prosodic features, and Parrish is most attentive to the manner of unfolding of Wordsworth's experimental ballads; but no one has yet treated all three topics in terms of their common function. In the next section, pulling together their insights and Wordsworth's accounts of those features of his work, I shall try to advance the discussion of these three aspects of form by showing how together they guide our reconstruction of the tones of Wordsworth's speakers.

Bakhtin and Wordsworth both have the most to say about that aspect of form which has the most obvious relation to tone, the selection of epithets and metaphors. Bakhtin writes:

> Value judgments . . . determine the author's *selection of words* and the reception of that selection (the coselection) by the listener. The poet, after all, selects words not from the dictionary but from the context of life where words have been steeped in and become permeated with value judgments. Thus, he selects the value judgments associated with the words and does so, moreover, from the standpoint of the incarnated bearers of those value judgments. It can be said that the poet constantly works in conjunction with his listener's sympathy or antipathy, agreement or disagreement. Furthermore, evaluation is operative also with regard to the object of the utterance—the hero. ("Discourse in Life," p. 107)

In these terms, Wordsworth's preference for the real language of men as it is manifest in the language of low and rustic life can be seen as a preference for the associations likely to be attached to words by a certain community of "incarnated bearers of . . . value judgments" and against the associations probably attached to them by another community, specifically a preference for the associations of his heroes over the associations of his sophisticated readers. But it is also clear in these same terms that he is not like the romantic writer Bakhtin characterizes who *"concludes an alliance, as it were, with his hero against the listener"* ("Discourse in Life," p. 112) but rather is a writer who invites his reader to participate in a community which the writer already professes to share with his hero. Writing in an unhealthily divided community, he is forced to make explicit to his potential readers the position from which his language and the language of his characters must be taken if it is to appear not as a trivialization of serious poetic diction but as a realization of significant responses to the enduring conditions of human life. He calls attention to the need to reconstruct the language of his poems as *someone's* language and to the speeches he represents as the expressions of their speakers' value judgments toward their subjects and their auditors in a context of common experience of important subjects and common knowledge of the grounds of their importance.

John Danby's path-breaking reading of "Simon Lee" shows a clear grasp of this approach to Wordsworth's use of language. It achieves much of its power from Danby's attention to the evaluative tonal aspects of such seemingly commonplace epithets for the hero as "old," "poor," and "little," such subtle differences of expression as that between "Ivor-hall" and "the hall of Ivor," and such apparently conventional gestures as his address to the reader as "gentle." Danby recognizes the traps into which this language may lead the reader who brings conventional literary expectations to the poem, and he sees that the act of recovering its speaker's tone leads the reader to reconsider seriously his assumed relation to poets and to poor old men. He hears the sentimental and the comic, the jacobin and the tory, possibilities the language permits and recogizes the choices they compel the reader to make. He shows how the speaker's unseemly insistence on the swelling of Simon's "poor old ancles" aborts the reader's hope for a ballad and forces him to rely upon his own "reality of experience and judgment" instead of upon his literary expectations. In reaching his own judgment of what has left the speaker "mourning," "the reader is restored to independence: independence of the 'poetic', and independence (a more difficult thing) of the Poet—of the writer, that is, as the provider of new 'attitudes to life', of novel patterns and formulae of response" (*Simple Wordsworth*, pp. 38–47).

Danby's general observations and detailed recoveries of tone show a sensitivity not only to the evaluative context of human relations in which to read epithets and metaphors but also to the possibilities of relationship among author, hero, and reader which are opened in a model where their positions are taken as independent in principle. Bakhtin's explicit elaboration of this model and his recognition of the significance of the choice of language in its poetic realization grounds those aspects of Danby's approach in a theoretical framework which allows us to understand what Danby taught us, teach it to others, and recognize its relation to other aspects of form which share the same function. It permits us now to consider how the disposition of epithets and metaphors in metrical arrangement helps us to estimate more precisely the tone in which we may imagine them to be spoken.

Critical examinations of "rhythm and other formal elements of verse" in Wordsworth have frequently not even gotten to the function of meter in his poems, confining themselves instead to the question, raised originally by Coleridge's attacks on Wordsworth's views, of "who disparaged and who defended meter" (Parrish, *Art*, p. 24). Wordsworth's own most prominent discussion of the topic addresses the threshold question,

"[W]hy, professing these opinions have I written in verse?" (*LB*, p. 262) rather than the interpretive question of how in this poem or group of poems meter embodies the evaluative interrelations of poet, hero, and reader. In answer to his own question in the Preface to *Lyrical Ballads,* Wordsworth concentrates almost exclusively on one dimension of the larger question, namely, on how the poet's use of meter affects the reader differently than would a presentation of the same subject in prose. His focus is on the "complex feeling of delight," complexly roused in the reader by the "perception of similitude in dissimilitude" in "language closely resembling that of real life, and yet, in the circumstance of metre, differing from it so widely." Even when the subject of verse enters the discussion, it does so in ways that concern the reader's probable re-sponse—first, the subject may be either too painful or too familiar to the reader, whose interest and pleasure in it the superaddition of meter manipulates and, second, the subject may receive less wide circulation and less frequent perusal if it is presented to the reader in prose rather than in verse. All the effects Wordsworth here considers are effects of verse in general as distinct from prose and not of this or that kind of versification or this or that local metrical effect within a given line or stanza, and all of them bear on the poet's manipulative relation to his reader, not on his relation to his subject.

In his 1815 Preface, where Wordsworth makes explicit a more active role for the reader than he had emphasized in the Preface to *Lyrical Ballads,* he represents the reader's relation to versification of the poem in a different light: "I require nothing more than an animated or im-passioned recitation, adapted to the subject. Poems, however humble in their kind, if they be good in that kind, cannot read themselves; the law of long syllable and short must not be so inflexible,—the letter of metre must not be so impassive to the spirit of versification,—as to deprive the Reader of all voluntary power to modulate, in subordination to the sense, the music of the poem;—in the same manner as his mind is left at liberty, and even summoned, to act upon its thoughts and images" (*Prose,* 3:29–30). Here the poet is no longer thinking of himself as working pleasurable effects on the reader through subliminal manip-ulation of metrical devices but imagines the reader to realize the versi-fication in the same way he realizes the thoughts and images of the poem, through a free and active interpretation to which the poem "sum-mons" him. Wordsworth does not, however, here any more than in the earlier Preface, give much help to the reader who would discover how the letter is to be animated by the spirit of versification, how the music is to be subordinated to the sense of the poem in specific lines, stanzas, poems, and groups of poems.

Paul Sheats, the modern critic who most explicitly recognizes the importance of meter in Wordsworth's ballad experiments, conflates the attitudes of the 1800 and 1815 Prefaces in the direction of the earlier pronouncement (*Making*, pp. 185–87). In elaborating his claim that the "lyrical" of the title *Lyrical Ballads* "emphasizes an aspect of the poems that the reader was likely to take for granted, their meter, and encourages him to yield to its influence and to give these poems the 'animated or impassioned recitation' that Wordsworth requested in 1815," Sheats draws entirely on the 1800 context where "the pleasure that we blindly associate with meter, or the sound effects that cluster with far greater intensity in stanzaic forms, mitigate and transfigure the pain evoked by the poet's imagery." The emphasis of 1815 on the reader's exercise of a "voluntary power to modulate" the meter in his "animated or impassioned recitation" is here submerged in the earlier emphasis on his submission to the "influence" of meter.

Sheats's development of his point through a contrast between the effects of a blank-verse passage in which, he says, "feeling tends to generate form," and a ballad-stanza passage, in which "feeling . . . is not allowed to generate form," states as an *opposition* between the effects of different metrical forms what would be better recognized as a *relation* between the feeling (the sense or spirit) and the form (or the letter of the meter) which the active reader modulates in reading different metrical forms according to the special formal expectations each establishes and the ways in which the sense works over and through those expectations. In these terms Sheats seems to me to overstate the contrast between the "psychological implications" of blank verse, where he thinks Wordsworth treats "subjects that can be mastered without the aid of extrinsic guarantees," and "the lyric" (including the "lyrical ballad"), in which he "may confront fears that in contemporary blank verse he represses." Certainly the choices of such forms, as well as of others like the rhyming pentameter of the "Lines written near Richmond, upon the Thames" or the anapestics of "The Convict" and a host of poems in the 1800 volume, may be taken to imply different relations of the poet to his subject and his reader, but none of these forms, not even the blank verse Sheats cites, lacks either the power to control or the power to give emphasis and intensity to feeling. The passage from *The Ruined Cottage* which Sheats cites to illustrate how in "the relative freedom of blank verse, feeling tends to generate form" is not characterized, I believe, by the threat of feeling overcoming form but by the flexible use of form at once to regulate and to intensify our sense of Margaret's feeling:

> "I am changed,
> And to myself," said she, "have done much wrong,

And to this helpless infant. I have slept
Weeping, and weeping have I waked; my tears
Have flowed as if my body were not such
As others are, and I could never die."

Sheats is of course correct here to note the "relative freedom" of the
form, which allows for enjambment without a sense of violation of the
line and for placement of the caesura at various positions besides after
the fourth syllable, where some have regularized it. Within this flexible
framework, however, a significant order emerges both among the lines
and within certain lines. The emphatic parallel position, rhythm, and
syntax of "I am changed" and "I have slept" call attention to Margaret's
present awareness of her passivity to processes which have worked on
her even as she was unconscious of their working. The similar parallels
between "And to myself" and "And to this helpless infant" at once
provide the double object of "have done much wrong" and subtly identify those distinguished objects not only through their parallel form and
place but through the assonance in the same line position of the "self"
and "help" in "myself" and "helpless," a significant echo that reinforces
the effect of the syntactic distance between the initially stated subject
"I" and the act—"have done much wrong"—for which it takes responsibility. The "I have slept" at once stands alone and enjambs with the
"Weeping" of the following line; the whole "I have slept / Weeping" is
balanced by "and weeping have I waked," with its reversal of the subject/
verb order; and the two clauses are combined in and balanced against
"my tears," which itself, like "I have slept," works in its own line and
also flows into what follows. The enjambment of "my tears / Have flowed,"
linking subject and its verb, is stronger than that of "I have slept /
Weeping," where a statement seems completed until the modifier
"Weeping" is introduced, but not as strong as the final enjambment of
"as if my body were not such / As others are" where the statement of
a relation of her body to some unspecified other is suspended in the
middle, with the relating "such" given with nothing yet to relate to.
The force of these enjambments is to build across the regular pattern of
the last three lines another stronger pattern: the dimeter "my tears /
Have flowed" followed by the alexandrine "as if my body were not
such / As others are," ending on the trimeter "and I could never die."
Though these phrases are of such differing numbers of feet, they take
up roughly the same time and emphasis with the long vowels on stressed
syllables in the first and last (Tears, flowed//I, die) contrasting with and
equalling in weight the sequence of stressed short vowels in the intervening segment (if, body, were, such, others, are). The unaccented syllables are all short, as well, except for the "my" whose rhyme with the

powerful "I-die" rhyme of the last phrase may help to explain why
Sheats hears in the passage "a despairing wish for death," even when
its overt theme is Margaret's awe at her own capacity to endure suffering
and her distance from the suffering being she thus perceives (I/myself;
my body//and I). It may in some sense be correct to say from the point
of view of the writer, which governs Sheats's study, that in this passage
feeling generates form, but it is more accurate to say from the active
reader's position that form orders and suggests feeling, that even the
underlying suggestion of the form-destroying desire for death in the
relatively free form of blank verse appears through the poet's control
and the reader's realization of the suggestive powers of rhyme, assonance, meter, enjambment, and caesura.

Sheats is right to observe that the effects of these prosodic resources
in a stanzaic form in rhymed iambic tetrameter will not be the same as
those in blank verse, but he is mistaken, I think, to imply that the same
powers are not in operation in both cases, that the one regulates pain
while the other, lacking its resources of regulation, must minimize or
understate the pain instead. Just as blank verse orders *and* intensifies,
so even the most regular stanzaic patterns may be exploited to intensify
and emphasize as well as to regulate passion. In this connection, I would
like briefly to take up "Simon Lee," the stanza form of which has been
described by one critic as "simply two ballad quatrains run together,"
though Danby suggests that there are "no mechanical ballad-metrics . . .
[but] a genuine and unaffected music in them" which moves from a
"jaunty . . . near-jocularity" at the outset to a "full seriousness of tone"
in the end.[3] Sheats, who discusses the poem at some length, makes only
one subordinate prosodic observation concerning it—that in the last
stanza "the unobtrusive metaphor 'to run,' which constitutes the poem's
only 'run-on' ending at this point in the stanza, recalls the physical
activity of Simon's youth, when he was a '*running* huntsman
merry' " (*Making*, p. 192). The pattern of "run-ons" or enjambments in
this poem is indeed interesting in ways that go beyond this punning
association of sense and prosodic device.

The poem divides into two parts, the first seven and a half stanzas,
in which Simon Lee is described in his past and present conditions, and
the last four and a half stanzas, in which the poet-narrator first addresses
the reader to correct his expectation that "Some tale will be related,"
enjoins the reader that, if he *thinks*, he will find a "tale in every thing,"
and then goes on to relate a personal anecdote of his encounter with
the old man, which concludes with his declaration of his present attitude
toward the kind of situation he has just recounted. In the most recent
and the most lengthy essay on the poem, Andrew L. Griffin sees the
relation among these parts as ultimately heterogeneous, "thrust apart

by the narrator's surprising abdication of his responsibilities as a storyteller." Especially in the 1798 version with which I am concerned, Griffin sees a speaker who "clearly could not tell a story if he would, but seems to draw at random from the unsorted contents of his mind." Griffin finds no connection of the speaker's early attention to "Simon's exact age," "the precise extent of his early fame," or the fairness of his livery coat both "behind" and "before" to the ultimate nontale which he tells ("Imaginative Story," pp. 392, 399). Since I discuss the poem as a whole and Griffin's argument in Chapter 3, I wish here only to suggest that close attention to the formal workings of the poem and the emphases implicit in them begins to reveal ways in which, from the very start, the poet is providing the necessary orientation to his "tale" and its hero for the reader who will realize it.[4]

An examination of the formal workings of the first stanza will be sufficient for my present purposes:

> In the sweet shire of Cardigan,
> Not far from pleasant Ivor-hall,
> An old man dwells, a little man,
> I've heard he once was tall.
> Of years he has upon his back,
> No doubt, a burthen weighty;
> He says he is three score and ten,
> But others say he's eighty.

In general, the syntax here stays much more within the bounds of the lines, whether tetrameter or trimeter, than did the syntax of my last example, but within those bounds, and between them, some interesting relations are suggested. Though the opening two lines have been taken to suggest the scene and manner of common ballad narration and so to establish a misleading orientation to the poem, the first whole syntactic unit is four lines, the first two on the scene, balanced and even over-weighted by the next two lines on the hero who "dwells" there. The first strong caesura in the poem, in the middle of the third line, balances "old man" and "little man," and the second phrase here, while repeating "man" and adding the quality "little," which occasions the qualification of the fourth line, also relocates the metrical stress from the "old" of the first phrase to "man" in the second—a slight move, granted, but prosodically interesting and thematically significant to the whole poem. In the text of the poem, Simon is introduced to us not as a huntsman but emphatically as a man. One may dismiss the next line's introduction of the first-person narrator and his second-hand knowledge of Simon's former height as irrelevant (the metrical weight here falls on "I've heard," "once," and "tall"), but if one reserves judgment he may find that this seemingly trivial bit of information, combined with others like it, builds a picture of the man whose reduction to abject gratitude could well lead the provoker of that gratitude to "mourning," in the thoughtful aftermath of his thoughtless act of charity.

The oddly inverted and interrupted fifth and sixth lines may seem less inconsequent if we recognize that they are connected, almost as an explanation, to the preceding two lines and link the three attributes to which those lines call attention—old, little, and once tall—through a metaphorical idea of the years of his great age as a weight bearing down, thus accounting for the otherwise inexplicable discrepancy of the little old man who was once tall. In the light of this connection, the emphatically set off and metrically emphasized "No doubt" may represent the speaker's gesture not so much toward the reader as toward his own puzzlement of a moment before; "no doubt," he may think, the burden of years which Simon Lee carries on his back can explain this discrepancy between the man as he is and the man as he is said to have been. For as the last lines go on reasonably to add, he is indeed old, though he, significantly I think, will say that he is younger than he is. These last two lines and the third and fourth lines, pairs which occupy parallel positions in the two ballad quatrains that compose the stanza, work in similar ways. In the first pair the hearsay of the second line modifies the speaker's present impression in the first, opening him to his discovery in lines five and six, while in the second pair the "others" again modify an impression, this time correcting Simon's account of himself, and possibly opening us to a discovery of a vanity, of a desire in him to diminish the burden or at least others' impression of the burden of age he carries.

Such discrepant accounts of the same subject may be recognized, if we do not settle down to amusing ourselves at the incompetent poet's expense, as classic invitations to thought. None other than Socrates in establishing the criteria for a philosophic curriculum in *Republic* VII provides the pertinent concept along with an instance that makes the first stanza of "Simon Lee" a paradigmatic instance:

> If you observe, some things which the senses perceive do not invite the intelligence to examine them, because they seem to be judged satisfactorily by the sense; but some altogether urge it to examine them because the sense appears to produce no sound result. . . . I mean by those which do not invite thought . . . all those which do not pass from one sensation to its opposite at the same time. Those that do, I put down as inviting thought, that is when the sensation shows two opposites equally, whether its impact comes from near or from far.[5]

Socrates goes on to explain that the recognition of a finger as a finger does not invite thought but the judgment of a finger's "bigness or small-ness," changeable as it is by the way in which it is seen in relation to other fingers and the distance from which it is viewed, does invite thought. A man, yes, but a little man who once was tall—hmmm. The poet's explicit appeal to his reader to think is not the first invitation to thought he provides.

It would not be far-fetched, I think, to suggest that the same kind of invitation is present even in the quantitative judgments of the prosodic differences we have been examining, the difference between óld mãn and líttle mán, for example. Our eye recognizes the word *man* in each case as the same word, as we see a finger as a finger or a man as a man. But when we come to judge its tone, its stress or emphasis and its meaning, we must think not just about the laws of iambic tetrameter, though we must think about those, but also about everything else that is given us in the utterance and in the context pertinent to it—the speak-er's "gratitude of men" in the last stanza and Wordsworth's stress on the idea of man in the Preface of 1802, for example. The senses alone will not be able to judge the question for us just by what they see on the page or even by what they hear in another reader's oral interpre-tation. The "perception of similitude in dissimilitude, [or] dissimilitude in similitude," is for Wordsworth, even in discussion of meter in 1800, "the great spring of the activity of our minds and their chief feeder," and "the pleasure which the mind derives" from this perception is an active and an intellectual pleasure, not a passive aesthetic one (*LB*, p. 265). The play of differences made possible by the metrical setting of words makes them at once like and unlike themselves, and is, to the attentive reader, itself a provocation to thought.

I must extend this already extended elaboration of the topic of meter to note how Wordsworth's treatment of it again implicitly answers the Platonic treatment of the same topic. I mentioned in my last chapter that the structure of Plato's discussion in *Republic* III divides along the same lines as Wordsworth's in the Preface to *Lyrical Ballads*—subjects, diction, and meter—but I did not there consider how Plato or Words-worth handles the last of these topics. Plato's position is simply stated: "[W]e must not seek for complex rhythms or variety of metrical steps, but consider what are the rhythms of a manly and orderly life; then with this in view we must compel the foot and the melody to follow the words of such a life, not let the words follow the foot and the melody." We have here terms similar to those which I have examined in Sheats's argument, only coming from another direction. Sheats argues that met-rical forms may either subdue a disorderly emotional sense to order or follow the disorderly direction that feeling takes and become themselves disorderly. Plato argues that the form should strictly conform to the tendencies of an orderly, rational, and manly sense, and that a rational and manly sense should not alter itself to fit the patterns of an essentially irrational metrical and musical form. What the positions share from Wordsworth's point of view is an interpretation of the relation between meter and matter as an *opposition*, which will end in one of the opponents subduing the other whether for the calming benefit of the overwrought emotions or the educational discipline of the irrational soul, on the one hand, or for the expression or liberation of passions on the other. Neither Plato's classic nor Sheats's romantic interpretation of meter allows that the interaction of sound and sense is interesting *as* an interaction to the mind, which finds in the similitudes in dissimilitude it discovers provocation to interpretive thought. Wordsworth's understanding of meter here may perhaps be his most radical implicit answer to the Platonic critique of poetry, for he finds in the poetic element which for Plato is most irrational a power to move the reader of the poem, not to automatic sympathy or to subliminal pleasure merely, but to the thoughtful interpretation which for Plato is the chief criterion of the philosopher's education. To read metrically set language aright, the reader must read it dialectically, critically, thoughtfully. Or perhaps I should say, to return to the context of Bakhtin's topics, he should read it dialogically, construing and reconstructing from its differentiated emphases the values of and relations among the diverse but similarly human narrator, hero, and reader it represents.

I have already considered how this construal and reconstruction is summoned and guided by the poet's choices of epithets and metaphors and by his arrangement of his words, sentences, and paragraphs within the formal patterns of metrical feet, lines, and stanzas. It remains to consider how Bakhtin's third topic, what he calls "the manner of the unfolding," contributes to these activities, though Bakhtin does not elaborate it at all. Neither does Wordsworth, whose best-known statements about what he is doing do not give the explicit recognition to this topic that they give to his choice of words and his use of meter. While he devotes major sections of the Preface to each of the latter, he publicly acknowledges our present topic in nothing more than the language in which he restates the purpose of his poems. Having first written that his purpose is "to illustrate the manner in which our feelings and ideas are associated in a state of excitement," he restates his purpose in "less general language": "[i]t is to follow the fluxes and refluxes of the mind when agitated by the great and simple affections of our nature" (*LB*, p. 247). Though it is not immediately clear how the language of the second formulation is "less general" than that of the first or how it relates to the manner of unfolding of the poems, both questions will bear further consideration.

The two formulations each break down into three grammatical parts, (1) an action expressed in both cases by a transitive verb ("illustrate" and "follow"), (2) an object of the action expressed in the more general formulation by a single noun ("manner") modified by a subordinate clause ("in which feelings and ideas are associated") and in the less general one by a compound of two nouns ("fluxes and refluxes") modified by a prepositional phrase ("of the mind"), and (3) a condition under which the object becomes an object of the action, expressed in the first by a prepositional phrase ("in a state of excitement") and in the latter by a subordinate clause ("when agitated by the great and simple affections of our nature"). At first the two actions in question seem only different but not more or less general, for to clarify by exemplifying something is one thing and to attend to the successive stages of something is another. Further, the different force of the two verbs in Wordsworth's use of them is reinforced by the difference in their objects as well as by the parallels between each of them with its object and the other verbs and objects he uses in the same context to show how his purpose is manifest in some of his poems. He speaks of illustrating a "manner," just as he speaks below of "shewing . . . the perplexity and obscurity which in childhood attend our notion of death" and of "displaying the strength of . . . moral attachment." In each case it appears that one condition or characteristic is revealed. But he also speaks of following the "fluxes and refluxes of the mind" in the same way that he does of "tracing the maternal passion through many of its more subtle windings" and of "accompanying the last struggles of a human being at the approach of death." In each of these cases the act of attention must go through a number of fluxes or windings or struggles.

I do not think that there is a contradiction or a paradox involved in the difference between these two sorts of expressions, but I am sure that there is plenty of room for misunderstanding. The tendency to minimize the illustration in comparison with a general truth it illustrates, to ignore the order and articulation of its parts for the sake of a general idea to which it contributes may seem authorized by the first set of formulations, if the second set is not taken into account, just as the opposite tendency to turn process into an end in itself, to celebrate an endless fluxing and refluxing may be fed by the second set taken alone. Neither the didactic and doctrinal reading of the first tendency nor the experiential and indeterminate reading of the second has been unknown in interpretations of Wordsworth's poems.

But Wordsworth's view of the two formulations as essentially equivalent though of differing generality and his elaboration of both their

tendencies in his subsequent choice of words should not be too easily
set aside. To follow the specific steps of a given process may be to
illustrate that process, even though things other than processes may be
illustrated more immediately by simply introducing or pointing to them
by name. "Follow" in this sense may specify "illustrate" for those cases
like plots and passions (and life) in which a thing is knowable only by
going in a given case through its successive phases and recognizing
them as the phases of the thing in question. We illustrate, show, or
display (a word etymologically equivalent to "unfold") the passions by
following, tracing, or accompanying them.

What we follow, Wordsworth's second and less general formulation
tells us, what the manner *is* in which our feelings and ideas are associated, is a series of "fluxes and refluxes," flows and ebbs, risings and
fallings, comings in and goings out metaphorically linked to the movements of the tides to which the original pair of terms is most commonly
applied. The mind then (not just the imagination, as Parrish suggests,
but I would say also the fancy, the attention, pleasurable interest, sympathy, affection, pride, fear and other activities of the mind subject to
quantitative variation in time), the mind is like the ocean flowing in and
out, rising and falling over a ground of objects on the shore whose
relative solidity and sameness make its movements perceptible.[6] At its
most roused it may inundate objects or wash them away, but even in
its more ordinary comings and goings it may make its risings felt in the
shine on a pebble or the bubbles on the sand and its fallings equally
discoverable in the dull stone and the dry sand. It may uncover treasures
and bury them again, record its ebbing in ripples of sand or hollows in
rock and obliterate them again in its next flowing. There is no clearer
illustration of these movements of mind in relation to its objects in
Wordsworth than the one Parrish cites (*Art*, pp. 30–32), Wordsworth's
explication to Lady Beaumont of his sonnet "With Ships the sea was
sprinkled far and nigh." I will take the liberty to quote it and the sonnet
again here to show how Wordsworth describes the unfolding of this
apparently trivial poem:

> With Ships the sea was sprinkled far and nigh,
> Like stars in heaven, and joyously it showed;
> Some lying fast at anchor in the road,
> Some veering up and down, one knew not why.
> A goodly Vessel did I then espy
> Come like a giant from a haven broad;
> And lustily along the bay she strode,
> Her tackling rich, and of apparel high.
> This Ship was nought to me, nor I to her,
> Yet I pursued her with a Lover's look;

This Ship to all the rest did I prefer:
When will she turn, and whither? She will brook
No tarrying; where She comes the winds must stir:
On went She, and due north her journey took.

Stating the general principle this poem illustrates, Wordsworth follows its unfolding in this way:

There is scarcely one of my Poems which does not aim to direct the attention to some moral sentiment, or to some general principle, or law of thought, or of our intellectual constitution. For instance in the present case, who is there that has not felt that the mind can have no rest among a multitude of objects, of which it either cannot make one whole, or from which it cannot single out one individual, whereupon may be concentrated the attention divided among or distracted by a multitude? After a certain time we must either select one image or object, which must put out of view the rest wholly, or must subordinate them to itself while it stands forth as a Head.

Having laid this down as a general principle, take the case before us. I am represented in the Sonnet as casting my eyes over the sea, sprinkled with a multitude of Ships, like the heavens with stars, my mind may be supposed to float up and down among them in a kind of dreamy indifference with respect either to this or that one, only in a pleasurable state of feeling with respect to the whole prospect. 'Joyously it showed,' this continued till that feeling may be supposed to have passed away, and a kind of comparative listlessness or apathy to have succeeded, as at this line, 'Some veering up and down, one knew not why.' All at once, while I am in this state, comes forth an object, an individual, and my mind, sleepy and unfixed, is awakened and fastened in a moment . . . this Ship in the Sonnet may be said to come upon a mission of the poetic Spirit, because in its own appearance and attributes it is barely sufficiently distinguish[ed] to rouse the creative faculty of the human mind; to exertions at all times welcome, but doubly so when they come upon us when in a state of remissness. The mind being once fixed and rouzed, all the rest comes from itself; it is merely a lordly Ship, nothing more:

This ship was nought to me, nor I to her,
Yet I pursued her with a lover's look.
My mind wantons with grateful joy in the exercise of its own powers, and, loving its own creation,
This ship to all the rest I did prefer,
making her a sovereign or a regent, and thus giving body and life to all the rest; mingling up this idea with fondness and praise—
where she comes the winds must stir;
and concluding the whole with

On went She, and due north her journey took.
Thus taking up again the Reader with whom I began, letting him
know how long I must have watched this favorite Vessel, and inviting him to rest his mind as mine is resting.[7]

Several features of this passage deserve comment. First, Wordsworth
takes the terms in which the objects in the poem are described as indications of his state of mind as the hero of the poem. The speaker's
description of the sea indifferently sprinkled with ships reflects his former state of "dreamy indifference"; his description of the sea's showing
"joyously" reflects his then generally "pleasurable state of feeling with
respect to the whole prospect"; his presentation of the ships' "veering
up and down, one knew not why" suggests the "comparative listlessness and apathy" he felt at the time. It is especially striking that Wordsworth expects us to imagine him as he is "represented in the Sonnet"
"casting my eyes over the sea" from the line "With ships the sea was
sprinkled far and nigh" in which no one is *described* standing on the
shore looking at the sea at all. Here a speaker's description of a past
appearance implies the hero who saw that appearance, and the language
in which that appearance is presently described gives evidence of the
mood in which it was formerly seen. Only the tense of the poem establishes a distance between these two perspectives, a distance which is
closed momentarily in the poem in the twelfth and thirteenth lines with
free indirect discourse that identifies the speaker's and hero's perspectives, and closed again in the explication of the poem by the shift from
past to present tense at "all at once, while I am in this state, comes forth
an object." The speaker's relation to himself as the hero of his narration
is complicated by his recovered interest in the hero of the experience he
narrates, the ship which engaged his mind then and engages it again
now so intensely that the distance between him then and him now as
well as between him later telling about the poem and him earlier composing it collapses.

These complex relations between the perspective of the telling and
the perspective told about are further complicated by another feature of
the poem which is especially crucial for our present topic—the states of
mind reflected in the speaker's descriptions of the scene are to be thought
of not just as contributing to the portrait of a static feeling or attitude
but as *developing* successively from line to line. Wordsworth is so strongly
oriented to movements of mind that he does not allow even the first
quatrain to establish a constant state of mind, a situation from which
what follows can depart, but insists that the initial description of the
scene already reveals dynamically modulating attitudes. As his narration
proceeds, the modulations become more pronounced until in the next
to the last line the power he attributes to the ship ("where she comes

the winds must stir") reveals the most powerful transformative exertion of his mind. As the mind rises, the ship "in its own appearance and attributes . . . barely sufficiently distinguish[ed] to rouse the creative faculty of the human mind" takes on its attributes from that faculty, like the pebble taking its shine from the rising sea.

Finally, it is worth emphasizing that Wordsworth imagines the *reader* to follow the progression of states of mind (perhaps "follow" here in the sense of "imitate" is most apt), as they are reflected in the speaker's description of his own changing attitudes in the scene, and to respond to an invitation, implied in the unfolding of the poem, to rouse his faculties and then to rest them. Following at once the shifting distance between the speaker and himself as hero and the changing moments of the hero's relation to *his* hero would be a task from which the reader might well turn with grateful acceptance to the poet's invitation in the last line "to rest his mind as mine is resting." A call to activity in response to the active depiction of a movement from listlessness to active perception—this is the relation among speaker, hero, and reader Wordsworth imagines in his account of the "fluxes and refluxes of the mind" in this poem.

The same general description could well apply to many of his other narrative poems, for all such poems call the reader actively to reconstruct a narrator's active reconstruction of some hero's excited movement of mind, but the recognition of this common pattern will only direct the reader's attention, not exhaust his interest. To expect to "follow" some "fluxes and refluxes" of some mind or minds is to know what to look for but not what will be found. Though all such minds will be in a "state of excitement," there is no telling which of the "great and simple affections of our nature" will move them or what objects will cause those affections. Even Wordsworth's statements of the laws or passions his poems illustrate will not preempt the discovery of those laws or passions in operation in a given poem, for the activity the poems invite is not naming or classifying but following, tracing, or accompanying certain passions through movements that reveal them. To trace such movements and recognize (not merely identify) such passions in the "incidents of common life" is, as Wordsworth says in his statement of his principal object, to make those incidents interesting.

We will do well to remind ourselves, however, that the incidents or events which gain interest from the passions they unfold are not interactions of disembodied passions but of persons with their temporal, spatial, and social worlds. The manner of unfolding the passions which Wordsworth follows, like his choice of words and his disposition of them in prosodic structure, permits us to infer how his speakers imagine their subjects and their listeners. We cannot rest in psychological characterization of a particular speaker's or hero's passions any more than we can be satisfied with an abstract formal analysis of diction or prosody for its own sake. We may recognize the fear and transference of anger that leads to the "lie" in "Anecdote for Fathers," but we have not understood the poem unless we see that these are a young son's responses to his father's perverse, persistent questions. We may read "The Thorn" as a "psychological study" (Parrish, p. 99) designed, as Wordsworth himself says, "to exhibit some of the general laws by which superstition acts upon the mind," but we will miss its interest as a portrayal of "human passions, human characters, and human incidents" if we do not also notice the old bachelor's fascination with his idea of a betrayed and guilty woman's interminable, constant misery, or the old sea captain's attempt to understand the human relations, passions, and stories of the landlocked society into which he, a stranger to all of them, has retired. His peculiar eagerness to have his auditor confirm what he has seen, combined with his reluctance and compulsion to tell what he has heard, make his relation to his listener almost as interesting as his obsession with his heroine, and both relations more interesting than his exemplary perfection as a case study of superstition's effect upon the mind.

Here Bakhtin's sociological terminology can help us correct the clinical tendency of Wordsworth's predominantly psychological language and at the same time help us notice functional features of the poems which that language does not bring to the foreground. Holding that "consciousness, as long as we do not lose sight of its content, is *not just a psychological phenomenon* but also, and above all, *an ideological phenomenon, a product of social intercourse,*" Bakhtin calls attention to the ways in which social or ideological content is manifested in the stylistic tone of public utterances as well as in the unvoiced selections of inner speech. Again introducing a useful distinction, he says that such tones and selections reflect both the relations among the "evaluative rank[s]" of speaker, hero, and listener and their "degree[s] of proximity" to one another. The evaluative rank of the participants, whether one is "higher or lower than or equal to" another "on the scale of the social hierarchy" defined by such names for social relations as "king, father, brother, slave, comrade, and so on," shapes the style and significance of an utterance ("Discourse in Life," pp. 110–11). A son will speak to his father of a brother's actions differently than he will speak of a friend's behavior or differently than he will speak to a judge or teacher of his brother's acts. Not only the relative social standing of speaker and hero but also the speaker's perception of his relation to his listener and of his listener's relation to his hero will shape his language and its meaning. All of the experimental poems in which Wordsworth presents himself querying another person reveal relations in which he can take the liberty to ask because he enjoys a social superiority to the shepherds, vagabonds, beggars, and children he addresses, and the qualities and effects of their answers are colored by the expectations their positions entail—the sailor's mother begins and ends her speech with "Sir." Frequently Wordsworth also recognizes in the poems the probable social distance between his heroes and his listeners as well as their expectations concerning his status and his duties toward them. Informed attention to what is implicit in all these relations is necessary to the thoughtful realization of the poems.

Similarly, attention to the signs of shifting degrees of proximity among the participants in a poem, or of the "distance" among them, as we are more accustomed to name this feature, is crucial to following its unfolding. The most familiar signs of distance are the pronouns of person, which indicate, for example, the presence or absence of the hero by the speaker's second- or third-person reference to him or the speaker's identification with or alienation from his listener in the range of relations implied by first-person plural, second-person informal, and second-person formal pronouns. It has been less commonly recognized, I think, that shifts in tense may suggest the same shifts in the proximity of relations among our trio of participants, as we saw in the twelfth and thirteenth lines of "With Ships," where the shift from past to present tense identifies the previously distinguished perspectives of the narrator and himself as the hero of the anecdote he narrates. Present tense may also be used to include the reader in an immediate experience of the speaker's, only to distance him from that experience with a shift to past tense, as in the beginnings of "Old Man Travelling" or "Resolution and Independence," or *The Prelude*. Wordsworth's tense shifts frequently function in these ways, almost always implying some change in the relations among speaker, hero, and listener.

Such changes in the relations between persons, not just changes in the direction or quantity of passions abstracted from persons, can constitute the unfolding of a poem. In fact, the signs of shifting passions *are* the signs of shifting relations among persons (or personified beings), just as shifting interpersonal relations are themselves evidence of shifting passions. The father's shift in "Anecdote for Fathers" from speaking of his son as "my boy" to calling him "the boy" marks a momentary distancing between them that is also a momentary ebbing of love. The old man's revelation in "Old Man Travelling" of a situation which is not exempt from human suffering brings him closer to the narrator, who had imagined him otherwise, and also dispels the envy which the young narrator had felt at the image of the old man he had created.

I believe that the unfoldings of these poems are more readily intelligible and memorable described in the language of human relations than in the abstract psychological language of feelings rising and falling, appearing and disappearing by themselves. Even the sonnet we have seen Wordsworth explicate in terms of the law of mind it displays makes more sense when we imagine that its narrator presents himself as having become a lover and the ship his momentary beloved, in relation to whom he has experienced the whole course of his passion so suddenly and arbitrarily that he is moved to recount the episode in wonder. His mind has transformed his relation to a thing into an emotionally charged interpersonal relation, revealing itself in doing so. It may not matter to the accuracy of our account of what has happened in the poem whether we describe it in terms of the psychological laws it illustrates or of the human relations it enacts, but I think it does matter to the ease with which we can activate our "human and dramatic Imagination" (*Prose*, 3:34) to realize what has happened. Our minds, after all, work the way the poet shows his mind working, responding personally to persons— Wordsworth says, "delighting to contemplate similar volitions and passions [to our own] manifested in the goings-on of the Universe"—and, to paraphrase and interpret him, habitually creating persons where we do not find them, as he does when he contemplates the sea sprinkled with ships (*LB*, p. 256). Endowed with such dispositions, we will enjoy his poems more and know them better if we take their represented speeches to imply persons involved in human relations instead of passions running their courses.

We can now turn to that special relation of persons embodied in narrative speech. The relation I have in mind is not just that of narrated characters to one another—of Michael to Luke, for example—nor simply that of the "two parties" to narrative viewed as a "social transaction," the narrator and the listener. Though Barbara Herrnstein Smith fruitfully conceives of narrative within a poetics of speech "as verbal acts consisting of *someone telling someone else that something happened*,"[8] Bakhtin makes us sensitive to the "third participant" her definition overlooks. Narrative may be better defined as someone telling someone else that *someone said or did or experienced something.* The defining speech-act of telling remains in effect in this definition, and the listener's necessary presence is not lost; but the object of the utterance is acknowledged as a third potentially speaking person whose relation to the other persons, to the narrator who tells about him and the listener who is interested in hearing about him, shapes the narrator's utterance. The introduction of this third person highlights possibilities that Smith underplays in her account of the "structure of motivation" that shapes the features of individual narratives and characterizes the common properties of sets of narratives, for it recognizes the hero's influence on the narrator's telling, while she concentrates on the listener's.

The surest signs of the listener's influence on a speaker's utterance are tacitly observed conventions, but the most noticeable signs are his explicitly voiced reflections of a listener's probable expectations. The utterance that begins "Once upon a time . . ." acknowledges the listener's conventional expectation that "some tale will be related" by conforming to one conventional way to establish such a transaction. The listener need not be invoked explicitly because his expectations have been directed by a conventional sign, and as long as the utterance that follows satisfies those expectations, his interest in the form of the utterance can remain tacit. If, however, as is most often the case with Wordsworth's experimental narratives, the speaker departs from what he takes to be a conventional arrangement, he must explain himself or somehow acknowledge the disappointment he has provoked, unless he is prepared to lose his listener or is involved in a form of utterance not aimed at an external listener. The narrator who violates conventions of communication will make explicit appeals to his listener that reveal both the role in which he imagines his auditor and the point at which the auditor's interests impinge on his tale.

The hero's influence on an utterance may be gauged by the degree to which he is presented as the source of his own meaning, that is, as an articulate being whose own way of understanding and explaining himself is respected and related by the narrator. The hero whose meaning is entirely a function of the narrator's account of him may not be presented as speaking at all or only be presented as speaking words that illustrate the narrator's claims about him. The hero who influences the narrator's account of his meaning may command large parts of the narration for his own words or shape the narrator's language or judgment to reflect his own. The narrator's handling of the hero's words—manifest most often in what I have called "narrative diction"—is the chief index of the hero's influence on the narrator, revealing the narrator's preservation of the hero's words and his modifications of them, his adoption of his hero's accents and his invasions of the hero's accents with his own.[9] To condemn some of Wordsworth's uses of such diction as "unevenness" of style or "ventriloquism," or to blame his narrators' explicit negotiations with their listeners as "intrusions," is to miss the significance of these parts of his represented speeches. Far from showing him having "trouble with the tone" of his poems (Hartman, *Wordsworth's Poetry*, p. 148), they reveal the shaping influences that account for his represented speakers' utterances. His narrative experiments acquire their individual meanings and their similarities and differences from one another as one of these influences predominates or as the relations between them are variously negotiated.

The two sets of experimental narratives that I will consider in the next two chapters illustrate two relatively stable configurations of these influences. The "tales" I take up in Chapter 3 all acknowledge (though in very different ways) a listener's expectation that "some tale will be related." Though almost all of them raise questions about this expectation and introduce other shaping considerations from the speaker's relation to his hero, they cannot be understood without taking into account a listener's habit of recognizing and responding to those "distinctly framed and conventionally marked tellings that we are inclined to call 'tales' or 'stories' " ("Narrative Versions," p. 232). In the "personal anecdotes" that will concern us in Chapter 4, the narrator's personal encounter and exchange of words with his hero motivates his attempt to tell what took place between himself and the other person. The narrator's relation to the hero in all these poems takes precedence in shaping his utterance over any expectation that a listener might have. The two sets are distinguished, as Smith would put it, by the "differences in the specific conditions that elicit and constrain them" ("Narrative Versions," p. 234), and they raise different problems as they bring one formative relationship into prominence and leave the other to be assumed or inferred. These differences will compel us, as we examine these sets and the individual poems within them, to elaborate further our poetics of speech, but we have now outlined it sufficiently to begin exploring them.

Chapter Three

O reader! had you in your mind
Such stores as silent thought can bring,
O gentle reader! you would find
A tale in every thing.

Wordsworth, "Simon Lee"

Tales

Like the author writing in verse, the speaker telling a tale in effect "makes a formal engagement that he will gratify certain known habits of association" (*LB*, p. 23). As the one signals his reader to mobilize some set of expectations—though different ones at different times—by setting his compositions in verse, the other arouses expectations that "some tale will be related" by invoking certain conventional signs. Though various gestures have been used to identify an utterance as a tale, two procedures may be the surest signs—the introduction of a person in a place and the introduction of a person at a time. Thus "In the sweet shire of Cardigan / Not far from pleasant Ivor-hall / An old man dwells" has already roused the expectation of a tale that the narrator of "Simon Lee" later acknowledges, and the narrator of "Michael," who announces his tale as such before he begins it, fulfills his promise by beginning, "Upon the Forest-side of Grasmere Vale / There dwelt a Shepherd." The narrator of "Peter Bell," discouraged from beginning in medias res—a convention of a more sophisticated narrative form than the "tale"—announces emphatically that he has "reached at last the promised Tale" when he says, "ONE NIGHT . . . Peter was travelling all alone," and the narrator of "Ruth" simply begins, "When Ruth was left half desolate." Our habit of processing tales is so strong, however, that even when only one of these elements is introduced by itself—a time, place, or a person, we may still expect a tale and await the introduction of the other necessary elements. Thus "It is an ancyent Marinere" and "There is a thorn" and " 'Tis eight o'clock, a clear March night" all already seem to point to a time or place when or where the mariner did something, to a person who has some significant connection with the thorn, or to someone doing something that night. Though these words could all lead to different kinds of utterances, though some of them do so in fact, they all rouse expectations of tale-telling that are not easily put to rest. The expectation of a tale is so easy to rouse that speakers may have to be at more pains to avoid it when they do not want it than to raise it when they do; it is so powerful that to introduce the signs of it far into a discourse of some other kind may transform that discourse into a tale.

It is one thing, however, to say what makes us expect a tale and another to say exactly what we expect when we expect one. When a speaker introduces us to a person in a place or at a time, we seem to expect to hear that he or she did or said or experienced something significant then or there, and we expect to hear it related in an utterance that will tell us what happened and what we need to know to appreciate its meaning. We expect, that is, a complete utterance organized to relate a complete significant happening as significant. We may, however, be more or less eager to get to the point, more or less willing to infer the point for ourselves, more or less concerned that the tale is true, more or less practical in our judgment of what tales are worth telling. We will be disappointed in our expectation if we cannot figure out what happened or what it is supposed to mean, or if the telling seems to diverge from the intent to tell us these things, but we may be induced to accept departures from any or all of these expectations if the telling holds our interest in other ways. The narrator, Barbara H. Smith writes, "always has the option of subverting the conventions" by which we are accustomed to recognize and process a tale. "The result may be a tale that provides for its audience an increased measure of cognitive interest at the expense of the smooth and efficient access to information" ("Narrative Versions," p. 231).

The conventions of tale-telling, then, establish a framework of expectations which may be met or modified by other interests and constraints that affect the speaker's sense of himself and the others.[1] The speaker's relation to the listener may not be what it was at first thought to be, the speaker's intention in telling may not be what it at first appeared to be, or the speaker's knowledge of or interest in his hero may raise problems for his telling of the hero's tale. "The Old Cumberland Beggar" illustrates the first of these constraints. Beginning with the narrator's presentation of a person in a place ("I saw an aged Beggar in my walk, / And he was seated by the highway side"), the represented utterance seems to promise a tale to an interested general listener, but when it turns to declare, "But deem not this man useless.—Statesmen! ye / Who are so restless in your wisdom," it specifies its audience more narrowly and reveals a persuasive purpose toward that audience that shapes the rest of the utterance. There is, of course, a specification of intention here as well as of audience, but intention may be announced independent of audience as it is in "Hart-Leap Well" when the narrator declares "The moving accident is not my trade." The speaker's knowledge of what has happened to the hero may alter the shape of the tale if the narrator makes a point of not being sure of what happened, as does the narrator of "The Thorn," or of not being allowed to tell what happened, as does the narrator of "The Idiot Boy," or of telling how he learned what happened, as does the narrator of "Hart-Leap Well." Finally, his interest in his hero will modify his telling as his sense of what the story means takes into account what it means to those who took part in it or those who transmitted it to him as an already significant tale. The narrator of "Simon Lee, " as we will discover, is constrained in his tale-telling by his recognition of the difference between Simon's meaning to him and Simon's meaning to himself, and the narrator of "Hart-Leap Well" must come to terms with the "small difference" between what the shepherd's account of Sir Walter's hunt means to the shepherd and what it means to him.

In *Lyrical Ballads* the conventions of tale-telling rarely govern a represented speaker's utterance without being modified by one or more of these constraints. Indeed, in all but the "rudest" tale in the collection, the notion of a tale is an explicit topic with which a narrator must come to terms, not a pattern to which he conforms. The relating of a tale or of a certain kind of tale becomes part of what the speaker talks about as he tells his story, part of the theme of his utterance, not an assumed form in terms of which he relates other content. Wordsworth's narrators make tale-telling an issue for themselves and their implied listeners and readers, just as Wordsworth makes the subjects and language of metrical composition an issue for his imagined audience. But if his narrators sometimes present themselves as failing or fearing failure by the conventions they imagine their listeners and readers to read by, he hopes in setting their utterances to meter to interest his readers. He declares his own pleasure in what he has represented and, in spite of his readers' "pre-established codes of decision" and habitual ways of taking poetic pleasure, he aims to please. We will see, in examining the one poem he identifies as a "story" and the group of poems whose narrators consider their own tellings in light of the idea of a tale, what "sort of pleasure" and what "quantity of pleasure" we can find in them.

"Goody Blake, and Harry Gill: A True Story" has not given its readers great difficulty, but it has not excited great interest either. Wordsworth helped to limit his readers' interests by saying that the poem is "founded on a well-authenticated fact" (*LB*, p. 8) and that he wished in composing it "to draw attention to the truth that the power of the human imagination is sufficient to produce such changes even in our physical nature as might almost appear miraculous" (*LB*, p. 267). He minimized their difficulties in reading by arranging a narration which readers have testified "approximates to straight narrative with a neutral narrator" (*Simple*

Wordsworth, p. 36) whose "speaker plays a relatively straightforward role" (Sheats, *Making,* p. 188). These judgments note the narration's straightforwardness relative to the narrations of other poems in *Lyrical Ballads,* especially that of "The Thorn," with which it has most often been compared, and they echo Wordsworth's remark that "the Tale of GOODY BLAKE and HARRY GILL . . . is one of the rudest of this collection" (*LB,* p. 267).

Readers have been able to enter and leave the narration with relative ease because it begins and ends with recognizable gestures that orient them to the tale it relates. The first lines, "Oh! what's the matter? what's the matter? / What is't that ails young Harry Gill?" voice a question from a listener's point of view that any reader can easily adopt: Mary Jacobus casually speaks of it as "our opening question" (*Tradition and Experiment,* p. 237). The final lines, "Now think, ye farmers all, I pray, / Of Goody Blake and Harry Gill," sound like a moral to the story and leave readers with the sense that the meaning of the tale has been wrapped up. Jacobus points to them as containing "Wordsworth's humanitarian lesson" (*Tradition and Experiment,* p. 237). One must take the lines' advice, however, and "think" for a moment before realizing that they do not say *what* to think of Goody Blake and Harry Gill. Like similar gestures in the middle of "Simon Lee" and at the end of "Resolution and Independence," this admonition to "think" leaves the task of making meaning unfinished. Though it sounds like a packaged lesson, it is in fact an open invitation, and Wordsworth's more explicit statement elsewhere of what he was trying to illustrate should not be allowed to close it and take the place of the poem.[2]

The tale unfolds as an answer to the question that opens it, but first it amplifies the condition that ails Harry. His teeth chatter, the neighbors reliably report, without regard to changes in time and circumstance, no matter how many blankets and coats he has, no matter what the season, what the time of day or what the ascendant heavenly luminary. " 'Tis all the same with Harry Gill," the narrator reiterates. He tells us then that young Harry once was lusty, stout, ruddy, and of powerful voice, but before proceeding further to explain whether the cause of Harry's chattering teeth has changed these attributes as well, he begins to contrast them to those of a certain Goody Blake—old, poor, thinly clad, ill fed, and poorly sheltered. We learn all of this about her condition and continue to hear about it for five more stanzas (we have had only two and a half stanzas of Harry, two of them nothing but chattering) before we arrive at any connection between Goody and Harry Gill, and were it not for the title of the poem (which I do not take as part of the telling), all of this would seem completely unexpected, out of place. Even with knowledge of the ultimate connection between Goody Blake and "what's the matter" with Harry Gill, we may find that much of what the narrator tells us to extenuate Goody's taking sticks from Harry's hedge is beside the point we have been engaged to hear about. Does Goody, after all, have to be shown to be so justified in her occasional forays to Harry's hedge for her words to have the effect they do on Harry? Harry, at least, is not shown to be any more or less aware of her condition than her other neighbors, and he may not need to be aware of it to be affected as he is, but the narrator is still concerned to establish it and we are taken along.

He establishes it, indeed, with a care that makes Goody's poverty as well authenticated and manifest as Harry's chattering. If "The neighbours tell, and tell you truly" that his teeth are always chattering, "any man who pass'd her door, / Might see how poor a hut she had," and "every man who knew her says" her wood supply never was enough for three days. The listener is even brought in as a hypothetical witness to the effect of winter on "her old bones": "You would have said, if you had met her, / 'Twas a hard time for Goody Blake." Goody is said to have been as oppressed by night and winter and as enlivened by summer as Harry is now unaffected by either seasons or times of day. Witnesses confirm that, though these circumstances now make no difference to him, they once made all the difference to her.

All of this leaves no possibility that a listener will take an interest in seeing Goody's theft punished and justice done, or sympathize with the claims of property against the claims of age, poverty, and misery on a source of survival and minimal comfort of which the owner (with his "warm fire" undoubtedly fueled by the imported coal that Goody cannot afford) has no need. Harry, however, unlike the young farmer in the source from which Wordsworth draws, is not concerned with legal justice (Erasmus Darwin's farmer is "determined to watch for the thief" and waits as she gathers the sticks so "that he might convict her of the theft") nor is property specifically the object of the "trespass" he vows to avenge.[3] Harry's motives, introduced at the end of the long account of Goody's condition, are presented in terms that make them seem strangely intense and personal, and his long-held suspicion and his frequently repeated desertion of his warm fire on winter nights to watch "to seize old Goody Blake" also cannot be dismissed merely as justice-seeking or property-preserving behavior.[4] Everything we have heard of the perfectly understandable conditions that have compelled Goody occasionally to steal Harry's wood makes the motives for Harry's vendetta against Goody and his comfort-denying, persistent pursuit of her seem all the stranger. The disproportion between Goody's "trespass" and Harry's response, the difference between her occasional expeditions to the hedge under pressure of necessity and his nightly stalking of her under vow of vengeance point to a mad concentration of Harry's mind on Goody Blake.

Our recognition of Harry's madness at this point in the narration depends upon our taking the narrator's words as indicative of his hero's thoughts and feelings, not just of his manipulations of a listener's responses. Paul Edwards, who brings Danby's concept of the manipulation of a narrator's "masks" to bear on the poem, hears "emotions being heightened beyond their true importance" in the use of the words "trespass," "vowed," "detected," and "vengeance" to describe a response to "an old woman stealing sticks from a hedge," but he attributes the heightening to the narrator's "comic inflation" of the action, not to his use in his diction of Harry's own words for what he is doing.[5] This view leads Edwards to read the next stanza, in which Harry's discovery of Goody at the hedge is related, as more "clownishly melodramatic heating up of the emotional climate." But this stanza, even more than the previous one, shows that the narrator is involved in Harry's perspective, sharing the intensity of the avenger's discovery of the object of his vengeance:

> He hears a noise—he's all awake—
> Again?—on tip-toe down the hill
> He softly creeps—'tis Goody Blake;
> She's at the hedge of Harry Gill.

The narrator here is caught up in Harry's act of attention; he is not just playing to his audience, and the emotional heat of this stanza and the previous one come from *Harry's* overheated imagination.

The narrator continues to participate in Harry's fixation on Goody through the first half of the next stanza where he reports Harry's gladness in beholding Goody as he watches her take "stick after stick," filling "her apron full." A moment when, in Darwin's account, the justice-seeker assures himself of the evidence he needs to convict a thief becomes here the moment in which the avenger relishes the sight of his object enacting the trespass that calls for vengeance. "Stick after stick" confirms his suspicion and builds his passion until both Harry and her apron are full. As she turns to leave, he, "with a shout," springs upon her, "fiercely" grabs her, "fiercely" shakes her, and cries, " 'I've caught you then at last.' "[6]

At this moment of fulfilment of a desire long delayed (" 'at last' ") with all of Harry's attention concentrated on the object of his vengeance, with his words opened to her as a "you" from whom a reply might be expected but with his hands on her as one completely subject to his power before whom she could not possibly have anything to say for herself, Goody speaks, not to Harry, as Darwin's old woman addresses the farmer who has caught her, but to " 'God! who art never out of hearing,' " praying " 'O may he never more be warm.' " There is not the least hint of witchcraft in the prayer nor of superstition in Harry's being affected by it. He, at the moment of his fulfilment, is rebuffed by the object of his vengeance, who does not even speak to him or acknowledge his power over her but appeals to a power beyond him. The avenger wants his victim to squirm, to beg for mercy, so that he can experience his power over what in his mind has such power over him, but Goody freezes Harry out of his fulfilment and prays that he remain fixed in his coldness. All his being has been madly concentrated on an object who refuses to assume the role he has prepared for her, and like a rejected lover, he becomes fixed in his moment of disappointment.[7]

Having related the climactic encounter between Harry and Goody, the narrator fills in the steps we can already infer from there to the image of Harry's chattering teeth that provoked his opening question. Harry's condition gradually emerges in the week after his meeting with Goody, and still "all who see him say 'tis plain / . . . / He will never be warm again." He, who shouted his triumphant capture of Goody with a voice "like the voice of three," is reduced to inarticulateness, never speaking "word to any man" and muttering to himself, "Poor Harry Gill is very cold." His life has been reduced to the effect of the single episode the narrator has related. His condition is the emblem of his tale, his tale is the meaning of his condition, and the narrator is the sole source of the account that connects them.

This last point is not immediately apparent, for the narrator, as we have seen, is careful to attribute much to the neighbors, to those who have seen Goody and Harry. But the distribution of his citations shows that, while he is careful to verify Harry's present condition and Goody's former poverty (she unlike Harry seems no longer to be alive and available for observation)—he says nothing of how he has learned what happened the night of their meeting. Harry speaks to no one, Goody is gone, no one else was present, no one is even said to have speculated about it, as Old Farmer Simpson speculates about Martha Ray in "The Thorn." The narrator has *imagined* it without making an issue of doing so, and his account stands or falls on its verisimilitude alone. His answer to the question he has posed depends entirely on his presentation of a plausible course of human passion, and our acceptance of his answer depends on our recognizing its plausibility and being satisfied with it, without any further irritable reaching after fact or reason.

Wordsworth thus has chosen to have the truth of his "True Story" verified imaginatively and the facts of Goody's and Harry's conditions verified with testimony. Wordsworth has in fact made his narrator cite evidence for conditions not given in *his* source for the tale and has left the narrator on his own imaginative authority just where Wordsworth's source has been most explicit. There is nothing of Goody's poverty in Darwin, who presents his old woman only as "like a witch in a play," and there is no need for neighbors to confirm the present chattering of Harry's teeth or to speculate on its permanence, for Darwin's young farmer has died after spending twenty years under his blankets "for fear of the cold air." On the other hand, while Darwin suggests that the farmer's motive is to bring Goody to justice and that he is affected by her words because "he lay many cold hours under a hay-stack" and heard what she said while "already shivering with cold," Wordsworth makes his narrator imagine different motives and causes without citing any source, either to differ with it or depend on it. Though Wordsworth chooses in "The Thorn" to have what really happened at the thorn become a thematized issue for his narrator, as he chooses in "Hart-Leap Well" to make his narrator's differences from the shepherd's account of Sir Walter's tale a thematized issue, he chooses in "Goody Blake and Harry Gill" not to raise these issues, leaving the truth of his narrator's tale "standing not upon external testimony, but carried alive into the heart by passion" (*LB*, p. 257). Like so many of the passions Wordsworth represents, however, it does not have its impact immediately, but reveals itself to us only when we follow his admonition and tread "the steps of thought" (*Prose*, 3:83).

"Simon Lee" more than "Goody Blake and Harry Gill" overtly and emphatically asks for thought, and its narrator's appeal to his reader to "think" has not gone unheeded. The poem has provoked more critical inquiry than any of the *Lyrical Ballads* tales except "The Thorn" and "Michael": its structure and tone have been fruitfully explored, and its centrality to Wordsworth's experimental project has been firmly established. The present state of understanding of the poem, however, clearly illustrates the limits of the concepts of tone and of narrative that critics have had to work with. Even in its most ambitious and sophisticated recent treatment, Andrew Griffin's "Wordsworth and the Problem of Imaginative Story: The Case of 'Simon Lee'," the poem's parts remain disconnected, its narrator's gestures (in the 1798 version with which I am concerned) appear as "random and unsorted," and its meaning finally emerges not from narrative but from lyric conventions.

The accomplishments and limits of Griffin's argument deserve close attention because he has so thoroughly and thoughtfully assimilated the available critical conceptions of Wordsworth's experiments and shown what each can make of "Simon Lee." Griffin sees the poem (and "The Idiot Boy" and "The Thorn" to which he links it) as "actions . . . in which the principal characters are not old men, women, and boys, but

speaker and hearer, or poet and reader—and a third party: that mys-
terious place, or moment which has the power to prompt a poem, in
which 'some tale' is felt (rightly or wrongly) to reside. The real concern
in these poems is tale-telling and tale-listening, in confused conflict with
the poetic imagination: in other words the problem of imaginative story"
("Story," p. 393). This formulation provides the outline for the three
parts of Griffin's argument: his explorations of the poem, following
Danby and Sheats, as "a manipulation [of the reader] and a rhetorical
tour de force" (p. 394); following Parrish, as "the revelation of [its narrator's] character through [his] troubled speech" (p. 398); and finally,
following Hartman, as a poem that moves from the ineffectual bustle of
narrating toward the "silent thought" of visionary lyric, the "full stop
. . . before a kind of picture . . . on which the mind can feed, from which
the mind can slowly withdraw into its own place" (p. 406). What Griffin's
formulation and his argument set aside, what the critics from whom he
draws give him no way of handling, are "the principal characters" of
the poems, their heroes. The "third party," besides narrator and listener,
in whose mind's workings he looks for the resolution to the difficulties
of "Simon Lee" is not Simon Lee himself but the poet. Griffin's argument
short-circuits the hypothesis we have been developing, that tone always
involves gestures in two directions, toward the listener and toward the
hero, and, after exploring the poem from the points of view of listener
and speaker, moves directly to a lyric poet's perspective outside of the
human relations the narrator has been involved in and outside of time
and the sublunary world. Simon Lee is transformed into an "image—
single, silent, still"—"the mute invitation of the lonely, separated figure
beside the stubborn root," whose meaning, beyond anyone's words, is
"a mood of [the poet's] mind that seeks no thing because it feels itself"
(pp. 405–6).

For the narrator of "Simon Lee" the old man he has met does not
easily reduce to such a significant image, nor does he for Wordsworth.
The old man's resistance to meaning what the narrator wants him to
mean is what the poem represents not just in its first part, in which the
narrator cannot settle the conflict in his mind between Simon as "a
running huntsman merry" and Simon as an impoverished and decrepit
old man, but also in its concluding anecdote, in which the narrator tells
of having acted to help Simon on the basis of the last of these images,
only to recognize something more to the object of his charity, something
that not only has left him mourning at the old man's gratitude but has
also compelled him to tell the man's story and to appeal to his reader
for help in making his telling a "tale." The telling Wordsworth represents
may be taken as a response to the episode with which it concludes, and
the question we may then ask is, what sort of response is it and what

is it really responding to? Why should the narrator who has thought what he has thought of Simon Lee and done what he has done for (to) him, try to tell what sometimes sounds like a ballad of the old man's former prowess as a huntsman when the tale that would account for his act of charity is simply the tale of the old man's present misery and incompetence? Why does he expose himself in his failure to make one tale of the two mutually interfering tales he tells to a reader he knows expects one meaning and one story to emerge in his telling? Why, instead of resting in "silent thought" after his meeting with Simon Lee, does he launch into such a troubled and risky verbalization? What is the tale in his telling and why can't he just tell it?

The only part of the narrator's utterance that he presents as a response to his encounter with Simon Lee is the reflection with which he concludes:

—I've heard of hearts unkind, kind deeds
With coldness still returning.
Alas! the gratitude of men
Has oftner left me mourning.

This reflection raises the issue of the just-reported encounter to a general level and makes it for its speaker an instance of a kind of situation to which he appears to have responded in this way more than once ("oftner" suggests that he has sometimes mourned at the ingratitude of men but that more frequently he has mourned at their gratitude). The generality of this reflection draws attention away from its specific implications for the situation out of the account of which it has just arisen, and a number of critics have found its specific bearing impossible or unnecessary to formulate, but a simple transformation makes its import graspable. If the ingratitude of men that sometimes provokes the speaker's mourning is defined as "hearts unkind, kind deeds / With coldness still returning," the gratitude of men at which he mourns in this case may be provoked by a kind heart, returning with warmth an unkind deed. The warm thanks are evident enough in the way Simon's "thanks and praises" are described running "So fast out of his heart," but the narrator's sense that his own deed was unkind is not so obvious. It can be heard, however, in the impatience with which he says he received the old man's thanks and praises ("I thought / They never would have done"), for his embarrassment may be imagined to be not just that what the old man is so grateful for has cost him so little effort but also that he has put another man in a position of such abject gratitude. He is not only forced to see another man reduced to making so much of so little, but he must also take responsibility for having exposed the other's weakness and dependency as it was not exposed by the persistent if ineffectual labor in which he discovered him. This is not to say that it is wrong to help another but that it is wrong to do so in a way that wounds his self-respect and that the narrator has seen Simon Lee and his own relation to him in a way that did not bring Simon's self-respect into consideration until after the damage to it was done.

Taking the concluding anecdote as containing all of the narrator's account of how he saw himself and Simon Lee when he was moved to help him, we may recognize that the narrator saw Simon as an "old man" who "might have worked forever" without being able to cut loose "an old tree, / A stump of rotten wood." The repeated epithet "old" links man and tree in the narrator's mind (cf. Averill, p. 160) and further links the man's vitiated condition to the rottenness of the tree stump (no other epithets complicate this stanza). Furthermore the narrator imagines that the man's labors are not just hard or time-consuming but "vain" and that (though as he tells us earlier the old man has "Few months of life . . . in store") "He might have worked forever" at his task. These exaggerations of the man's situation may well show the narrator's imagination at work turning the old man into a significant image of the futility and decay to which we are brought in our old age (cf. Griffin, pp. 397, 403; Averill, p. 166) and his gesture of aid may indeed be taken as a "powerful and liberating release of protective energy, a gesture of defense, and even revenge, on behalf of a humanity caught in the inexorable process of natural law" (Sheats, p. 192), but the exaggerated image does forget the old man who is standing in front of the young poet-narrator and turn him into an archetype at the expense of his self-respect for the little time he *does* have left. The image also leads the young man to forget his own strength in the vehemence of his rebellion against it and to strike his "single blow" without thinking about the effect it will have on the old man who "so long / And vainly had endeavor'd" to cut the root himself. If he imagines himself striking a blow against the bitterness of our mortal deterioration, he does not think, until too late, that he is also severing the artery of Simon's self-respect and leaving the "thanks and praises . . . to run / So fast out of his heart" that they seem to flow from a mortal, unstanchable wound. Realizing only after striking the blow that he has had this effect upon Simon and standing helplessly and embarrassedly listening to the excessive thanks and praises he had provoked, the young poet might be left with confused wishes to restore to Simon what he had taken from him (even to give back the mattock now is to give back something compromised) and to justify the impression under which he was moved to do what he now recognizes to be an unkind deed. The confused narration which he produces can be explained as the product of these unresolved and incompatible wishes.

That narration begins, as almost everyone since Danby has recognized, as if it were a ballad in the manner of Percy's *Reliques,* and it returns to this manner, as Wordsworth's revised final version makes clear, in about three stanzas over the course of the next six stanzas. This tale of Simon's prodigious feats in the days of his youth and of his continuing identification with the man he was then restores a dignity and meaning to Simon's present condition that the young man who met him had not seen. The "long blue livery coat" which he has kept "fair behind, and fair before" testifies to the piety with which he keeps his later days bound to his earlier ones. The appearance of his cheek—still "like a cherry"—preserves a physical resemblance to the flushed triumphant huntsman, "reeling" after outrunning "all the country." Most important, the one thing in the course of the poem that he is said to love, the one thing "At which his heart rejoices," is the cry of the hounds that (despite what the narrator declares to be the total annihilation of "men, dogs, and horses" at Ivor-hall) still reminds him of his twenty-five years as "a running huntsman merry."

This "tale" I have made from the materials given in "Simon Lee" does not emerge uninterrupted, however.[8] The opening stanza does not get three lines finished before the "old man" who "dwells" "In the sweet shire of Cardigan / Not far from pleasant Ivor-hall" becomes diminished as "a little man" who, the next stanza goes on to say, the narrator has heard "once was tall." The building of a heroic portrait is momentarily aborted here, and the theme of continuity (and proximity—"*not far* from pleasant Ivor-hall") between young and old Simon is countered by the observation of discontinuity between his present and former statures. A similar interruption qualifies Simon's preservation of his fair livery-coat in the next stanza, for despite the fairness of this appearance, the narrator assures us: "Yet meet him where you will, you see / At once that he is poor." We may begin to expect a narration here in which the narrator introduces appearances of continuity with the world of Simon's youth only to undercut them with the reality of Simon's present condition, but this is not exactly how the telling works. Even the two instances we have already considered work in different ways, for the first undercuts the manner of ballad narration by observing the present fact of Simon's littleness only to disturb that fact by introducing hearsay of a previous condition—his tallness; the second undermines an apparent continuity with the past (the fairness of the livery-coat) by noting a presently observable condition—his poverty. The second stanza goes on to make matters more complicated by seeming to shift its emphasis back to continuity despite the existence of present deterioration: "Full five and twenty years he lived / A running huntsman merry; / And though he has but one eye left, / His cheek is like a cherry." In the last two lines it is the lost eye that is conceded and the continuing redness of his cheek that is asserted, though both conditions are presently observable. Two stanzas later, however, the narrator points out only that "His hunting feats have him bereft / Of his right eye, as you may see." The narrator is not maintaining a consistent attitude toward what is apparent and what is real about Simon Lee.

Neither does he see steadily and comprehensively what persists from the past and what is irrevocably lost. The third stanza begins celebrating the prowess, joy, and fame of Simon in his prime but shifts midway to declare the final demise of the world in which his feats had meaning:

> His master's dead, and no one now
> Dwells in the hall of Ivor;
> Men, dogs and horses, all are dead;
> He is the sole survivor.

This declaration is followed by two stanzas shifting attention among present physical conditions, childlessness, and economic straits as if it had put the ballad world of the hunt out of the way once and for all. But the development of these topics is interrupted by the sixth stanza, the only whole stanza devoted to celebrating Simon's feats and establishing the continuity of his past and present pleasures. Its last four lines read:

> And still there's something in the world
> At which his heart rejoices;
> For when the chiming hounds are out,
> He dearly loves their voices!

Even if Ivor-hall is deserted, and its "men, dogs, and horses, all are dead," the hunt still lives and dogs still cry out. The institution that organized Simon's life, that unsuited him for "husbandry or tillage," that exacted the sacrifice of his right eye and ruined his ankles persists in the present and remains a source of joy to Simon Lee. The narrator's exaggerated report of its death is countered by his report of its persistence for Simon. Even if we did not have Wordsworth's testimony to Isabella Fenwick that "the expression when the hounds were out, 'I dearly love their voices' was a word from his own lips" (LB, p. 284), we would recognize that this perspective must come not from seeing Simon Lee or from hearing what others say about him but from hearing him tell what his life means to him. Though the narrator does not relate Simon's words directly anywhere in his narration, he speaks here under their influence and grants Simon that dignity which comes from participating in the "grand elementary principle of pleasure" in the light of which his own view of his life is "accompanied by an overbalance of enjoyment" (*LB*, p. 258).

The narrator, however, has seen, as he insists his reader may see, the poverty Simon's livery coat cannot cover and the decrepit limbs his hunting "feats have left"; he has heard Simon tell, as he says his readers can hear him tell, that "Few months of life he has in store"; he has ineffectually attempted, as he says his reader could ineffectually attempt, to "wean" Simon from his labor. He cannot shake the impression of futility that the sight of Simon's and his wife's efforts has left him with, and he cannot help but move from recognizing that " 'tis very little all / That they can do between them" to imagining that they can do nothing: "But what avails the land to them / Which they can till no longer?" Though he has related the perspective from which Simon's suffering takes its place in a still vital framework of meaning for Simon, he cannot participate in that perspective to the exclusion of what he saw and imagined that made him take the mattock from old Simon and strike the blow at the tangled root. He cannot choose between telling the romantic ballad of Simon's continuing pleasure in the disappearing world that gives meaning to his condition and telling the "tragedy of infirmity and poverty [framed] in the larger social tragedy of the decaying countryside" (*Simple Wordsworth*, p. 43) against which he struck his own futile blow. Neither is merely the appearance of which the other is the reality; both tales reveal the meaning of Simon Lee, the old huntsman, to the narrator who has seen him, heard him, and tried to help him.

They do not, however, add up to a single tale, at least not without our knowing what motivates the narrator to tell them as he does. As they stand in the edition of 1798, they fail to satisfy the expectation that "Some tale will be related," not so much because they do not issue in the relation of some "moving accident" (cf. Hartman, *Wordsworth's Poetry*, p. 149, and Averill, p. 164) as because they do not resolve into a single point or meaning the change in Simon Lee that both tales reveal. If the "running huntsman merry" is now an old man barely subsisting on a scrap of land, is the point that he and his human meaning have been so tragically reduced or that he still takes pleasure in the cry of the hounds and finds meaning in the wounds he has incurred following them?

Unable to decide this question and aware that his conventional responsibilities as a tale-teller obligate him to decide it, the narrator appeals for his reader's cooperation:

My gentle reader, I perceive
How patiently you've waited,
And I'm afraid that you expect

Some tale will be related.

O reader! had you in your mind
Such stores as silent thought can bring,
O gentle reader! you would find
A tale in every thing.
What more I have to say is short,
I hope you'll kindly take it;
It is no tale; but should you think,
Perhaps a tale you'll make it.

Though this gesture has been taken as "almost slily calculated" (*Simple Wordsworth*, p. 44), I think it is more plausible to see it as the mark of "a poet in difficulties, exposed before an audience that he would like to please" ("Imaginative Story," p. 399). Griffin, who takes the gesture in this second light as "a characteristically fumbling apology" (p. 399) does not, however, recognize the cause of the difficulties or their pattern. Far from drawing the conflicting stories he tells "at random from the unsorted contents of his mind," the narrator tells the story as he does because of what he has done to Simon, why he has done it, and what he has recognized in doing it. His point is not, it turns out, a general one but a personal one, and he must beg the reader's kindness in taking it and his thoughtfulness in making it a tale, not, I think, because he knows what the tale is and is not telling but because he knows that there is a tale in what he has done and said and cannot tell it himself. His turn after his impassioned appeal[9] to relating his own ambivalent encounter with Simon Lee puts the reader in the position of judging not just the tale he has told but the deed he has done. He puts himself on the line not just as a poet but as a man and appeals for the kindness and thoughtfulness of others after recognizing his own thoughtless unkindness. If he is vehement in valuing "such stores as silent thought can bring" and their power to make one discover "A tale in every thing," it is not merely to shift the burden of responsibility for making his tale to his reader but to acknowledge his own failure to think and recognize the tale in Simon Lee's condition. In responding to the decrepitude and poverty that is there for all to see, he overlooked the tale of Simon's meaning to himself and treated him unkindly. In urging his gentle reader to think and discover the tale that even such brute facts as Simon's "poor old ancles" tell, he urges on his reader a thoughtful kindness that, in recovering Simon's meaning, redeems the narrator's deed and his tale.

The reader who has taken the place of the invoked reader of "Simon Lee," who has learned to find a tale in every thing by thinking, will be prepared to find a tale in a thorn and to contribute a share of thought to making it but will not be prepared to assume the role in which the narrator of "The Thorn" casts his listener. One who has begun to take thought at the discrepancies involved in a little man's once being tall or in an old man's saying he is seventy while others say he is eighty will be reluctant to take the position of one who thinks an old thorn so old that he would find it "hard to say / How it could ever have been young." One who has been sensitized to the way the narrator of "Simon Lee" transforms his subject by calling Simon's effort "So vain . . . That at the root of the old tree / He might have worked forever" will have no trouble recognizing the imaginative transformation of mosses which "clasp" a tree "So close, you'd say that they were bent / With plain and manifest intent / To drag it to the ground," though such a person may have difficulty identifying with the "you" who is supposed to say it.

The speaker who is imagining that his listener would find it hard or easy to say these things is not only investing these objects with his own imaginative energy but also projecting the product of his imaginative work on his listener. He is not calling for a listener who fills out the meaning of what the speaker says with his own thought and imagination but for a reader who will own the products of the speaker's imagination as unselfconsciously as the speaker has produced them. Indeed, he expects his listener to respond to these products of the speaker's excited mind as if they were not products of a mind at all but descriptions of things charged with meanings independent of the mind that has characterized them, as if what the speaker says about them is what "you'd say" or what anyone would say in seeing these things. The superstitious narrator does not recognize or expect his listener to recognize his or her mind's contributions to his descriptions, as if what the narrator had half-created were wholly perceived.[10]

The reader who has learned to discriminate the mind's products from the objects on which they are based already shares with the poet, who makes this discrimination and represents some of his narrators and lyric speakers making it, a "vantage ground" from which to view the narrator of "The Thorn" and his interlocutor.[11] The narrator can distinguish what he "knows" from what he has been told, but he cannot and does not ever distinguish what he has imagined from what he has seen and heard. The interlocutor, who questions the narrator vigorously and repeatedly about the why's and wherefore's of the things he has mentioned, never thinks to ask him, "But what's the thorn, and what's the pond, and what's the hill of moss to *you?*" As much as the narrator upon whose accounts he depends, he takes the narrator's imaginative perceptions as givens from which further inquiry can proceed, not as objects of critical examination. The critical reader, who has learned from Wordsworth (or from Shakespeare or from introspection or from some other source) to attend closely to the way the mind selects and transforms objects in characterizing them, can no more find himself in the interlocutor than the poet who represented himself speaking in "Simon Lee" or "Tintern Abbey" can be identified with this narrator. Even without Wordsworth's care from the beginning to inform his reader that "The Thorn" "is not supposed to be spoken in the author's own person" (*LB*, p. 8), it should be impossible to imagine an author identified with the narrator of this poem who could have written any of the rest of Wordsworth's ballad experiments.

Far from being impossible to imagine, however, the identity or at least the analogy of poet and narrator has been a compelling topic for many readers of the poem, who have returned to it in essay after essay almost like Martha Ray returning to the thorn. Not only does the narrator's imagination seem to them to reveal Wordsworth's imagination, but the poem seems to reveal in its starkest outlines the pattern of Wordsworth's relation to the suffering human subjects in his other poems, no matter how those relations may elsewhere be decorously prettified and fictionalized.[12] It is ironic that the one poem whose speaker Wordsworth made a point to distinguish from himself has been taken more frequently than any of the other experimental ballads as a paradigm of his mind's handling of its objects. And though there are familiar psychological patterns that could make such an irony plausible, there is far less evidence of telltale vehement denial of the identification on Wordsworth's part than there is evidence of strained, gratuitous insistence upon it on the part of his readers. Far from taking the trouble to protect himself from the connection, he provided in his note on the poem the link between its narrator and the imagination that suggested it, and in the Fenwick note many years later he revealed the exciting fact that there *was* a thorn that impressed him and provoked him to invent the poem in which there *is* a thorn that impresses his narrator and provokes him to tell about it. This has been enough for his readers to build their tales on, as the sight of Martha Ray's face was enough for the narrator, but the resemblance thus established between poet and narrator should not be allowed to obscure what distinguishes them. Wordsworth knows the difference between his impression of the thorn and his invention of a vehicle to convey it; his narrator does not. Wordsworth presents for his readers' enjoyment a "picture" and a "character" to describe it; the character he invents can only share the impression he does not know he has modified and urge his listener to go where he has been and see what he imagines he has seen.

The narrator of "The Thorn" speaks as neither poet nor tale-teller but as one who has been impressed by something it would be "worth your while" to see, an extraordinary appearance to which he directs his listener's attention and anticipates his listener's responses. He presents the thorn and the mound as things of such unusual wretchedness and unusual beauty that "you" would want to see them and would in seeing them share his estimate of their unusualness. He presents the "little muddy pond," however, without embellishment and exaggeration. It is as prosaic as the other features of the scene are significant; he has measured it, but he has not perceived it in terms of the intensifying metaphors and similes that heighten his description of thorn and mound.

He goes on to introduce "A woman in a scarlet cloak," who sits between this pond and the hill of moss, as a reason to choose carefully "your time" to cross the mountain where the scene is located, and he dwells on her and her cry as if they were the most important features of the extraordinary scene he recommends to his listener's attention. Like thorn and mound she is heightened by his descriptions to an extraordinary figure who haunts the spot at all times and seasons, known to all the personified stars and winds that observe her there. The narrator's description of her and repetition of her cry is so compelling that it provokes a response from a represented listener, who takes her not just as the most extraordinary feature of an extraordinary scene but as a "poor woman" whose persistent returning to the "dreary mountaintop" and sitting by the thorn and repeating her "doleful cry" calls for an explanation. From the qualifying adjectives the listener adds to "woman," "thorn," and "cry," and from the kinds of questions he asks, it seems that his interest is not so much in seeing the scene ("dreary") as in understanding the woman, whom he takes not as an amazing sight but as a pitiful human being.

In response to this interruption the narrator clarifies his purpose in mentioning the woman and in telling of the spot. He did not intend to divert interest to her (though certainly he has done so by dwelling on her and her cry), and he "cannot tell" the tale that explains her condition, "For the true reason no one knows." In any event his concern was with his listener's seeing "The spot to which she goes," and his point in mentioning her was to teach him not how to find her there but how to *avoid* finding her: "I never heard of such as dare / Approach the spot when she is there," he adds. His listener, however, confirming his human interest by adding the adjective "unhappy" to the woman, still wants to know why she goes there more than he wants to go himself, and he compels the narrator to take a new approach to his subject. Though the narrator says it is "all in vain" to "rack your brain" with such questions, he agrees to "tell you every thing I know." He keeps his original focus at the same time, however, by expressing his wish that his listener "would go" to the thorn "and to the pond / Which is a little step beyond" since being there he "may trace" something of "her tale," more of it, he implies, than he is able to tell. All that he can tell is no more than a "help" to prepare his listener for the journey up the mountain (see Owen, " 'The Thorn,' " pp. 4–5).

It is important, I think, that the narrator does not here or elsewhere accept the responsibility for telling a tale or acknowledge the expectation that a tale will be related, though he has created that expectation by introducing a person in a place and in a condition that require explanation. He does not presume to explain why the woman is reduced to the condition she is in, as the narrator of "Goody Blake and Harry Gill" sets out to explain Harry's chattering teeth, nor does he invite his listener to make a tale of his telling, as does the narrator of "Simon Lee." What "tale" there is his listener must "trace" for himself at the place the narrator has told him about. He cannot "make" anything of all he knows, however much he thinks (racks his brain) about it, and he does not imagine that his reader can make out any more than he can by thinking any harder or better.

What he offers to share is not a meaning for the woman or the thorn but a sense of meaningfulness he finds in them, and the help he goes on to give his listener in the remainder of his utterance does not violate that sense by providing a plausible tale to account for the woman's or his own fascination with the spot. Though the village sources on which he draws are sure enough of what happened to try to bring the woman to justice, the narrator repeatedly "cannot tell" or "cannot think" that their story is adequate to his impression. And though he reveals that he has been to the spot and seen the woman's face and heard her cry, he turned to flee the spot and did not ask her to explain her cry and tell her own story, as the narrators of so many of the other poems ask the sufferers they meet to tell what ails them. Instead of imagining the meaning of her cry or finding out what it means to her or accepting what it means to the others, he repeats it as a thing fascinating in itself; instead of explaining the thorn and why she goes there, he returns to affirming his original impression of its being "bound / With heavy tufts of moss that strive to drag it to the ground."

Despite his listener's final outburst of questions, the only hope the narrator holds out for a gain in understanding is in the listener's going to the pond, for "Some say" that if you go to this one part of the scene which has so far escaped the narrator's amplification

And fix on it a steady view,
The shadow of a babe you trace,
A baby and a baby's face,
And that it looks at you;
Whene'er you look on it, 'tis plain
The baby looks at you again.

This response of the pond to the observer's glance has apparently so far escaped the narrator, who has described it only as "a little muddy pond / Of water, never dry," and the intensity with which he urges his listener to go to the spot must be connected with his hope that the tale the listener "may trace" there will include his tracing this shadow of a baby's face ("you . . . may trace" in X becomes "you trace" in XXI—the word "trace" appears nowhere else in the poem). The listener might be the one to trace the tale that the narrator with his ruler and the villagers with their shovels have not been able to discover.

The form of this anticipated discovery, as others have noticed, sub-stitutes the baby's face and his actively returned look for the onlooker's own reflection in the pond, as he intently views it.[13] Though this emblem has been subjected to elaborate and ambiguous allegorization, I think its shimmering can be steadied if we distinguish the narrator's per-spective from those of the villagers and the poet. While the narrator hopes for a confirmation of the uncanniness of the spot in another's discovery of portentousness where he has so far found none, the vil-lagers take the baby's appearance as confirmation of their case against Martha Ray; the poet, however, can be imagined to take this unrecog-nizing recognition scene as a model of the imaginative process by which the narrator and the villagers have filled the scene with meaning without recognizing their own roles in doing so. For Wordsworth, anyone who thinks he sees something other than his own reflection looking back at him from the pond has informed that reflection with his own imaginative activity and fails to see his own mind where it is most active. To see your face reflected in the water requires no particular thought, but to see your mind reflected in the uncanny transformation of your image into a baby's face requires active self-critical awareness. As much as the narrator lacks this awareness and does not imagine it in his listener, Wordsworth has it and requires it of a reader who would appreciate his poem. His steady view does not uncritically share the narrator's self-titillating superstition or the villagers' willingness to believe and act on what they imagine; rather it makes available what they have made and the power by which they have made it, even what Wordsworth has made and the power by which he has made it, to our own critical participation.

Wordsworth's experimental tales pose a double problem even for the critical reader he requires. Not only do they depart as a group from satisfying conventional expectations but they also depart individually from satisfying the expectations raised by reading other poems in the group. As we have seen, the reader who has accustomed himself to think at the urging of the narrators of "Goody Blake" and "Simon Lee" must be disconcerted by the demands of the narrator of "The Thorn" to share his obsessions and trace the images he desires. Generalizing in the other direction, from "The Thorn" to the other poems—the more common procedure, as we have seen—produces equally strange results. Attempts to characterize a typical Wordsworthian paradigm to replace the conventions he has challenged seem to founder on the range of his experimental works. Too often our legitimate efforts to carry expectations from better-known to less well known poems in the collection have led us either to reduce the unknown to conformity or to reject it for non-conformity to the paradigm we have applied. At the level of the collection of poems as well as at the levels of meter and diction, "the accuracy with which similitude in dissimilitude, and dissimilitude in similitude are perceived" (*LB*, p. 265) is the life of our reading, and we may recognize by now that each new poem we bring under consideration will resemble and differ from the others we have examined with unpredictable richness. Though we may become familiar with the lines along which the poems differ from or resemble each other, or the variables as a function of which they vary, we cannot establish the true Wordsworthian pattern of those lines or the typical Wordsworthian determination of those variables. His experiments are too radically diverse to reduce to a formula—to an unconventional convention by which we can return to the comfort of familiar expectations on a higher ground than before.

In the present context, having read the first three tales from the 1798 *Lyrical Ballads* in the order in which they appear (and ignoring for the moment all the complications that would have affected us had we read the poems that are *not* tales), we arrive at "The Idiot Boy" and discover interesting departures from most of the expectations we may have formed. The narrator of this tale is so involved in his characters and in his telling that he makes almost no overt demands on his reader like the very different demands made by the narrators of "Simon Lee" and "The Thorn." He is so close to his heroes that he cites no testimony of neighbors, of specified or unspecified others, of the characters themselves, or of his own to establish what happened or what is the case. Indeed, it seems wrong through most of the poem to talk about what *happened*, because the events of the poem seem to be happening as they are told. They are not offered to account for a phenomenon or a figure or an object that "you may see" or that others testify to having seen; they are not tied to a place at all but occur only on the "clear March night" on which the narrator may also be telling them.

His telling, furthermore, is not just a function of his relations to his readers and to his subjects and of his individual intentions, for his declared intention to tell his reader a "delightful tale" of his hero's adventures is thwarted by the muses to whom he appeals to let him tell it. In language reminiscent of the narrator's appeal to his reader in "Simon Lee," the narrator of "The Idiot Boy" appeals to his "gentle muses" for "kind" treatment, but the transfer of this language and of the appeal itself to this new object raises plenty of questions. We have not, after all, run across muses before in this collection, and the muses we do know from elsewhere are not customarily addressed in such human terms. If the appeal for kindness from gentle *readers* implies, as Danby suggests, a recognition of the claims of shared humanity for "an equality that stands not on rightful demands so much as on reciprocal indulgences" (*Simple Wordsworth*, p. 45), these muses must be more like the narrator and like us than we are accustomed to imagine.

Their powers do seem limited, though not inconsiderable. They do not bestow omniscience on their apprentice or give him license to invent delightful fantasies, but they seem to give him an immediate relation to the actions of his heroes and a heightened sensitivity to their significant words and gestures that allow him to participate in their joys and fears. Though he imagines that the account of Betty Foy's movements and words he gives us "Would surely be a tedious tale" compared to the "delightful tale" of Johnny's "strange adventures" that he is not permitted to give us, his gift is to call attention to just those movements and words that communicate Betty's passion and to preserve those "very words" of Johnny's that epitomize the real strangeness of his adventure.[14] His muses are kinder than he imagines them to be in giving him a sensitivity to "human passions, human characters, and human incidents" (*LB*, p. 7) of greater interest than the stock-in-trade of supernatural balladeering for which he pleads.

Indeed, the range of human passions, characters, and incidents reveals itself to be greater than the narrator realizes, for it includes powers not only to transform perception but to work cures on the body, powers that are not any less wonderful because we recognize them to be our own (see Easson, p. 16). Old Susan's cure "As if by magic" reveals unexpected powers in the intense concern for others, and Johnny's account of his adventures produces as strange a reversal of normal situations as the narrator's fantasy of him turned backwards on his horse "All like a silent horseman-ghost." Betty herself would not have been any more moved had she seen a "goblin" or a "ghost" than she is to recognize "Him whom she loves, her idiot boy." Even the narrator, who made his appeal to tell supernatural adventures before all these marvels in his human tale revealed themselves, seems content in the end to report all Johnny's "travel's story" as if it were enough to satisfy him and the reader he is wishing to please. If the narrator of "The Thorn" gives his listener less than all his supernatural portents seem to promise, the narrator of "The Idiot Boy" gives his reader more than the supernatural adventures with which he hopes to please. Wordsworth, of course, gives his reader both poems to think about.

"Hart-Leap Well," the first poem of the 1800 volume of *Lyrical Ballads*, internalizes the sort of shift in expectations that we have recognized in moving from tale to tale in the 1798 volume. At the end of its first part its poet-narrator divides his telling into two related tales ("But there is matter for a second rhyme, / And I to this would add another tale") of two different kinds. Having related a tale of a romantic hunt in which a lone hunter, Sir Walter, follows a hart to its death and commemorates the spot where it died by building a pleasure house, the narrator begins his second tale disclaiming the intention to tell adventurous tales and identifying himself with the pastoral:

> The moving accident is not my trade,
> To freeze the blood I have no ready arts;
> 'Tis my delight alone in summer shade,
> To pipe a simple song to thinking hearts.

Leaving behind his tale of adventure, he begins his pastoral by telling of coming upon a scene which raised "various thoughts and fancies" in his mind and of seeing "one who was in shepherd's garb attir'd." The shepherd, it turns out, is the source of the tale of Sir Walter that the poet-narrator has just told. The poet tells of eliciting the tale from the shepherd to discover "what this place might be" in which nature seemed "willing to decay" and man had left behind unmistakable signs of his former presence (" 'Here in old time the hand of man has been' ").

If the shepherd is the source of the adventurous tale and the poet-narrator has more affinities with the pastoral tale he is now telling than with the adventures he has just told, we might have expected the narrator to present the adventure as the shepherd's tale, keeping the romantic adventure subordinated within a pastoral framework. However, as Parrish has noted, "the story of the chase (Part I) is not put into the shepherd's mouth but is related directly by the poet—the shepherd is allowed to speak only afterward." Parrish, who thinks this poem abandons some of the "more daring and original" techniques of the 1798 poems, goes on to suggest that in the first part "our interest focuses on its incidents, not on the speaker's psychology" (*Art*, p. 132). His dramatic presuppositions lead him to focus interest on the motives of the dramatized character and to lose interest in "psychology" when the narrator speaks; but if we attend, as we have done before, to the motives of the narrator as well, we may see Part I not as an unmediated presentation of events but as a telling with its own emphases related to the emphases that follow in Part II. The question we may then ask is, what difference does it make that the poet-narrator is made to "rehearse" the shepherd's tale of Sir Walter in his own words instead of reporting it as the shepherd told it?

What we hear of the shepherd's attitudes in the second part of the poem suggests that the tale of Sir Walter as we are given it in Part I has been significantly altered from any version he could have told. The shepherd's sympathies are all with " 'that unhappy Hart,' " the victim of Sir Walter's chase, and his attitude toward the memorial remains of Sir Walter's triumph and the Hart's prodigious leaps is one of superstitious horror. The work of Sir Walter's hand has, to the shepherd, polluted the natural scene, poisoning its waters and destroying its plant-life, and the scene will not recover its life and health until, as he has often said, " 'trees, and stones, and fountain all are gone.' " All signs of man's work upon the scene must be completely obliterated before its purity can be restored. The human power and purpose and will which altered the scene must be to him fearful violations of the pastoral values he celebrates—the love of place associated with early memories of rest, drink, music, mother, and birth.[15]

It would hardly be within the power of such a speaker to recount Sir Walter's hunt and his founding of the pleasure house with the sympathy the poet's narrative reveals. The poet's references to "that glorious day," "this glorious act," "a joyful case," and "that darling place" assume his hero's attitudes toward the events of the hunt without explicitly distinguishing them from his own, and his imagining of the knight's words of triumph and determination, like the words Wordsworth's speaker later attributes to the little girl in "The Pet-Lamb," show that he has "almost receiv'd" his hero's "heart into [his] own." It is the poet-narrator, after all, who embroiders Sir Walter's motives with the feeling of having seen something never seen " 'by living eyes' " before, with the desire not only to commemorate his own deed and the hart's prowess but to provide an arbor where travellers, pilgrims, and lovers may take shelter, and with the hubristic expectation that his " 'mansion with its arbor shall endure . . . till the foundations of the mountains fail' "—motives not unlike those which in other contexts at other times Wordsworth himself expressed about the originality of his perceptions, the intended readers of his poems, and the permanence of his achievement. That Wordsworth had already in the first version of *The Prelude* discovered sources of his poetic power in his youthful lone pursuits of the woodcock or the raven's nest only corroborates the internal evidence for the sympathy which a poet such as he was might have for a hero like Sir Walter. His poet-narrator's "small difference" from the shepherd is not merely that he, "as a member of the educated class, . . . cannot really accept the Shepherd's superstitious belief that the place is cursed" (Averill,

Suffering, p. 221) but that he sympathizes with and in part resembles the Sir Walter he invents, while the shepherd has nothing in common with such a figure.

Indeed, the poet-narrator as a pursuer of natural energies and a constructer of artificial objects meant to memorialize those energies and provide future pleasure, takes a kind of interest in Sir Walter's story that the shepherd, a man of unaltered nature, does not take. He values the ruins, which the shepherd wishes were not defacing the natural scene, as signs of a human activity like his own, calling for imaginative reconstruction, and yielding knowledge of "what we are, and have been," and he envisions a Nature which takes an interest not only in the death of "quiet creatures" like the hart but in the preservation of monuments made by noisy creatures like us who act upon and alter the face of what the shepherd takes to be nature.[16] Though he shares with the shepherd a sensitivity to the pathos of the hart's situation (he speaks of the "poor Hart" even in his account of Sir Walter's hunt, while Sir Walter himself is made to imagine only a " 'gallant brute' " like himself), his more comprehensive vision allows Nature both the power to overgrow the evidences of human action and the intent to preserve the memory of it for those contemplative men who, like the poet, herald the "milder day" when even such recollections will not be necessary.

But his ability to herald that day does not make him a man of that future only; he can see too clearly into the motives of a man like Sir Walter to be free of them himself. When he offers to "divide" with the shepherd the lesson, "Never to blend our pleasure or our pride / With sorrow of the meanest thing that feels," one may suspect that the poet-narrator would end up with the larger share. Like the speaker of "Nutting," who warns the "Maiden" to "move along these shades / In gentleness of heart with gentle hand / Touch," he admonishes one who does not know the temptation as he does and needs the lesson less. Only if we have seen that the narrator's character and sympathies are as evident in the first part of this poem as in the last will we recognize this motive in his moral and appreciate the need he has to utter it. The division of his tale represents a division of his mind that a report of the shepherd's tale alone could not have revealed, and his declarations of intention to shepherd and reader alike express his wishes for a simpler tale and purer pleasure than he in fact enjoys.

The complexity of the narrator's interest in the "unhappy Hart" and the hunter who pursued it to the death in "Hart-Leap Well" is matched by that of the narrator's interest in "Ill-fated Ruth" and the young man who betrayed her to madness in "Ruth."[17] In both poems a narrator sympathetically portrays a simple victim closely associated with nature and a hunter or wooer of the victim moved by the complex human motives of pleasure and pride. Indeed, in both poems the narrator devotes the greatest part of his imaginative energy to realizing the motives of the pursuer and thinking about the portrait he has imagined, while consigning the fate and ultimate care for the victims to divine powers who love them and will help them. The narrator of "Ruth" is as thoughtfully sympathetic with the "Stripling" who betrays Ruth as the narrator of "Hart-Leap Well" is with the knight who hunts the deer, and he is as pious in his disposition of Ruth to Christian burial as the other is in his leaving the deer to "sympathy divine."

The final appeals to a power beyond humanity to care for the victims in these poems does not, however, preclude sympathy with them as suffering beings, animal and human. The narrator of "Hart-Leap Well" has presented the hart's humanized suffering through the shepherd's account of the hunt, and the narrator of "Ruth" follows Ruth through the period of her weeping and mourning, from the six months of her developing madness to the time of her imprisonment when, "exulting in her wrongs / Among the music of her songs / She fearfully carouz'd." The narrator of "Ruth" acknowledges this woe, even enters into it, but his emphasis is as much on the amelioration of it as the emphasis of the narrator of "The Thorn" is on the unrelieved suffering of Martha Ray. After the one stanza in which he vividly imagines Ruth's fearful carousing, he goes on in the next five stanzas to emphasize that "Sometimes milder hours she knew," that "There came a respite of her pain," that "Among the fields she breathed again," that she still loved the natural objects with which she grew up "Nor ever tax'd them with the ill / Which had been done to her." In the next stanza he claims ("And in this tale we all agree," he adds) that in the summer months "She sleeps beneath the greenwood tree / And other home hath none." As if Wordsworth were producing a counterimage to that of Martha Ray beside the stunted thorn, he has his narrator present Ruth here peacefully sleeping beneath a tree associated with the green world of revitalization. These villagers are in as much agreement about Ruth's peaceful sleep there as the others are about Martha Ray's burial of her infant under the hill of moss, and they hear the self-consoling notes of her flute as the villagers in "The Thorn" claim to hear Martha's inconsolable cry coming from the mountaintop. The narrator here is at pains to establish Ruth's return to the same pastimes she enjoyed as "A young and happy Child," not without recognition that "she had wept" and "she had mourned" since then, but with a clear emphasis on the comfort she takes in nature, not on her fearful woe.

Yet the comforts of nature that the narrator emphasizes seem to be insufficient for him, even as the "thoughtless freedom" of Ruth's life as an "infant of the woods" seems to have been insufficient for her before her suffering. The young man who betrays her has made his entire appeal to her in terms of natural pleasures and natural bonds, but Ruth, in the one speech that seems to belong to her in the whole poem, adds to her acceptance of his invitation to "drive the flying deer" the condition that she join him in "lawful joy, and bear / His name in the wild woods." She says,

> "And now, as fitting is and right,
> We in the Church our faith will plight,
> A Husband and a Wife."

She is not satisfied to join him solely in terms of their shared participation in nature but wishes for the legitimation of civil and religious ordinances. She wants not just the pleasure of the chase but the security of a shared name and recognized bond—a family to replace the one she has lost. Ruth has come to nature late (four years later than the Lucy of "Three Years She Grew") and on the rebound—a slighted child in flight from a stepmother—and though she behaves "As if she from her birth had been / An Infant of the woods," she has not been. Nature to her even at the first is not "all in all" but a refuge from half-desolation.

In the end, after all she has been through, the narrator seems to take on her attitude to the sufficiency of the natural comforts he has so fully described. In bidding her farewell after presenting his last image of her still playing her childish games at the riverside, he declares:

> Ill-fated Ruth! in hallow'd mold
> Thy corpse shall buried be,
> For thee a funeral bell shall ring,
> And all the congregation sing
> A Christian psalm for thee.

The care of "Nature," which seems to have been sufficient for the poor hart to the narrator of "Hart-Leap Well," is not sufficient for the human sufferer Ruth to the teller of her tale. A sanctioned burial—not the un-hallowed burial of the suicide—with proper ceremony and psalm by the church family seems necessary to put her suffering to rest. Though nature soothes and eases her pain, it does not satisfactorily place it in a framework of meaning. Though nature has not betrayed the heart that loved her and has remained a source of pleasure and love even in her grief, man has betrayed Ruth more than once and seems unable to help her or make sense of her pain without appealing as an unidentified voice in the poem does, when her pains begin: " 'God help thee Ruth!' "

If the narrator has found nature important to Ruth's comfort but in-adequate to make sense of her suffering, he has also found it central to

her last betrayer's attractiveness (to him as well as to Ruth) but insufficient to prevent his corruption of his soul and his desertion of Ruth.
This young man seems to have had all the benefits of an upbringing in
nature:

> —While he was yet a Boy
> The moon, the glory of the sun,
> And streams that murmur as they run
> Had been his dearest joy.

He has the beauty and gaiety of natural beings and has the "hues of
genius on his cheek" and in his speech. His attractiveness to "any Maid"
is clear enough, and his attractiveness to Ruth, who herself has lived
close to nature "In thoughtless freedom bold," would seem even clearer.

When the narrator turns from presenting the youth's successful court-
ship to explaining his betrayal of Ruth, he takes some pains to isolate
the cause of the corruption of "a Youth to whom was given / So much
of earth so much of Heaven." Nature, which has been so much a part
of his life, may have been a contributing cause, but the narrator is careful
to say that if "The beauteous forms of Nature" might "feed voluptuous
thought," they do not themselves form the disposition to that thought.
Though the irregularities he found in the "tropic" climes

> Did to his mind impart
> A kindred impulse, seem'd allied
> To his own powers, and justified
> The workings of his heart

those workings seem to be the prior condition that found affinity in "the
tempest roaring high, / The tumult of a tropic sky." The narrator, indeed,
cannot imagine that someone so close to nature even "in his worst
pursuits" did not sometimes experience

> Pure hopes of high intent:
> For passions link'd to forms so fair
> And stately, needs must have their share
> Of noble sentiment.

And he believes that the young man wooed Ruth "with no feign'd
delight," for "What could he less than love a Maid / Whose heart with
so much nature play'd"? Finally the narrator locates the source of his
corruption not in the natural forms that may have fed it but in the
company he kept and the choice he made to receive their vices:

> But ill he liv'd, much evil saw
> With men to whom no better law
> Nor better life was known;

Deliberately and undeceiv'd
Those wild men's vices he receiv'd,
And gave them back his own.

His genius and his moral frame
Were thus impair'd. . . .

Nature that has given him so much does not make the choice he makes to use his gifts to "seek what the degraded soul / Unworthily admires," and so nature does not corrupt him or betray Ruth through him, though it is powerless to save her from him.[18]

Of all the narrators we have considered so far, the narrator of "Ruth" is the only one who unambiguously identifies in his portrait of Ruth's betrayer a domain of human choice with tragic implications. Harry Gill's obsession with Goody Blake is presented as sui generis and its fixation in his chattering teeth completes its course without symbolizing a choice he has made. The narrator of "Simon Lee" presents himself as coming close to a tragic recognition of what his apparent act of charity has meant to Simon, but his response to what he has done is to appeal for a thoughtful kindness that can redeem his deed. The narrator of "The Thorn," not knowing his own responsibility for what he imagines but thinks he sees, is no better at recognizing moral responsibility. He presents a counterpart of Ruth's betrayer in Stephen Hill, but he penetrates Stephen's condition no more than to call him "Unthinking" and responds to him no more thoughtfully than to wish that "he had died, that cruel father!" He dissociates himself from the villagers' efforts to treat Martha Ray as responsible for her actions, preserving the exciting uncertainty on which his mind thrives. The narrator of "The Idiot Boy" comes near to framing Betty Foy's foolish risk-taking with her idiot boy in moral terms, but when he seems about to say that "There's not a mother, no not one, / But when she hears what you have done" would be quick to blame you, he says instead, "Oh! Betty she'll be in a fright." Judgment is deflected and anxiety for another's welfare prevails, anxiety which before the poem is over reveals itself to have curative powers. The muses that govern this poem keep matters well away from moral terms that would interfere with the flow of sympathy and from tragic events that might call for judgment. Finally, in "Hart-Leap Well" the narrator, who presents himself as closer to the shepherd than his tale of Sir Walter's hunt suggests he is, manages to enjoy his identification with Sir Walter without taking responsibility for it and gets off with no more than a slap on the wrist, a "lesson" of which he takes the lion's share. Nature in any case is powerful and immanent enough in his creed to register and take care of the hart's death—a wronged human being would be another matter.

In such a case, as we have seen for the narrator of "Ruth," the gifts and compensations of nature, though valuable and important to insist upon, do not take care either of Ruth's suffering or her betrayer's flight from the commitments he made to her. This narrator, entering sympathetically into the minds and characters of his hero and heroine, finds a point in both where nature alone does not account for what is there and where man on his own has failed. In response to this recognition he turns, as bearers of tragic vision have always done, to appeal in the midst of the action to God and to end with a congregation singing in chorus at his heroine's funeral. Implicated in the human failings he is able to imagine, subject to the limits of natural comfort he perceives, he cannot redeem Ruth's suffering with his own song. The "Christian psalm" he imagines is needed to let her story rest.

"Michael," the last poem in the second volume of *Lyrical Ballads* and the last one whose speaker is concerned to tell a "tale," seems set apart from the rest of the collection, and even more from the other tales we have examined. It appears in closest proximity to the five "Poems on the Naming of Places" with which it shares its blank verse and its concern for rural places "where little Incidents will have occurred, or feelings been expressed, which will have given to such places a private and peculiar interest" (*LB*, p. 217). Its blank verse also links it to the inscriptions with which it shares epitaphic and commemorative gestures, to "Tintern Abbey" which has the analogous place at the end of the first volume, to "The Brothers" with which it shares the author's designation of "pastoral poem," to "Old Man Travelling" and "The Old Cumberland Beggar" whose poet-narrators similarly dignify their aged heroes, and to "There was a Boy" and "Nutting" which are linked as is "Michael" to the themes and emphases of *The Prelude*. Its association with the other tales is not the first one it evokes, especially since it has enjoyed a success with critics unmatched by any of them. When it is not celebrated entirely without connection to them, it is usually distinguished from them in terms that attempt to explain its success and their failure. It is "cleanly told with the least intervention of the author" and proceeds in "a straightforward manner" with "only the shadow of a narrator" or one who only "unobtrusively reminds the reader that the story is, so to speak, second-hand."[19] It is thought to conform, as the other tales do not, to the Aristotelian canons of minimal narratorial presence that so many of the other poems egregiously violate, and its exceptional success is found both in this conformity and in the superior dignity which its blank verse has over the "arch jog-trot of the ballads."[20]

Though I have made a point of distinguishing the other tales from one another and of denying any single pattern to which all of them can be reduced, I think it is necessary to argue the similarities between them and "Michael." To do so is not just to discover the special achievement of this poem but also to recognize it as an achievement in the same kind as the others. It is not a uniquely fine poem that alone subordinates its teller to the tale he tells but a fine poem that realizes one integral and interesting relation of teller, hero, and listener among several that Wordsworth represents. "Michael" is not the *telos* against whose achievement the other tales can be measured any more than it is one more work whose artistry can be undressed by reduction to the pattern of "The Thorn." It is rather the longest, the most elevated, and the last-presented of a series of experiments in *Lyrical Ballads* that represent attempts to tell tales of other people's joys and sorrows. If its narrator seems to succeed in his attempt more than with some of the others we have examined, it is not because he absents himself from attention but because he presents himself as subject to different constraints. Because he stands in a different relation to his hero and his listeners than the narrators of the other tales, he can present his "Tale" with a capital "T" with more assurance and poise than some of them display. But to represent assured telling is in itself no more interesting than to represent anxious telling. Both are interesting as they reveal the conditions that constrain them and the dynamic interrelations of speaker, hero, and listener they involve.

The narrator of "Michael" can identify his telling as a "Tale" at the outset because he stands at a greater temporal distance from his hero than any of the narrators we have considered, except, in one respect, the narrator of "Hart-Leap Well." The narrators of "Ruth," "The Thorn," and "Simon Lee" have all seen the heroes or heroines of their tales; the latter two have even encountered them, though the one flees from interaction while the other actually speaks to, acts upon, and registers the response of the old huntsman. The narrator of "Goody Blake" is a contemporary of the still living Harry Gill, though he does not claim to have seen or met him. The narrator of "The Idiot Boy" enjoys the immediate presence of his characters through the agency of his muses so that the question of his actual familiarity with them as neighbors or village figures or people of whom he has heard does not arise. Only Sir Walter of "Hart-Leap Well" is more distant in time from the narrator of his tale than Michael is from the narrator of his, but the narrator of "Hart-Leap Well" has recently come upon the scene of Sir Walter's adventure and met the shepherd who told him the tale. The narrator of "Michael" recalls a tale that touched him while he "was yet a boy" so that not only the hero of his tale but also the source of it do not immediately impinge upon his telling. He must be thought to recall it and the place to which it "appertains" for a conscious present purpose and not under the fresh impression of the place (like the narrator of "The Thorn") or the person (like the narrator of "Simon Lee") or of the source (like the narrator of "Hart-Leap Well"). Indeed it is likely that while he "was yet a boy" and first heard this tale, he was more impressed by the fortunes of the boy in the tale, Luke, whose motives and fate he now minimizes to concentrate on the father with whose position he presently analogizes his own.

The analogy he sets up—one implying a comparison between his attempt to leave this tale as a legacy to "youthful poets, who among these hills / Will be my second self when I am gone" and Michael's attempt to leave his portion of the hills themselves to his son Luke—introduces a conscious design on at least one group of his readers that further constrains his telling into the formal shape of a tale.[21] Property cannot be passed on to others if its boundaries are not delimited. It must be mastered and possessed by someone before it can be handed on to someone else, demanding a self-possession in the one who receives it and passes it on that few of the other narrators exhibit. The narrator of "Simon Lee" is not in control of his tale and appeals to his reader to help make it; the narrator of "The Thorn" is possessed by a scene and wants his listener to be possessed by it too; the narrator of "The Idiot Boy" is possessed by his muses; the narrator of "Hart-Leap Well" is possessed by his imaginative sympathy with Sir Walter to tell the sort of tale it is not his "trade" to tell; the narrator of "Ruth" is prepossessed by her unfaithful lover to devote the bulk of her story to him. Only the narrator of "Michael" in effect announces that "some tale will be related" and then goes on to relate it, confining himself to Michael's story (again property enters in) and sacrificing Luke's, though the latter raises many of the same interesting questions that Ruth's lover's story raises.[22] The narrator of "Michael" minds his trade better than Wordsworth's other narrators and makes a product he can offer for his readers' pleasure. Aware of what he has put into it, he is the only narrator who can speak of "my tale" in the satisfaction of deliberate craftsmanship.

It is not surprising that readers still waiting after two volumes to be pleased as they "have been accustomed to be pleased" (*LB*, p. 272) by narrative poetry arrive at "Michael" with relief and imagine that it is the "cleanly told" "straightforward" tale they have been wishing for all along. More satisfied with this than with all the other tales, such readers ignore or minimize the importance of its narratorial gestures after the opening verse paragraph.

The poem, however, is as rich in those gestures as any of the ballads except "The Thorn." In some ways it is even less sparing in its resort to them, for its gestures of substantiation take several lines of leisurely blank verse to accomplish something very close to what is managed in a brief tetrameter line in the ballads. Thus "I have convers'd with more than one who well / Remember the Old Man, and what he was" functions much like "As every man who knew her says" in "Goody Blake." Again "I may truly say, / That they were as a proverb in the vale / For endless industry," works like "To say the least, four counties round / Had heard of Simon Lee." The much praised "And never lifted up a single stone" is not usually read as part of a longer gesture of appeal to the testimony of Michael's neighbors, but that is what it is:

> 'Tis not forgotten yet
> The pity which was then in every heart
> For the Old Man—and 'tis believ'd by all
> That many and many a day he thither went,
> And never lifted up a single stone.

In its context this view of Michael is much like the narrators' presentations of their neighbors' unanimously held beliefs in "The Thorn" ("But all and each agree / The little babe is buried there / Beneath the hill of moss so fair") or in "Ruth" ["(And in this tale we all agree) / She sleeps beneath the greenwood tree"]. I do not present these parallels to argue the superior compactness of the ballad lines—I do not believe that the quality of lines can be meaningfully compared apart from the poems in whose represented speakers' utterances they function—but to show the common practice of narration in which "Michael" participates with the other experimental tales, even well after its prologue at the moments where its narrating is most admired. The narrators of all the tales we have examined except the muse-inspired "Idiot Boy" make some such gestures of substantiation, placing at least some of the facts and images they relate on common verifiable ground.

If the narrator of "Michael" departs from the practice of the other narrators in his manner of verifying aspects of his subject, he does so by completely excluding claims to direct personal experience that show up in all the others except the narrator of "The Idiot Boy." He presents his telling of the "Tale" of Michael as neither occasioned by a specific personal encounter with the ruined sheepfold nor validated by a personal sighting of or meeting with the hero but as told to him by others and confirmed by conversations with them. It is even told in part for the sake of those from whom he has learned it, for he acknowledges (until 1805 when Wordsworth cuts the passage) that he speaks so "minutely" of Michael's lamp to give pleasure to the many people "Whose memories will bear witness to my tale." He seems here to be consciously rendering back what he has received not indirectly to the next generation of poets but reciprocally to some of those from whom he has received it.

The passage I have just cited occurs at line 131 of the 1800 poem, reintroducing ninety lines after the prologue an additional audience to the two specified at the outset and an additional intention of the narrator's to please them. The gesture is made, however, not toward the audience it mentions but toward those readers who would otherwise imagine that the narrator's minute attention to the lamp was "a waste of words." The narrator does not tell his story primarily to his neighbors who already know it but to the "few natural hearts" and the "youthful Poets" he anticipates in the prologue, and he must explain to them what the neighbors already know and apologize to them for indulging those who still remember Michael.

His explanations to his uninitiated audience are numerous. He gives explicit directions to the unfinished sheepfold, for his listeners are strangers who might mistakenly "suppose" that the path up Greenhead Gill is a formidable one, and he calls attention to the "straggling heap of unhewn stones" they otherwise "might pass by, / Might see and notice not." He warns them that it would also be a mistake to "suppose / That the green Valleys, and the Streams and Rocks / Were things indifferent to the Shepherd's thoughts," though he politely avoids the second person this time and says only that "that man errs" who should suppose it. He mediates the language of Michael's community to listeners who might not understand it or might think the narrator himself talks it, calling attention to the "Shepherd's phrase, / With one foot in the grave," to what "in our rustic dialect was call'd / The CLIPPING TREE," to how "the House-wife phrased it" in describing Luke's letters as "The prettiest letters that were ever seen." He gives his listeners credit, however, for understanding "the general passions and thoughts and feelings of men" (*LB*, p. 261) if not the peculiar passions and thoughts and feelings of shepherds, allowing that "you will divine" that the five-year-old Luke was "Something between a hindrance and a help" to his father and acknowledging that there is really no need to relate (though he does so anyway) that Luke's presence made "the objects which the Shepherd loved before" dearer to him than they had previously been. All "natural hearts" should recognize this effect of a child on its father without being told, though they may not understand without assistance the peculiar language and passions of a shepherd like Michael.

The narrator of "Michael" is thus tactful in his explanations, though certainly not unobtrusive. He does not presume as does the overbearing narrator of "The Thorn" that his listeners will see what he sees or say what he would have them say. He does not confront his listeners directly with their mistaken suppositions as do the narrators of "Simon Lee" and "Ruth" but indirectly combats the suppositions of "that man" who should make the mistake. Perhaps most importantly he does not urge

anything on his listeners or share any wishes with them. He does not
tell them to think, as do the narrators of "Goody Blake" and "Simon
Lee," or to take care and choose carefully the time to go to the sheepfold
as does the narrator of "The Thorn." He does not express the wish to
tell a certain kind of story like the narrator of "The Idiot Boy" or the
wish that his listener would go to the spot of which he speaks like the
narrator of "The Thorn." He makes the possibility of seeing the spot
available in the last line, but that it "may be seen" compels no one to
see it nor even makes it worth their while to see it. The listeners, given
what the narrator has told them, must judge for themselves.

The narrator of "Michael" more than any of the others except the
narrator of "Hart-Leap Well" treats his listeners as people who can be
expected to understand the human interest in what he relates, people
who do not need to have the point of his tale explained.[23] It cannot be
the absence of his intrusions that pleases those who admire the poem,
but it may be the tactful respect his intrusions express. The narrator of
"Michael" is not flattering to his listeners, but he is considerate and
undemanding. He gives more than he asks, makes allowances for what
they do not know and leaves decisions up to them. The role he creates
for his listeners is easier to identify with than those created by Wordsworth's other narrators and more gratifying to our sense of ourselves
as people capable of judging his meaning on our own.

The impression of his tact toward and respect for his listener gains
by comparison not only with the narrators of the other tales but also by
comparison with his hero, who tells a tale to his son in the central episode
of the poem. Michael, on the scene at the sheepfold, turns to Luke to
relate "some little part / Of our two histories" in the confidence that
" 'twill do thee good / When thou art from me, even if I should speak /
Of things thou canst not know of." His tale is a tale of what Luke has
meant to him and what he has done for Luke that attempts to bind his
son to him and to the ongoing transmission of the gift of love and land
from generation to generation. Michael, however, is not passing the
land to his son in this speech, and his overbearing emphasis on love—
on his love for his son—may come from its being the only heritage he
can give to Luke as he sends him away from the land of his fathers.
With nothing else to appeal to he does not restrain himself from picturing
even that part of his relation to Luke that he knows Luke knows, and
he acknowledges that he has said "things of which I need not speak"
only after he has brought his son to tears. He goes on to press Luke,
despite signs of his hesitation, to do his part in creating an explicit symbol
of his bond to his father, a "covenant" that formalizes his commitment
to "the life thy Fathers liv'd" beyond the "links of love" which bind him
to his father and bind his father to both the land and his son. The

covenant is supposed to do for Luke at eighteen away in "the dissolute city" what seventy years of daily association with the scene of his labors has done for Michael, and it is not surprising that, even as he declares the meaning of the covenant, Michael imagines the contingency of Luke's fate and declares his love "whatever fate" may befall him.[24] The overbearingness of his attempt to determine Luke's meaning with story and symbol is directly related to the unlikeliness of his succeeding, as he seems himself to know.

The narrator who tells his tale with "fonder feeling, for the sake / Of youthful Poets, who among these Hills / Will be my second self when I am gone" hands on his heritage to them without insisting on what it or he should mean to them. His tale is in good order and has meant something to him and to others, but whether it will matter to his listeners, whether it will affect what they mean to themselves is up to them to decide. Property in land and love of kindred have an unavoidable literalness that leaves the man committed to them open to the "real and substantial action and suffering" (*LB,* p. 256) of a Michael, but property in meaning, while not completely independent of the conditions that bind and hurt Michael, is nevertheless voluntarily appropriated as it is voluntarily produced in accord with the "grand elementary principle of pleasure." The narrator's confidence in handing down the tale of Michael may be grounded in the pleasure with which he tells it, a pleasure that gives him reason to hope that others will find it too and in finding it accept the heritage he offers. Unlike Michael, who sends Luke off with the memory of a symbol but separates him from the sources of pleasure that are its ground, the narrator of "Michael" hands on a tale bound up with and capable of providing the pleasure of its meaning.

Chapter Four

What then does the Poet? He considers man and the
objects that surround him as acting and re-acting upon
each other, so as to produce an infinite complexity of
pain and pleasure; he considers man in his own
nature and in his ordinary life as contemplating this
with a certain quantity of immediate knowledge, with
certain convictions, intuitions, and deductions which
by habit become of the nature of intuitions; he
considers him as looking upon this complex scene of
ideas and sensations, and finding every where objects
that immediately excite in him sympathies which,
from the necessities of his nature, are accompanied by
an overbalance of enjoyment.

To this knowledge which all men carry about with
them, and to these sympathies in which without any
other discipline than that of our daily life we are fitted
to take delight, the Poet principally directs his
attention.

Wordsworth, 1802 Preface

Dialogic Personal Anecdotes

While the poems I have called "tales" identify themselves by invoking if not by fulfilling the convention of story-telling, the poems I call "personal anecdotes" do not invoke any specialized convention either to meet it or to argue with it.[1] Their narrators are usually as unselfconscious about the form in which they speak as the narrators of the tales are self-conscious in defending or criticizing their tellings. It is perhaps for this reason that the personal anecdotes have remained relatively neglected even as the growing interest in self-conscious narration during the last twenty-five years has brought some of the more self-conscious tales under consideration. The narrators of the personal anecdotes do not raise questions about themselves and their readers have not been moved to discover questions to ask about them.

The neglect of these poems has also been perpetuated by the low critical estimate in which they have been held since Coleridge first identified four of them (and one poem containing a personal anecdote) as poems that would have been more delightful to him in prose.[2] With a few interesting exceptions the poems in this group have borne, more than any others, the brunt of critics' contempt and supported the commonplace judgment of the experiment's failure.

Only recently have they been recognized as members of a group defined by common formal features. Richard Henry Haswell is the first critic, I believe, to call attention to those features, identifying the group by Wordsworth's use of first-person past-tense point of view to narrate "a specific event as it once happened to the speaker."[3] Entering the debate provoked by Robert Mayo's claim that *Lyrical Ballads* reflected the poetic conventions of its day, Haswell argues not that this point of view itself is original but that the use of it for this purpose departs from its conventional use in pastoral or ghost complaint or in allegorical and gothic vision.[4] In those eighteenth-century genres, a narrator who begins to tell in his own person of something that once happened to him is likely to have met a ghost, an abstraction, or the Scottish Muse, but not an actual shepherd, an old man, or a sailor's mother. Mayo himself compared under the genre of "anecdote" Wordsworth's "Expostulation and Reply" and "The Tables Turned" to a pair of poems entitled "Reason's Expostulation" and "Answer to Reason," in which " 'Reason' chides 'Love' " and " 'Love' rebukes 'Reason,' " but he did not notice that Wordsworth presents himself as reporting a conversation he had with a friend, not a dialogue of allegorical figures. Haswell's discovery of Wordsworth's consistent use of the personal anecdote to relate naturalistic human exchanges rather than artificial or visionary encounters is more than a clear argument for Wordsworth's originality. Though Haswell stops with his case against Mayo, he has effectively identified the common genre of the most troublesome group of Wordsworth's experimental poems.

As Haswell enumerates it, this group includes " 'Simon Lee' ('One summer day I chanced to see / This old man'), 'Anecdote for Fathers' ('One morn we stroll'd on our dry walk'), 'We are Seven' ('I met a little cottage girl'), and 'The Last of the Flock' ('But such a one, on English ground, / And in the broad highway, I met'). 'The Thorn,' though basically a dialogue, also contains an extended first-person past-tense account ('one day . . . I climbed the mountain height'), and 'Old Man Travelling,' though beginning apparently as a present-tense description, reveals itself as a specific event from the speaker's past ('I asked him whither he was bound')" (pp. 197–98). One need only bracket "Simon Lee" and "The Thorn"—which include personal anecdotes in the course of telling tales—and add three belated lyrical ballads of the same kind—"The Sailor's Mother" ("A Woman in the road I met"), "Alice Fell" ("And there a little Girl I found"), and "Beggars" ("Before me begging did she stand")—to recognize the infamous set Haswell's criteria sort out: butts of parody, candidates for *The Stuffed Owl*, poems better written in prose, better if their first part had not been written, better if their second part had not been written, better if they had not been written at all. "Expostulation and Reply" from *Lyrical Ballads* and "Resolution and Independence," associated in composition with the last three poems, have close affinities with this group, though they are usually treated in other contexts and have not shared the fate of the other poems.

These are not the only poems in *Lyrical Ballads* which use first-person past-tense to present personal experiences—there are epitaphic anecdotes and anecdotes of experiences in nature this list ignores—but it includes all such poems that present recent encounters between their narrators and other persons—in all but "Anecdote for Fathers" and "Expostulation and Reply" total strangers. All the narrators of these poems tell of their own experiences not in the role of story-teller from whom a tale is to be expected or of memorializer from whom an epitaph is in order but simply as people to whom something has occurred that is "significant because memorable and worth retelling" (Haswell, p. 202). All of them, furthermore, find it significant to recall and report something that was said by themselves, by the person they met, or by both.

This last feature, the report of an exchange of words, not just of an event or impression, leads me to call these personal anecdotes "dialogic" with two senses of the word in mind. In the first sense they are dialogic because they report dialogue in narrative diction, but in a more interesting sense they are dialogic because they continue the dialog they report. The narrators, that is, relate these anecdotes in response to the exchange of words in which they have been involved and so continue the dialogue after the other party is no longer present. Something in the exchange has been significant to them and left them wishing to share what they have learned, to preserve something of value, or in some cases to have the last word in an exchange in which the narrator did not come off as well as he would have liked. The narrators in every case are motivated to say more by what has already been said and, unprovoked by another's questions or by any additional external compulsion, tell, for their own pleasure, what they have said and heard another say.

Their account of the exchanges they narrate will thus be shaped by a continuing interest in the exchange itself, and that interest will be discoverable not just in an extractable didactic lesson but in the whole pattern of their emphases. Those emphases, however, can color but not entirely obscure the independent emphases of the characters (including the narrators themselves as they figured in the earlier encounters) whose words the narrators now report, and they may also be colored by the independent emphases of the poet who has represented the narrators' accounts, juxtaposed their language with the languages of the characters they imitate, entitled the poems, set their words in metrical arrangements, and printed them along with explicit declarations of purpose and with other poems which may "serve as a commentary unostentatiously directing [the reader's] attention to [the poet's] purposes, both particular and general" (*Prose*, 3:28). The interest of reading such poems, like the interest of dialogic forms generally, should be not just in coming to share one of these several perspectives, not even the poet's, but in discriminating them, discovering their interrelations, and judging them from an independent human ground. No one has recognized this last point more clearly than John Danby, who calls the effect of reading such poems "irony":

> It is unfortunate that Wordsworth's irony has not been much
> remarked. If irony, however, can mean perspective and the co-

presence of alternatives, the refusal to impose on the reader a
predigested life-view, the insistence on the contrary that the reader
should enter, himself, as full partner in the final judgement on the
facts set before him—then Wordsworth is a superb ironist in *Lyrical
Ballads*. . . . The narrator, the characters involved in the story, the
poet himself as the finally responsible assembler—these are the
three main levels at which the voices work. By changing the voice
one can step from one frame to another and back again. Stepping
apparently out of the frame of mere "literature" altogether and into
the reader's own reality (his reality of experience and of judgement), confronting the reader with the need to be aware of what he
is judging with as well as what he is judging—this is, above all, the
Wordsworthian trick in *Lyrical Ballads*.

(*Simple Wordsworth*, pp. 37–38)

Critics have detected the "trick" of irony in the first two anecdotes I
propose to consider here, "Anecdote for Fathers" and "We Are Seven,"
but they have most commonly referred that irony for judgment directly
to limited contexts in Wordsworth's life and works, without passing
through or ultimately arriving at judgments based on what Danby calls
their "own reality."[5] Paul Sheats, for example, orienting himself in relation to earlier poems and the intellectual errors they enacted and over-
came, reads both anecdotes as criticisms of their adult narrators' efforts
"violently to impose demonstrative categories of thought and value on
their seemingly helpless but truly invulnerable victims" (*Making*, p. 196).
Other critics, with their eye on the Immortality Ode and the Fenwick
note in which Wordsworth linked it to the opening stanza of "We Are
Seven," have debated whether the poems present children with pre-
scient knowledge of immortality or children limited by "narrowness of
experience and imperfect conceptual powers."[6] In judging the poems'
irony by referring them to these ideas such readings reduce them to
simple instruments of a didactic point neatly separable from the poetic
representations themselves.[7] The poems remain isolated also from "the
reader's own reality" and offer no challenge to his human judgment so
long as they are treated as little more than expressions of stages in the
peculiar history of Wordsworth's ideas.

The very title of "Anecdote for Fathers," however, including as it
originally did the subtitle "shewing how the art of lying may be taught"
and ultimately the epigraph "Retine vim istam, falsa enim dicam, si
coges" ("Restrain that force of yours, for I shall tell lies if you drive me
to it"),[8] would appear to dispose of my fastidiousness about didacticism,
for the moral seems pointed before the poem even begins. The concluding stanza of the peom has been taken to reinforce the same point,
that the speaker of the poem has learned from the episode how the art

of lying may be taught, regrets having taught it, and resolves, as one critic has suggested, "not to badger other people, and still more not to badger himself, to find reasons for feeling as he does."[9] But the blithe and seemingly cheerful attitude with which the rest of the poem is narrated contrasts with its announced subject of "lying" and makes the interpretation of the last stanza into what Jack Stillinger has identified as a "special problem: either the speaker has suddenly and unconvincingly awakened to a new understanding, or the line represents a wooden attempt at sarcasm, in which, as at the end of 'We Are Seven,' the adult remains firm in his conviction that reason must prevail" (p. 506). The question, then, to which an examination of the poem should give us an answer is, what has the father "learned" and what attitude is he taking toward his son when he declares:

> Oh dearest, dearest boy! my heart
> For better lore would seldom yearn,
> Could I but teach the hundredth part
> Of what from thee I learn.

That final declaration, an apostrophe to a child who is not present at the time of the narration, is the narrator's attempt to express a concluding attitude toward the exchange he has just narrated, and it is in the emphases of his narration that the feelings and attitudes informing the final stanza must be sought. In that narration, the narrator begins with a description of the child in terms of his physical beauty and his special relation to his father. He mentions the child's fair face and beautiful limbs, his own possession of the child ("I have a boy of five years old") and the child's love of him, but none of the terms of that description hint at a moral identity of the child which might prepare for the poem's announced theme of his "lying." Rather they show that the narrator perceives the child as lovely and loving, and, significantly, not as loved but as owned. He again pairs his appreciation of the child's beauty and his sense of possession at lines 17–18 ("My boy was by my side, so slim / And graceful in his rustic dress!") and at line 45 ("At this, my boy, so fair and slim"), and he presents himself as using the possessive pronoun with the diminutive "little" to address the boy in line 25 and to address him by name in line 37. The complex of attitudes revealed here is close to that which Edmund Burke associates with the beautiful, a feeling of complacency aroused by the perception of objects flattering to our wishes, weaker than we are, and, though loved, also held in a kind of benevolent contempt.[10] This father sees his child as part of the delightful scene which has roused him to such careless delight, as an especially charming part not only lovely in appearance but lovingly receptive to himself and his own idle preoccupations. Wrapped up in this self-satisfied view of his relation to his son, he does not perceive his double assault upon him—his questioning him and his holding of the boy's arm—as an assault but as a kind of overflow of his feelings into an image of himself. Yet the gesture and the questions both assert power over the child and respect neither his physical nor his mental separateness. Having himself become engaged in recalling the pleasures of their former home, the father leads the son to prefer those pleasures by subtly loading the questions in favor of Kilve, describing it as "a pleasant place," "Kilve's delightful shore" and "Kilve's smooth shore by the green sea," while Liswyn farm remains merely "Liswyn farm." The child, held by the arm and sharing his father's "careless mood" answers as he has been led to answer, "At Kilve I'd rather be / Than here at Liswyn farm."

The father has his will, but he is somehow troubled to hear the answer he has brought the child to articulate for him, the bald statement of dissatisfaction with the scene where he and the child are, where *he* is, and feels, perhaps, that his presence ought to be sufficient for the child. "I'm happy to be wherever you are, Dad" may be the sort of answer wished for by the father who had declared at the outset how dearly his son loves *him*. Though the father himself has engaged in what he, in effect, insists is a safe flirtation with thoughts of former pleasure ("A day it was when I could bear / To think, and think, and think again; / With so much happiness to spare, / I could not feel a pain"), he senses some dissonance, I think a disloyalty, in his son's declaration in favor of those same former pleasures, and he puts the child on the spot to defend his choice: " 'Now, little Edward, say why so; / My little Edward, tell me why.' " His use of the child's name here for the first time subtly indicates a recognition of the child's separate identity consequent upon the difference in feelings which has suddenly opened between them, and his response to the child's confession that he knows no reason for his expressed preference, " 'Why this is strange,' said I," isolates the child, quite literally estranges him, by treating his predicament of unjustified preference as if it were inconceivable, completely outside the bounds to which the father can extend his sympathetic understanding. Having led the child to express a careless preference for Kilve he turns around and amplifies the reasons for preferring Liswyn farm, betraying the child by exposing him as defenseless in the position to which he has led him and by taking seriously the question which seemed at first an idle one, less important than the common pleasures of their walk and the common bond of their affection.

It should not be surprising that a child thus cornered should hang down his head and make no answer to the insistently repeated questions of his pursuer, but it is striking to me that the narrator as he turns to describe the child's attitude and his own questions should, having just revealed the distance that opened between them in the episode he is narrating, describe the child again as "my boy, so fair and slim," as if the attitude with which the poem began remains the governing attitude of the teller toward his son *in spite of* what he reveals has happened between them.[11] This attitude, however, does not remain consistent, for, having described in carefully analytical detail the process through which the child came to focus on the "broad and gilded vane," and before repeating the child's declaration that the presence of that weathercock is his reason for preferring to be elsewhere, the father refers to his child in the most distancing language of the poem as "the boy," and he represents himself for the only time in the poem as the object of the child's action: "Then did the boy his tongue unlock, / And thus *to me* he made reply" (my italics). He is at once impressed with the arbitrariness of the boy's answer—his careful description shows how closely he has observed the boy arriving at it—and by the fact that he is the recipient of this answer, that the boy will resort to such a blatant absurdity with him. I detect here not a recognition of what he has forced the child to do but a resentment of how the child has treated him, an understanding of lying not as something which he has taught the child but which the child has *tried* on him.

The word *lying,* however, is not used by the narrator in the poem, and we might find it strange if he did use it. What sort of lie is depicted here, after all? It is not a false report of an action done, not a misrepresentation of some known state of affairs. It is an arbitrary answer to a persistent question to which the child has virtually admitted he has no answer; indeed it is an answer to the persistence of the questioner, an attempt to tell him, "Get off my back!" The child cannot directly say, "I wish you would leave me alone"—a wish, by the way, which might confirm the fear which led the father to question him in the first place—but he can dissemble the wish and put an end to the questions by naming an arbitrary object and wishing for *its* absence. (That he calls it a "weathercock" instead of a "weather vane" may hint at his unconscious identification of it with his father.) His "lie" is his projection of his unexpressible wish for his father's absence onto an indifferent object.[12] It is consequential because it issues from a loss of that simplicity which makes the artless speech of child or rustic the direct index of his feeling. It is the holding of his real feelings in himself and the use of speech at once to relieve and to hide them.

His father, however, is clearly concerned with the fact of the lie. He attends to the process through which the child has arrived at it, as if he were gathering evidence to expose the arbitrariness of the child's answer, and he describes the vane in terms—"broad and gilded"—which he could have applied to a lie if he dared to name in such serious terms what his child had done. He dares not so name it, however, for to attribute moral responsibility to the child would be to introduce terms of moral responsibility much more applicable to himself. What the story revealed would then require a correction of the child but even more an apology to him. Instead the father declares his affection for the child and praises him for the unspecified "lore" he has taught him. He is neither reaching a new understanding nor satirizing the child; rather he is trying, in the face of what he has revealed and in part recognized, to recover his idealized relation to his son as one of affection and appreciation and to declare his heartfelt satisfaction in what has happened between them. Though implicit in the word "lore" is the idea of a lesson learned, implicit in the father's use of the word is also the idea of a clever or cute anecdote which his boy has provided for him. On the brink of a moral discovery and reversal in his telling of the tale, the father manages at the last moment to resolve his resentment of the lie and his guilt at having provoked it into an affectionate declaration that "kids say the darndest things." But his manner of declaring his final attitude manages at once to say "I learn a new one every day, so many I can only tell the smallest part of them," and at the same time to imply that there is only a small part of what he has learned or might learn from the episode that he can teach, that is, possess with the consciousness which would make it communicable to another.[13]

We, however, with the help of the poet's subtitle, can see it all, not merely a comic exposure of the adult's meddling reason by the child's superior wisdom, but the father's impossible wish of oneness with his son, his cruel response to the child's unwitting failure to love him as he wishes, the child's fear and resentment when his father turns on him, the child's desperate search for a way out of the corner in which his father has placed him and for an object on which to discharge his anger, the father's critical scrutiny of his strategy and resentment at its being used on him—all resolved not in exposure of the father or the child or in the poet's or father's moralizing but in an attempt to tell a story which will at once acknowledge the problem and resolve it. The manner in which the mind associates ideas in a state of excitement is here revealed in the encounter of father and son as well as in the narrative of the father as at once true to nature and evocative of sympathy. The discovery or recognition of what is happening and what it says about being human belongs to the reader, not to the narrator, giving the reader a pleasure in seeing that which, if the narrator fully recognized it, could for him be only a source of pain. We share the pleasure which the poet declares he took in all his compositions, while the pleasure of the narrator and thereby his very motive for telling is preserved through a merciful self-deception.

To call the father-son relations in this poem Oedipal might seem about as informative as to call the child's speech a lie, but like the use of that word, the identification of the Oedipal theme calls attention to other contexts, both psychological and poetic, in which the social relations the poem explores are treated more explicitly. The psychological context reminds us that Wordsworth had promised to reveal the "laws of our nature" in the manner in which the mind associates ideas in a state of excitement, and it leads us to remember that the child of the poem is five years old—right in the middle of the Oedipal stage. It also leads us to look for the other side of the Oedipal problem, the child's love of the mother and the father's jealousy, and to find it hinted in the son's attempt to share in the father's overt fondness for smooth and beautiful Kilve and the father's reaction against his attempt. Another interpretation of the father's abrupt reversal is discoverable here in his sudden perception of the child as a competitor, a would-be sharer in his fantasy enjoyments, not merely a reflection and extension of himself.

But the introduction of this psychological context leads too easily to the habits of unmasking, the discovery of the "real" and usually shameful motives under the surface of expressed ones. More interesting, I think, is to look to the poetic context of both Freud's naming of the natural pattern and Wordsworth's embodiment of it. Sophocles' *Oedipus Rex* is the paradigm not only for a psychological complex but also for a poetic kind: the story from which Freud names his theme is also the story which gives Aristotelian tragedy its form. I am less interested here in theme and form, however, than in the manner through which both are presented. Aristotle, we have seen, in finding the only pure mode of imitation in the dramatic manner, commits himself to a preference for poems in which, to use a Freudian phrase, the passions of the agents are "acted out." *Oedipus Rex* shows us the paradigmatic conflict of father and son in a form in which the son has already fulfilled unwittingly what Freud would see as his twin forbidden wishes, discovers he has done so, and suffers a reversal in his new knowledge of himself. The completion of the action—that is, Oedipus's discovery and reversal—produces a central figure who is consciously once and for all on the other side of two forbidden actions, one whose situation clarifies to the audience what it means to have done these things and how it feels to discover it. The spectators look on in increasing horror as the action reaches its fulfillment, shocked into recognizing the difference between themselves and Oedipus, between those who may have wished and the one who knows he has done a forbidden thing, and are cleansed by the recognition.

In choosing to treat the feelings connected with the father-son relationship as a narrative report of a dialogue, from the point of view of one involved in those feelings themselves, Wordsworth not only takes away the interest of fascinating action—the "gross and violent stimulants" characteristic of the great tragic spectacles as well as of the "sickly and stupid German Tragedies" he condemns—but he also makes the reader's pleasure a problem by requiring sympathetic interpretation of the speaker's situation as the price of discovering its nature and standing outside it. The active reader is closer to the narrator of "Anecdote for Fathers" than the spectator is to Oedipus; the reader must apply his imagination to what he is told, thus implicating himself, while the spectator watches from a distance that grows greater and greater as the action reveals itself. But of course the imaginative reader finally has understood not an incestuous patricide but a father's ambivalence toward his son and a son's toward his father; nothing has been done by either character in the poem to require a permanent transformation of their relationship, and the reader's discovery of what the father and son have felt would be misrepresented by the crude formulas—"wish to kill his father and marry his mother" or "jealousy of his son's threat to his masculinity and possession of his beloved." We have seen the feelings of mutual resentment arise in a context in which they have become clarified for us but in which each of the participants has found a way of deflecting them, of expressing them without recognizing them. The poem pleases by at once revealing to us potentially damaging emotions and showing us the fictional strategies through which those who have felt them can continue to live and affirm their love. We enjoy both superior understanding and sympathetic understanding, knowing the self-deceptions as such and affirming the self whose capacity for life and growth depends on its capacity to sustain them. Not the agonized cry of the tragically completed life, nor the mea culpa and didactic story of the converted life, but the self-sustaining, self-pleasing, awkward anecdote of the continuing life calls in this poem for our sympathetic understanding.

The unlikely comparison I have just made between "Anecdote for Fathers" and *Oedipus Rex* suggests another which will permit a novel perspective on its companion poem "We Are Seven," for as the social relations represented in the first poem are analogous to those in the play, so the relations presented in the second are like those in the play's counterpart, Sophocles' *Antigone*. The encounter between a grown man committed to an external rational order and a young girl committed to her personal relation to her dead siblings is a common subject whose different treatments in the tragic drama and the narrative anecdote help to clarify what Wordsworth is doing in this strangely intense and frequently parodied poem. Though I do not claim that Wordsworth had the parallel I am suggesting in mind, I am sure that the "perspective by incongruity" it provides will clarify the human situation at issue and reopen our interpretation of the poem.[14]

The difficulty of understanding what the narrator is after here has been frequently recognized, perhaps most clearly by David Perkins, though Perkins refuses to explore the difficulty because it seems to him to lie "outside the poem": "the dramatic situation seems a little grotesque. The speaker argues earnestly and at considerable length, laboring to convince the child as though some important issue were at stake. This earnestness is pedagogic in character, and for Wordsworth something serious is involved. The matter-of-fact speaker represents the adult world actively seeking to destroy the just confidence of the child in its own intuitions."[15] "Outside the poem" this will take us only if we head straight for Wordsworth, as Perkins here does, without considering the earnestness and the matter-of-factness of the strangely impassioned narrator who speaks here to his "brother Jim." Perkins sees a "dramatic situation" with a poet outside it, where we can consider a narrative whose telling is crucial to our understanding of the situation it relates. Our problem is not just to discover why the speaker had to prove to the child that she was mistaken in her inclusion of her dead siblings among the count of her brothers and sisters but even more why he must tell his own brother of his failure to convince her.

The question he poses in the first stanza of the poem seems to establish his attitude toward the story he is about to tell, but like the final stanza of "Anecdote for Fathers" it is open to conflicting interpretations that cannot be weighed without reference to the story itself. He asks:

> A simple child, dear brother Jim,
> That lightly draws its breath,
> And feels its life in every limb,
> What should it know of death?

Stillinger again points to two possible interpretations, this time focusing on the force of "should" in the last line: "The fourth line may be interpreted as either 'What can it be expected to know' or 'What ought it to know' " (p. 506). But within the first of these interpretations there are two possible emphases which significantly alter its force. Does the emphasis fall on the *it* in a way which deprecates the child's knowledge in contrast to the adult's superior understanding, or does it fall on the *should* in a way which takes the circumstances stated in the two preceding lines as mitigating any expectation that such a child would be expected to know what an adult knows? Is he diminishing the child for its ignorance or excusing it?[16] Here the stress patterns of these iambic tetrameter lines guide us toward weighting the *should* and softening the narrator's attitude toward the child, or at least they suggest that the other weighting is a deliberate interpretive choice we must make for reasons other than metrical ones.

Whichever the emphasis, the stanza also introduces the subject on which the difference between the child's and the adult's knowledge is in question—death—and the ground of the difference between their knowledge—that the child is simple, draws its breath lightly, "and feels its life in every limb" (the metrical weight on "simple," "lightly," and "feels" adds strength to our wish to weight "should" which follows them in the first stressed position of the line). At the same time these statements show us how the narrator interprets the life of the child as something experienced in its limbs, evident in its easy breathing, and reflected in its ideas on life and death and how his own ideas on the subject are presumably arrived at without reliance on the quality of his breathing or feeling. His idea of life is connected with the observable motions of the body ("That lightly draws its breath") but he attributes her idea of life to her way of *experiencing* life in the body ("and feels its life in every limb").

His behavioral idea of life informs his first argument to the child. After he has queried her about the number of her siblings, has asked where they are, and, having heard her say that two live at Conway, two are at sea, and two lie in the church-yard, has reiterated her count, omitting the last two, only to have her repeat the total number and remind him of the two he left out, he argues,

> "You run about, my little maid,
> "Your limbs they are alive;
> "If two are in the church-yard laid,
> "Then ye are only five."

He appeals here not to her feeling of life in her limbs but to the observation that she moves them and that they are consequently alive. Her dead siblings do not move their limbs and so, he concludes, the true count of her family must only be five. But on the speaker's premise, the only proper conclusion to be drawn from the difference between the child's animation and her siblings' lack of it is that those two are dead, not that the number of children is only five. The missing premise here is that the dead do not count for the living, that their loss of physical animation is at the same time the loss of their significance. This narrator, who is so frequently identified as the type of the rationalist, as the imposer of "demonstrative categories" on the child impervious to reason, is in fact a faulty reasoner. His stated premise shows a behaviorist interpretation of the concept of life, but his argument fails to link that premise to the conclusion he draws, and the child, far from clinging irrationally to the idea that her siblings are alive in his terms, admits their deaths, narrates how they died, and denies that those deaths have deprived her of a significant relation to them. She is in daily relation to them, working beside their graves, taking her meals there, and singing to them. Their graves are for her not merely a reminder of them but are the place where they have gone, and in going there they have not gone far from her. But her emphasis on a continuing relation to the locally present dead leads him to reiterate his question in terms which transport the dead to another place, utterly out of relation to the here and now in which she relates to her siblings. " 'How many are you then,' " he asks, " 'If they two are in Heaven?' " But her repetition of her original answer leads him to one last insistence on the difference between her life and their death and on her presence here and their presence elsewhere: " 'But they are dead: those two are dead! / 'Their spirits are in heaven!' " He ends by interpreting her refusal to change her mind as a waste of his presumably valuable and persuasive words on her obdurate will to hold her irrational position, but in fact he has shown us a conflict of wills in which he has given her no reason to change her mind.

We can now refine our formulation of the problem of the narrator's motives, for it becomes clear that his impassioned insistence on the difference between the living and the dead and on the unbridgeable distance between the living and the dead—and especially his unstated insistence on the absolute insignificance of the dead for the living—gives rise to his initial statement of the difference between the grounds of the child's ignorance and the basis of the adult's knowledge of death. After he fails to persuade her, he finds a ground peculiar to her on which it is possible to explain her holding to a view which so radically denies his own, lest his own view be shaken. She must as a simple and lively child have feelings peculiar to herself which give her her peculiar ideas, while adults, in the absence of such feelings, possess clear notions independent of feeling, given by objective definitions and religious revelations.

The narrator's strident appeals to these definitions and revelations in the face of the child's matter-of-fact relation to her dead siblings, like Creon's shrill appeals to the primacy of public duties in the face of Antigone's defiant clinging to the claims of her dead brother, reveal that the independence of personal feeling on which both men pride themselves is uneasily maintained. Both can be threatened in their certainties by beings they consider their inferiors (Wordsworth's narrator by a girl-child, Creon by a woman and by his own child), and both are driven to cling more and more irrationally to the foundations of their rationality. But while Creon, in the course of the actions in which his position has implicated him, discovers his vulnerability and is reduced to nothing ("My life is warped past cure. My fate has struck me down" [line 1342]),[17] the narrator of "We Are Seven" tries to tell the story of his encounter with the disturbing child to a sympathetic auditor—indeed to an auditor to whom he can acknowledge a filial bond—in a way that conceals his vulnerability and permits him to continue. That his view of himself as a man of reason and objectivity hides from him the fear of death and the uncertain ground of rationality which his story reveals to us, that his emphasis on the child's willful and irrational attitudes does not reveal to him the willfulness and irrationality we see in him, that his appeal to his brother implicates him in the kind of human bond he wishes to sever—these ironies only underline again that the discovery and recognition in this narrative mode belong to the reader, while the power to experience and to tell belongs to the narrator. We are liberated from the defenses which he cannot afford to give up, not as in *Antigone* by the spectacle of the horrid consequences to which Creon's clinging to them leads, but by the sympathetic discovery of their function for Wordsworth's narrator and the critical recognition of their fragile self-deceptiveness. The narrator does not learn from his encounter as Creon learns too late from his, but he does *register* the encounter in a way that allows us to learn.

Again, as in "Anecdote for Fathers," this ability to tell what has happened is bound up with an inability to realize it. Were the narrator more aware of what he reveals to us, he would be either more wise or more worried than he is. In either case he might have no story to tell, for a wiser man would lack the uncertainties that motivate the telling and a more worried one would fear the exposure that accompanies it. Both here and in "Anecdote for Fathers" Wordsworth has situated his narrators so that their ambivalent involvement in the episodes they narrate accounts for their need to interpret their experience, while the self-serving interpretations they invent permit them to tell to their own satisfaction stories in which the risk of self-exposure is high. This limitation of the narrators' understandings is the price of the extension of the readers', but the price we imagine they pay to become a lesson for us is, after all, less than we imagine Oedipus or Creon to pay. We, at the same time, must invest more of our imagination in discovering what we can learn from their stories, and so we associate the potentially painful lessons we have learned with the pleasure of uncovering them. If our knowledge here increases, it can be said to do so in accordance with the same "grand elementary principle of pleasure," which conditions both their self-pleasing limitations and our pleasurable sympathy with their pain.

There remains, however, a difference between our pleasure and the pleasures of the narrators with whom we have sympathized, a difference which, if unchecked, may undermine their common principle and open the way to an irony colored by our feelings of superiority to the limited narrators we have seen through. It is unlikely that this is the pleasure which Wordsworth invites us to take with him, nor do I believe that we are justified in taking it, by identifying him with his narrators, at his expense. But the poems by themselves will not prevent our taking it or fully reveal to us the point of view from which the poet judges his narrators and would have us judge him. We must finally return to his claims about our common humanity and the poet's relation to it to discover the point of view from which he is judging.[18]

As we have seen in Chapter 1, Wordsworth describes in his 1802 Preface the poet's sympathetic participation in the pleasure of human subjects who themselves are sympathetically and pleasurably contemplating the "complex scene" of their own pleasures and pains. The poet, Wordsworth writes, takes delight in considering

> man and the objects that surround him as acting and re-acting upon each other, so as to produce an infinite complexity of pain and pleasure; he considers man in his own nature and in his ordinary life as contemplating this with a certain quantity of immediate knowledge, with certain convictions, intuitions, and deductions which by habit become of the nature of intuitions; he considers him as looking upon this complex scene of ideas and sensations, and finding every where objects that immediately excite in him sympathies which, from the necessities of his nature, are accompanied by an overbalance of enjoyment.

The poet attends, that is, to the capacity of men in their ordinary life within the limits of their immediate knowledge and beliefs—what Bakhtin might call their "behavioral ideology"[19]—to resolve the "infinite complexity of pain and pleasure" of human experience into "an overbalance of enjoyment," the capacity to find upon reflection a pleasurable interpretation of the "complex scene of ideas and sensations" generated in immediate experience. This is the capacity we have seen exercised by the narrators of our two anecdotes, both of whom look back upon complex interactions with the objects of their immediate experience to discover self-pleasing interpretations, but neither of whom breaks through the limits of knowledge and belief with which he started.

The poet, however, considers the narrators he represents from a point of view which could not be inferred from the individual anecdotes themselves. If the narrators find in their experience particular objects the contemplation of which is accompanied by "an overbalance of enjoyment," the poet, as we saw in Chapter 1, considers the *pattern* of such pleasing contemplations under a general view of its significance. The narrator of any given anecdote need be represented only in terms of the predispositions and convictions in terms of which he finds satisfying significance in the specific encounter he relates, but the poet who represents the whole range of anecdotes does so with his own predispositions and convictions about the nature of such encounters: "He considers man and nature as essentially adapted to each other, and the mind of man as naturally the mirror of the fairest and most interesting qualities of nature." For him the individual instances of an isolated mind's pleasing interpretion of its experiences confirm his universal conviction that such interpretations are naturally to be expected. He takes his own pleasure not only in sympathizing with the narrator's pleasures but in recognizing how consistently various narrators with different knowledge and beliefs under different circumstances resolve ambiguous experiences on the side of their own pleasure. Such consistency confirms his predisposition to believe in the "grand elementary principle of pleasure" and thus grounds his confidence to represent whatever objects please him as objects of general meaning and delight. Encounters which are simple experiences for his narrators become for him illustrations of the kind of experience whose occurrence calls for a poet to cultivate and celebrate them. He confirms the ground of his vocation in the significant repetition of experiences which, for the narrators of his poems, were significantly unique, and he challenges his readers to judge those narrators in light of a belief more radical than any about the child's relation to immortality or the adult's relation to the child. For the poet, it is the human mind's relation to its experience in the world which is at stake in our judgment of his narrators, and our indulgence in an irony at their expense or his could, in his terms, cost us a world of pleasure.

But critics who indulge in such irony may only exclude themselves from appreciating Wordsworth's world of pleasure in order to include themselves among the instances Wordsworth collects—as the peculiar interpreters of human experience and human works who take pleasure in confirming their presuppositions that experience is tragic, that works must fail, and that it is heroic to face these truths. To interpret Wordsworth's poems in light of this modern (some would say Freudian) metaphysical pathos is to take a kind of pleasure in seeing through their maker's failure or the failure of their narrators to see the "real" truth of their situations and our own. This is a genuine pleasure, but it isolates the one who characteristically takes it from the subjects he examines and exposes him to the unmasking which he habitually performs on others, for it presumes an idea of reality which can easily be shown to be only "a certain quantity of immediate knowledge," just another ideology. Though some may even enjoy the game of stripping off their own masks before anyone else can touch them, such agility still is a pleasure mainly to the one who exercises it. It is kinder, I think, to trace the subtleties of our rationalizations and celebrate their power to sustain us than to expose them and ourselves to an unmasking which promises personal pleasure at the expense of human community. What Danby called the "irony of detachment and loving-kindness" (*Simple Words-worth*, p. 50) and what I have called "critical participation" may give us a better and more lasting pleasure in the speeches these poems represent than an irony which exposes their narrators' or the poet's intellectual pride through an assertion of our own.

While critics have recognized *some* ironic relation between the speeches of the narrators and those of the characters in the two poems we have just considered, they have usually not seen any coherent relation between those speeches in the two poems to which we now turn.

Unlike "Anecdote for Fathers" and "We Are Seven," whose narrators relate developing interchanges between themselves and the persons they describe, "The Last of the Flock" and "Old Man Travelling" each present a narrator who tells how a man he met appeared to him, what he asked the man, and how the man replied. The resultant division of the poems into two main parts—the narrator's description and the character's speech—has generally led critics to find the real poem in one of the parts rather than in the relation between them. Thus the narrator's opening description of the shepherd in "The Last of the Flock" has been treated as superfluous to the shepherd's monologue, and the narration of question and answer in "Old Man Travelling" has been considered as incongruous with the striking initial description of the old man himself. Wordsworth's composition of monologues with prose and verse introductions has supported critics in their reading of "The Last of the Flock" as another such poem, and Wordsworth's eventual omission of the last half of "Old Man Travelling" has confirmed their judgment of its extraneousness.[20] My hypothesis, however, should lead us to ask whether we can discover any motives of these narrators which would unify their utterances and guide our response to the characters and speeches they tell of.

In the poems themselves, the link which connects the narrator's description and the character's speech is a question, a simple device, but one which in other poems in the collection is pregnant with indications about the asker's state of mind. In poems like "Anecdote for Fathers" and "We Are Seven" the narrators' reports of their repeated questions call attention to the passionate concerns which led them to badger the children for the answers they desired, but in the two poems before us their account of an unrepeated question follows a description which tells us all we can know about why it was asked, and is immediately followed by the presentation of an answer from which our attention is never subsequently returned to the question and the questioner. The speeches of the shepherd and the old man apparently speak for themselves in answer to the concerns which the narrators' questions have expressed, so that the narrators, though they have reason for telling what they saw and heard, have had no reason either to pursue the matter further with the characters or to attempt to reinterpret their speeches afterwards in a more satisfying way. The point of each anecdote is not, as in "Anecdote for Fathers" or "We Are Seven," that the narrator has asked a question and gotten an odd or disconcerting reply which he must somehow explain to himself, but that he has asked a question to which the answer he has received was sufficient. His narration consequently prepares us for the question, states it, and then leaves us to share the answer he has received—"I met such and such a man whose appearance struck me in a way which led me to ask him this question, and *this* was his reply." We will establish the unity of the poems if we can discover how the narrators' visions of the characters motivate their questions and how the answers they receive put the questions to rest.[21]

The narrator of "The Last of the Flock" has been struck by an unusual public display of emotion. In all his experience in England and abroad he has rarely seen "A healthy man, a man full grown / Weep in the public roads alone," but on the occasion he is about to recount he has seen such a man, and "on English ground" too, in the "broad highway," he reiterates, displaying the unusual sign of emotion: "His cheeks with tears were wet." Why such a display of emotion is rare becomes evident when even the man who has given way to it attempts to wipe his tears away and to hide his condition from the narrator and when he begins his reply to the narrator's question about the cause of his weeping with the declaration, "Shame on me, Sir!" The public display of tears in such a figure is rare not because suffering is rare but because concealment is common, because a healthy, full-grown man is expected to have enough pride to keep his miseries to himself and usually does. The man whom the narrator has encountered does not reveal merely that men can be miserable in England but even more that they can be demoralized, and the narrator's question, therefore, "My friend / What ails you? wherefore weep you so?" may be taken to ask both "What is the cause of your misery?" and also "What accounts for your almost shameless public expression of it?"

The shepherd's answer is sufficient, I believe, because in answering the first question it so fully reveals the answer to the second. He begins his reply, "Shame on me, Sir! this lusty lamb, / He makes my tears to flow," and adds, "To-day I fetched him from the rock; / He is the last of all my flock." What this fact means to him that it should compel his tears unfolds in his narrative in stages that deepen both our impression of his character and our sense of what was implied by the question. Much more comes out than we or the narrator could at first have expected.

The first two stanzas of his narration recount the beginning of his flock in the casual purchase of a ewe and the issue of this purchase in the increase of a healthy flock. Along with this increase came his marriage, which for him is grammatically parallel to his purchase and nurture of his flock ("I bought . . . I raised . . . I married"). And though at his marriage the "full score" of sheep he owned made him "rich / As I could wish to be," his "stock" continued to increase to more than twice the number sufficient to that wish. His joy in his flock of fifty sheep is evident in his calling them "comely" and "sweet." He describes them in a manner that suggests the permanence and magnitude of the natural resources available to feed them ("upon the mountain did they feed"), and he links their vigorous and lovingly enumerated growth with the health, material well-being (and perhaps the increase) of his as yet unenumerated family ("They throve and we at home did thrive"). It is almost with a shock that we are returned to his present situation to discover that all but one of those lovely sheep are dead and that, just as his family throve in their increase, so now in the flock's demise they may "perish all of poverty." What jars us, however, at this stage in the narrative is the shepherd's declaration that he does not care if they and he thus perish. The basis of this attitude we have not yet discovered, but its expression suggests that the narrator was right to suspect the man's demoralization.

At this point in the shepherd's narration we do not know the cause of the death of his flock, which we might imagine was ravaged by disease or depredation. He has mentioned, after all, not the sale of the other forty-nine sheep but their death, while the lamb he carries (we do not yet know that it too is being taken to be sold) is described as "lusty," perhaps the only healthy one from so many which were sick. Neither do we know yet whether the loss of the others was sudden or gradual, though the hypothesis of natural causes which the narration so far would support makes sudden and shocking loss seem the more likely.

The stanzas which follow answer our questions in ways that force us to reject such probable hypotheses and confront an unexpectedly horrible situation. The thriving "we at home" of the previous stanza suddenly become "ten children" requiring food in an unexplained "time of need." The man who declared but a moment ago that he "was rich / As I could wish to be" has turned to the parish to ask for relief, only to have his own words of a moment before returned upon him: "They said I was a wealthy man; / My sheep upon the mountain fed." What earlier in the narrative had been conditions in which the shepherd declared his satisfaction and found his well-being become here the bitter conditions of his failure to qualify for help. Because of them, he himself is forced to carry out the sale of his beloved flock one sheep at a time in a manner and over a length of time that make the sudden natural destruction we might have imagined for them seem merciful. The correlative thriving of flock and family turns into the temporary sustaining of the one at the permanent expense of the other, a relation which the shepherd recognizes from the time he appeals for help and which deprives him thereafter of satisfaction in the sustenance of his children.

Indeed, it deprives him, as he confesses in the next to the last stanza, of his very love of his children. This climactic confession seems almost to raise his love of his flock to a pathological height, as he links both his increasing love of his children to the increase in his "store" and his diminishing love to its dwindling. This admission tests the limits of our sympathy by tempting us to refuse to recognize a common human feeling in what he admits. Here is a man, we may think, who loves his sheep too much if he loves them as much as his own children and lets the amount of his love for his offspring vary with the amount of his "store." But we can think this only if we hold him responsible for the natural increases of sheep and children that have conditioned his equally undeserved good and ill fortunes. He has come, as he tells the narrator, from a careless beginning to take "care and pains" for a flock which has grown of its own nature, but with all his care and pains he cannot make more sheep than he is given. The same biological processes beyond the shepherd's control have increased his flock and his family, and he can neither reduce the needs of his children nor increase the productivity of his flock by working harder or longer. His situation is determined by "permanent forms of nature" beyond his control, for surely the process of generation is such a form.

In compelling him to act as if he can make a difference, as if he is a man of sufficient means or sufficient power to supply his own means, the parish council judges reasonably in its own terms, for surely a man with fifty sheep is not one of "the poor," but it at the same time forces him to act a masquerade that makes him go about his work "crazily, and wearily," knowing as he does from the first that all that he has is not enough. From this masquerade the sale of his last sheep will free him, and we may imagine that his tears as he carries it away are not only tears of grief at the loss of the last of his flock but tears of relief at the final realization of what he has known all along to be his true position. From now on, he need not act the part of a "wealthy man" in providing for his family out of his capital, for he has finally proved beyond any public doubt that he is the poor man he, with tamed pride, had said he was from the beginning. At last he can give way to the despair which he has felt ever since he foresaw in the sale of his first sheep the gradual attrition of his whole flock; at last he has the wish which, he confesses, he "many a time" wished, that "they all were gone."

Through his speech the shepherd reveals himself to the narrator and to us not just as a particular man with a particular tale of woe but as the very type of the ruined man, perversely fulfilled in the completion of the ruin he has so long anticipated and public in his grief because his public display of his ruin is the ultimate vindication of the claim which no one would believe without such public proof—that he is one of "the poor." The narrator makes no gesture to help him, no effort to justify or condemn the laws which have turned his poverty into humiliation, no attempt to interpret his speech in terms of a theory of property or of the passions, though critics of the poem have suggested all these responses.[22] Rather he is absorbed, I think, in sympathetic contemplation of the complex state of mind and the tragic story which the shepherd has unaffectedly displayed. He is moved not to action or to argument but to recognition, to the discovery of unexpected meaning in his chance encounter and unexpected fullness in the answer to the questions he has asked. In this poem the narrator can be imagined to share in the discovery which his narration permits us to make; indeed he may be thought to tell the story of his meeting with the shepherd from the excess of the special pleasure inherent in such a discovery, the pleasure of seeing clearly and feelingly that *this* is what it is like.

Wordsworth might well have given the subtitle "Humiliation" or "Ruin" to "The Last of the Flock," as he gave the subtitle "Solitude" to "Lucy Gray" and "Poverty" to "Alice Fell" and "Animal Tranquillity and Decay, A Sketch" to "Old Man Travelling." Of this last poem the subtitle became the title in 1800, and eventually (in 1815) the concluding six lines, which make it a narrative, were omitted to leave the opening "sketch" in present tense as the whole poem. Influenced by the subtitle, critics have felt in the original version an incongruity between the sketch, which assimilates the old man to the silence and impassiveness of nature, and his speech, which reveals him not only as capable of speech but as affected by an unanticipated human woe. Most recently, Mary Jacobus has written: "Wordsworth's old man, as first conceived, *could* not have spoken. The man whose peace is that of the impervious natural world is given precisely those articulate human involvements from which he should be exempt" (*Tradition*, p. 181). That such judgments do not consider the narrator's point of view but treat his poem as a lyrical description interrupted by a narrative intrusion is understandable, for the poem does at first seem to be a lyric which aims to involve us in the speaker's

present vision, not a narrative which imitates a former vision in present
tense to involve us in it. After the dash which marks the break between
the immediate description and the framing narration, the reader must
reconsider the status of the opening lines and decide whether the new
point of view violates the old or transforms it; he must hold that a lyric
speaker has suddenly and inexplicably turned to narrative, or he must
see that the narrator of an anecdote has brought him to share immediately in a point of view which he is now asked to modify in light of
subsequent events.

The reader's judgment should hinge not on his disapproval of imitating a present description in the opening of a past narrative—the device
is familiar enough in Wordsworth and the sophisticated reader knows
how to take it[23]—but on his ability to discover a relation between the
beginning and the end of the poem and an effect to which the two
together contribute. In this poem as in "The Last of the Flock" the
unexamined link is the narrator's question: "I asked him whither he was
bound, and what / The object of his journey." Taken in itself such a
question addressed to such a person might express idle curiosity about
the man's journey or profound wonder about the ultimate end of life.
Taken in the context of the description in which the narrator involves
us, it expresses a more complex motive:

> The little hedge-row birds,
> That peck along the road, regard him not.
> He travels on, and in his face, his step,
> His gait, is one expression; every limb,
> His look and bending figure, all bespeak
> A man who does not move with pain, but moves
> With thought—he is insensibly subdued
> To settled quiet: he is one by whom
> All effort seems forgotten, one to whom
> Long patience has such mild composure given,
> That patience now doth seem a thing, of which
> He hath no need. He is by nature led
> To peace so perfect, that the young behold
> With envy, what the old man hardly feels.

The narrator whose vision of the man this is, attends closely to the
manner of the man's motion, assimilating all its aspects imaginatively
to "one expression." If the shepherd of "The Last of the Flock" was
striking for his overt expression of pain, this old man in motion is striking
for the absence of all such expression: he moves as if he were feeling
no pain, as if he were absorbed in thought. This interpretation of the
old man's motion leads the narrator to turn, at the dash in the seventh
line, to imagining his mode of being. In two clauses turning on the verb

is, he first posits that the man "is insensibly subdued / To settled quiet" and then elaborates that to be thus subdued is to be beyond both effort and endurance, or at least to *seem* to have forgotten the one and to have transcended the other. The apparent absence of pain in his movement thus becomes interpreted as the absence of painful struggle toward something or of painful suffering of anything. The expression of his motion makes him seem not to be going anywhere at all but already to be in a condition beyond desire and beyond irritation. He moves, but in his motion he expresses such "settled quiet" that he seems already almost to have arrived at the destination of his human journey, the "peace so perfect" to which the narrator imagines nature is leading him.

It *is* strange, then, that the narrator who has apprehended the old man's being in this way should turn to ask him where he is going and why, for he seems already to have answered his own question by imagining that the old man has arrived at that condition in comparison with which any ordinary destination would seem trivial. But the peace which the narrator has imagined the old man enjoys and which seems to place him beyond any ordinary human motives is not felt by the narrator himself, who has been moved not only to envision in this way the figure he has chanced to see but who has also been moved to hint, indirectly but I think unmistakably, that he beholds the vision he has created with envy, that is, with pain felt at the sight of a good which he believes he cannot share.[24] A narrator who envies such a figure must not enjoy settled quiet, be beyond effort, or be so patient that he no longer needs patience, and if he has created a vision of the old man which expresses his wish that such a state be possible (Jacobus, *Tradition*, p. 180), he has attributed that condition to a figure who appears to enjoy it by virtue of his place in the natural life-cycle, a place from which the young narrator is presently excluded by nature just as much as the old man is led there by her. The vision then is not stable from the point of view of the mind in which it has arisen, however unified and appealing it may be, for it does not fulfill the wish that has controlled its invention. The young narrator needs to bring the old man back down from the pedestal on which his wishes have placed him, for the basis of the old man's invulnerability, as the young man has imagined it, simply confirms to him that he must for many years struggle and suffer on the way to the perfect peace he wishes for.

His question to the old man, then, may express his need to dispel his vision, to achieve some communion with the old man he has imaginatively isolated from himself, to recover the old man as a traveller on the same human journey he is in the middle of. At the same time, to the extent the narrator is caught up in his vision, his question can be imagined to express surprise that the old man should be going anywhere or have any reason for remaining in motion and even resentment that the man should be still here in the movements of life and yet so far beyond him in the achievement of ultimate peace. The indirect narration of the question does not permit us to interpret the tone in which the question is asked, but the complex situation of the narrator at least allows us to imagine the range of his motives and to explore the possible effects of the old man's reply.

That reply is brief, controlled, and dignified, but its resonances for the narrator can be imagined to be both shocking and satisfying:

"Sir! I am going many miles to take
"A last leave of my son, a mariner,
"Who from a sea-fight has been brought to Falmouth,
And there is dying in an hospital."

This man, who has appeared so calm and thoughtful as to seem "exempt" from "articulate human involvements" (Jacobus, p. 181) reveals himself, calmly and thoughtfully, as the father of a dying son; this man who has seemed to have reached his journey's end must travel "many miles." At the end of his journey, he can expect to participate not in perfect peace, but, if he is fortunate enough to arrive in time (and he is too old to hurry), in the dying agonies of his son and in the narration of his fatal battle. If he is too late, he will find the body and not even a story to comfort him. The narrator could hardly have anticipated the "thought" with which the old man moves with such dignity and the feelings which must necessarily accompany such a thought, but the revelation of that thought and those feelings behind the motion which the narrator has so completely misinterpreted cannot but affect him. He must see that he and the man are fellow sufferers and fellow strivers, far from the completion of their lives' journeys, that the man whom he a moment ago envied for the peacefulness to which nature has led him is in fact being led to witness a turbulent and unnatural end, the death in war of a son before his father, the violent death of the young before the old. The narrator, far from the sea or from sea fights, cannot but be chastened for his self-pity over his own imagined strivings and sufferings by the fate of the old man's son and by the dignity with which the old man goes to face that fate and tells of his journey thither. He is after all alive and relatively safe, and the nearness to the end which he has envied but a moment ago is not only illusory but undesirable.

If there is some pain in being forced to relinquish the vision which he has formed of the old man (and the reactions of the critics seem to testify that there is), there is more pleasure in the vision which replaces it, the recognition that life is precious for the young and old and that pain, though intrinsic to life for as long as one is alive, can be borne with dignity. The old man becomes not an image of one who has finally achieved his exemption from the trouble which the narrator longs to escape but the image of both the worth and the possibility of living with that trouble. Though the narrator does not shout, "God be my help and stay secure; I'll think of the old man travelling!" his very telling of the anecdote, his careful preservation in the form of a story of the correction he has undergone, is evidence of his satisfaction in the lesson he has learned.

The reader's satisfaction here, as in "The Last of the Flock," is not caused by his superior insight into the narrator's situation, for the narrator himself has seen something and told of what he has seen because of his own gain in insight. Indeed, his use of the present tense in the first part of the poem is evidence that he has not only seen something in his experience but that he has designed a representation of it to make his reader go through the process of discovery he has gone through. "Old Man Travelling" is thus more artistically self-conscious than "The Last of the Flock." Our reading of it depends not just upon our human insight into its speaker but on our ability to deal with a narrative device as such. In using this device the poem lets the narrator's art show instead of revealing its point through the artlessness of its speaker. It exposes its "design" upon the reader and thereby becomes more than an anecdote of personal experience, for if its content reflects the lesson its speaker has learned, its manner of presentation reflects his wish to bring the reader through to the same lesson. Yet we ought not to resent this manipulation, for it issues not in the narrator's establishment of superiority to us but in his inclusion of us in the community of pleasure and pain into which his encounter with the old man has brought him. He uses our poetic expectations as does the narrator of "Simon Lee" only to disappoint them for the sake of a human recognition; he aborts his lyrical description as the narrator of "Simon Lee" aborts his narrative preparations—in order to reinforce an impression more salutary than the one we have expected. Critics of "Simon Lee" have accepted the challenge to discover the deeper "tale" for which Wordsworth's baffling of their narrative expectations prepares them.[25] They should recognize in "Old Man Travelling" that he has used their lyric expectations to the same disconcerting but humanly satisfying effect.

To consider "Expostulation and Reply" in terms of the "mould" in which it is cast is to remove it from the context in which it has always figured for Wordsworthians. This poem is traditionally taken, even by critics who elsewhere reveal formal interests, as one of the poems most pertinent to the question of what Hartman, summarizing a long-standing critical topos, calls "the creed of *Lyrical Ballads*" (*Wordsworth's Poetry*, p.

155). Under this heading "Expostulation and Reply" belongs first with its dramatic counterpart "The Tables Turned," then with the lyrics about nature from the 1798 volume, and then with any other poem or prose remark, published or in manuscript, which appears to bear on "wise passiveness" or "the One Life" or other topics of Wordsworthian doctrine. Paul Sheats is alone among the critics who have guided my inquiry in cautioning students of Wordsworth's philosophy that the "style" of these poems does not permit direct extraction of authoritative statements of the poet's beliefs. He warns that to quote the declarations of such poems as "Expostulation and Reply" and "The Tables Turned" as if they were "a sober summary of Wordsworth's doctrine of nature is to ignore the fact that the speaker . . . is a dramatic character, and that his language is appropriate to the debate, a genre that sanctions hyperbole, ellipsis, and condensation, all tacitly understood as the product of the contest dramatized." Conflating the two poems, Sheats goes on to claim that the speaker's enthusiasm in "The Tables Turned" about "one impulse from a vernal wood" is "acknowledged and corrected by the form of the poem, which balances it against the antithetical sentiments of the opposing speaker, Matthew. Although Wordsworth gives his namesake the last word, neither of the two speakers can be regarded as his philosophical spokesman." Elsewhere he treats the two poems as "a debate between two speakers who represent a formal opposition of types, such as *L'Allegro* and *Il Penseroso,* and who together generate a stable and comprehensive equilibrium" (*Making,* pp. 208–9, 188).

Sheats' insistence on "equilibrium" and his conflation of two poems into a single poem or a formally balanced pair follow from his attempts to correct the common attribution of the poems' most unqualified statements to Wordsworth himself, but they do not go so far as to take an interest in the difference between the narrative form of "Expostulation and Reply" and the dramatic form of "The Tables Turned" or to ponder the relation between these two formally dissimilar poems, always published together and in the same order, first the narrative anecdote, then the dramatic scene. The poems do go together, but in an asymmetrical relation that makes the second depend upon the first. In the context not of doctrine but of the other dialogic personal anecdotes we have examined, this relation can be clarified.

While "The Tables Turned" presents a "scene" spoken in the voice of a single character, "Expostulation and Reply" represents a narrator relating the words his friend Matthew addressed to him one morning and the words with which he answered him. The pair of poems is in no respect symmetrical, but "Expostulation and Reply" by itself almost is. The first three four-line stanzas report Matthew's question and exhortation to William; the fourth stanza, the narrator's only lines solely in his present voice, relate the time of the exchange, his mood at the time, his social standing toward Matthew, and the connection between their speeches; the next three stanzas present the substance of William's reply; and the final stanza, still part of the report of William's speech to Matthew, concludes the reply by telling Matthew not to ask what he has just asked. William gets four stanzas to Matthew's three in the reported exchange, and William gets to report it, too, but the shape of the poem overall, with the two speeches pivoted on the narrator's intervening stanza, comes closer to balance than any other poem in the 1798 collection ("A slumber did my spirit seal" in 1800 could be said to achieve balance, if that were what poems aimed at). If "The Tables Turned" is weighed into this balance, without consideration of the functional relations between the two poems, William gets more than the last word— his sixteen stanzas dwarf Matthew's three. To his expostulation there is no reply.

On the supposition that the two poems constitute a formal debate, with William and Matthew representing the opposing sides of nature and culture, critics have been correct to feel the weight in favor of nature, and, though Sheats is right on this supposition to caution against taking debating devices as real statements of Wordsworth's beliefs, he is mistaken to call the match a draw. An expostulation, however, is not a debate but an earnest attempt to dissuade, and the relation between good friends is not ordinarily that between opposing debaters. In the first poem at least there is every reason to think that the positions stated are not held merely for purposes of debate and little reason, I think, to characterize its mood, as that of the two poems together is often characterized, as "jocular." Neither Matthew's remonstrance nor William's answer indulges the exaggerations of the speaker in "The Tables Turned," whose extended and high-spirited utterance presumes upon a prior understanding the characters in the first poem do not immediately share.

Matthew in his expostulation perceives his friend's condition as a serious lapse from a human norm he presumes William to share, for the crucial difference between a debate and an expostulation is that a debate displays opposing positions not necessarily held by their advocates, but an expostulation addresses another with intent to move him by reasons to which he may be susceptible. Matthew blames his friend for wasting time, for isolating himself not only from the community of the living but from the community of dead authors the reading of whose works justifies our temporarily cutting ourselves off from those around us, and for absorbing himself in his dreams, figments of his own mind with no relation to the world outside. William's reply does not deny the importance of making good use of time or the value of being in touch with reality. He claims to be busy in his apparent idleness taking in the impressions that "powers" make on our minds whether we will or no. He is not idle and he is not out of touch with reality but taking it in through his eyes and ears and body. He shares Matthew's values on these points and is in conformity with them, though he may not appear to be.

The question of isolation he handles in another way. Most obviously, he claims to be in the presence of "things for ever speaking," "conversing" with them as he may, but this answer by itself does not meet Matthew's objection to William's isolation from the human world. More subtly but consistently and thoroughly he includes Matthew in the community he communes with, answering Matthew's addresses to "you" in terms of his beliefs about "our bodies" and "our minds," "the eye," and "the ear," not "my" body or mind or senses. William uses the first person singular only once in the core of his reply to claim as his own the beliefs he declares about the mind and the powers that work upon it (line 21), and he uses the second person only once (Matthew uses it eight times) to ask Matthew a crucial question about *his* beliefs:

"Think you, mid all this mighty sum
"Of things for ever speaking,
"That nothing of itself will come,
"But we must still be seeking?

Matthew must be imagined to indicate that he does not think this, for William concludes in his final stanza, set off from the rest of his speech by a dash, not that he is right and Matthew wrong but that Matthew knows better than to have asked. To tell Matthew "—Then ask not wherefore, here, alone, / "Conversing as I may, / "I sit upon this old grey stone, / "And dream my time away" is to remind him that he knows wherefore, that he participates in the community William has included him in and knows it. William may be imagined to report this anecdote not just out of the pleasure of winning in a debate (much less out of the dubious pleasure of reaching a stalemate) but out of the satisfaction of coming to an understanding with his good friend about a matter of serious concern to both of them, despite their apparent differences over it. Matthew's acknowledgment of the absurdity of the view William attributes to him binds them in a common faith that things will sometimes come of themselves, without seeking or questioning.

It is on the basis of this recognized common faith that the exaggerations of "The Tables Turned" can be imagined to be absorbed between friends without the need for Matthew to have his reply. The memory of the earlier exchange provides both Matthew's original position for his friend's parody and his assent to William's fundamental faith to make the parody friendly. Sheats is right when he says that Matthew's humanism "by no means supplies the target for the more serious attack on the 'meddling intellect' in the second poem" (*Making*, p. 188), for William at least imagines that he and Matthew have reaffirmed a friendship grounded in common values which can be distinguished from their exaggerated expression and directed against a common enemy. "The Tables Turned" is indeed a jocular and high-spirited poem, but it depends for its success on our imagining just that relation between its speaker and the butt of his humor which the previous poem represents as achieved. Without that preparation, its play might easily be taken not to confirm their friendship but to violate it.

Matthew's implied acquiescence in William's views not only establishes the basis for the dramatic monologue which follows "Expostulation and Reply" but also fulfills a wish variously represented in the nature lyrics with which that poem is often thematically linked. "Lines written at a small distance from my House," "Lines written in early spring," and "Lines written a few miles above Tintern Abbey" all present lyric speakers who appeal to another in different ways to recognize the values they imagine in nature; but in the single-voiced manner of these poems, none of these speakers receives an answer to his appeal or an acknowledgment of his views. The speaker of "Lines written in early spring" is the most isolated from his fellows, reviewing his past experience in nature and the regrets his interpretation of it raises about "what man has made of man" with no specified auditor. Located in first-person singular, unlike the William who replies to Matthew, he can only ask in the end, given *my* creed, "Have *I* not reason to lament / What man has made of man?" (italics added). The difference between this conclusion and the "then ask not wherefore" of "Expostulation and Reply" can be felt if we imagine William in the latter poem concluding with, "Have I not reason here to sit?" instead of with the gesture he chooses. The speaker of "Lines written in early spring," like the voice of the 1800 Preface, wants another to acknowledge that he has his reasons without presuming to bring the other to assent to them, but the speaker of "Expostulation and Reply" tells of an achieved consensus between himself and a friend on the same important matters.

In the other two nature lyrics the speaker addresses a specified person, his sister, about the value of his experiences in nature. In the "Lines written at a small distance from my House" he appeals to her to join him in a present moment of joy in nature, while in "Tintern Abbey" he recognizes that she now enjoys the passionate involvement with nature he enjoyed five years ago and anticipates that she will follow him in the process of development he has tried to account for earlier in his utterance. In the first poem the speaker desires her immediate participation; in the second he turns to her as a concrete embodiment of the values which, even if he were "not thus taught" to hold the creed he holds, would confirm his love of nature, and he appeals to her to witness his devotion and to look forward to a time when she will be pleased to remember his present exhortations, for she cannot yet share his understanding of the feelings and values he declares. Both poems in the immediacy of their lyric presentation do not allow for the dramatizing or the reporting of her response to the roles in which she is cast and leave us with the image of a speaker who has articulated his desires or his hopes but not even momentarily fulfilled them. Again the narration of "Expostulation and Reply" implies not only William's appeal but Matthew's assent to it, suggesting that its narrator enjoys the consciousness that his friend and intellectual equal has come to share the beliefs which the lyric speakers passionately urge on others inferior in age or experience.

"Expostulation and Reply" is also alone among the dialogic personal anecdotes in *Lyrical Ballads* in its report of an encounter between equals, for the other four poems we have examined present narrators' accounts of conversations with children or with social and economic inferiors who address the narrators as "Sir" and are willing to answer their impertinent questions. In "Expostulation and Reply" it is the narrator who is first questioned by his friend and equal to whom he in his turn addresses a question, and the footing of mutual understanding on which their encounter is reported to conclude is unlike the embarrassment with which the adult speakers of the encounters with children sense more in the children's replies than they had anticipated or the impressed satisfaction with which the superior narrators of the exchanges with the old man and the shepherd report their unexpected finds. As we will see, Wordsworth returns to explore these unequal relations in his final set of dialogic personal anecdotes. He does not again represent the friendship his narrator enjoys in "Expostulation and Reply."

Wordsworth's last dialogic personal anecdotes have received less critical attention than those published in the *Lyrical Ballads*, though they have received their share of scorn. Their close relation to one another has not gone unnoticed, however, and neither has their connection with the *Lyrical Ballads* enterprise. Dorothy Wordsworth's journals tell us that three of them, "The Sailor's Mother," "Alice Fell," and "Beggars," were composed on four consecutive days in March of 1802, the first new compositions after what Jared R. Curtis has called "nearly two years of silence."[26] Curtis, following Helen Darbishire, speculates that they were composed for the forthcoming new edition of *Lyrical Ballads* but were held back from that edition "in deference to the extensive additions to the Preface" (*Experiments*, p. 20), additions whose composition may well have immediately preceded what Parrish has called "a fresh outburst of boldly experimental writing." Parrish calls attention to the poems because Coleridge singled out all three of them along with "Simon Lee" and "Anecdote for Fathers" as "so plain that they would have been 'more delightful' to him in prose (2:53)." For Parrish the composition of these poems and of the 1802 additions to the Preface helps to explain the sharpening of Coleridge's disagreements with Wordsworth in 1802, and he considers them no further than they support (sometimes imperfectly) his thesis that those disagreements focused on "the dramatic passages, where the poet presented the thoughts of his characters or spoke with their voices, not his own" (*Art*, pp. 135–36).

Curtis, whose examination of the three poems is the most extensive I have found, sees them as the last efforts in a familiar kind before Wordsworth's achievement of a new lyric voice. The terms in which he characterizes and examines them show that their chief significance for him is their anticipation of the situation and the devices of one of the main achievements in that new voice, "Resolution and Independence." The "three poems," he writes, "depict a meeting between the poet-traveller and a counter-figure, a wandering and usually alien spirit, whose 'story,' either elicited from her or willingly told, stands in sharp contrast to the poet's experience, giving him pause. The emphasis in these poems falls on the startling self-sufficiency of the wanderers and their gift of effective speech" (*Experiments*, p. 27). Clearly there is a relation between these anecdotes and "Resolution and Independence," but Curtis's characterization of the narrators of the poems as poet-travellers and of the figures they encounter as alien, self-sufficient, and gifted with effective speech stand more appropriately as a description of the narrator and the leech-gatherer in the later poem than as precise generalizations about the figures in the other three ballads. Only in the later poem does the narrator identify himself as a poet; only there and in "Beggars" is he so overwhelmed by the speech of the counter-figure as to lose touch with the other's specific words.

In any event, the inquiry we have pursued so far commits us to move beyond generalizing the common features of the three poems or using them to set up another poem of greater interest to us. Since they are similar both in their form and in the incidents they narrate to the other dialogic personal anecdotes we have examined, we may wonder whether the strategies we have developed in reading those other poems will allow us to discover new pleasure in these. The formal analogies between these poems and the anecdotes of 1798 provide a place to begin. Two of the 1802 poems follow patterns we have seen before—the movement from initial vision of the narrator to the speech of the character in "The Sailor's Mother" and the narration of a dialogue between the narrator and a child he has interrogated in "Alice Fell." "Beggars" presents us with a new pattern—the narration of encounters with two different figures who are related in the mind of the narrator.

If "The Sailor's Mother" works as the anecdotes it resembles work, it should, like "The Last of the Flock" and "Old Man Travelling," provide some clue to how the narrator's initial vision of the woman he meets is completed or corrected or deepened by his hearing her speech.[27] His vision here is more emphatically identified as a vision by his mentioning the fog in which the figure of the woman (like the shepherd in *Prelude* VIII) appeared to him and by his saying that he "woke" from "lofty thoughts" before he noticed her concealed burden or inquired about it. He begins his account of how he saw her in terms which at first seem primarily descriptive of how she looked:

> A Woman in the road I met,
> Not old, though something past her prime:
> Majestic in her person, tall and straight;

and he goes on to compare her to a proverbial type of feminine dignity of character and bearing:

> And like a Roman matron's was her mien and gait.[28]

His next move at the opening of a new stanza drops description and comparison for direct declaration, and in doing so transforms the woman into the embodiment of the figure with whom a moment before she was compared:

> The ancient Spirit is not dead;
> Old times, thought I, are breathing there;
> Proud was I that my country bred
> Such strength, a dignity so fair.

To the narrator at the time of meeting, the woman was no longer *like* a Roman matron; she *was* an embodiment of a still living "Spirit" of strength and pleasing dignity which he had associated until her appearance with "old times" dead and gone. Now and in England this spirit stood before him, and moved him to a pride, in his country and in humanity itself, which even the woman's begging did not at once diminish. A "Woman" who a moment ago had only resembled "a Roman matron" became a "Spirit" whose begging made her only resemble "one in poor estate." His mind had become master enough of outward sense that even a second look at the figure after she begged alms did not abate his pride in what he saw in her.

How does the question the narrator asks her follow from this vision, and how does the answer she returns affect him? The question only arises when he has awakened from his vision and regained his power of speech, and it is occasioned not by her begging but by his observation of a detail that in his visionary state had escaped him. In that state he had watched her manner of moving toward him, but with her standing before him he noticed that she carried something concealed under her cloak. His question most simply understood expresses his curiosity at a feature of her appearance which until then he had failed to notice, but the form in which he stated it—" 'Beneath your Cloak / What's that which on your arm you bear?' "—places emphasis both on his wish to know what has been concealed by the outer appearance with which he has been absorbed and also on his sense that the thing concealed is some burden. The strength to which he has responded is after all impressive in relation to what it can carry; the dignity is moving when its uprightness is felt as a resistance to a powerful bending weight. He asked her, then, to reveal her burden, and she did so, taking it from under her cloak and calling it, " 'A simple burthen, Sir, a little Singing-bird.' " But, as if in response to the narrator's implied question about the moral or human burden she bears with such dignity, she went on to tell the tale of her son's death, his ownership of the bird, his uncanny separation from it before his last voyage, and her reason for keeping it with her:

"And now, God help me for my little wit!
I trail it with me, Sir! he took so much delight in it."

Coleridge has asked the rhetorical question which has shaped subsequent understanding of her reply's relation to the vision which preceded it: "I would further ask whether, but for that visionary state, into which the figure of the woman and the susceptibility of his own genius had placed the poet's imagination . . . whether he would not have felt an abrupt downfall in these verses from the preceding stanza?" (BL, 2:54–55). The answer he expects is of course "yes," but by the "preceding stanza" he means not the immediately preceding one in which the question is asked but the one before that in which the vision is at its height. Like those who have felt the old man's speech in "Old Man Travelling" as an "abrupt downfall," Coleridge ignores the narrative situation and the question which the narrator has asked. Here as in "Old Man Travelling," however, the woman's reply is not a downfall for the narrator but a more than sufficient answer to his question. What burden is she carrying? The burden of her son's recent death. And how is it that she carries it with such dignity? Because, for a reason she does not understand, her son has left this bird behind, and for a reason that embarrasses and confuses her, she finds pleasure in it because he "took so much delight in it."[29] She may be embarrassed, because, at the core of this Roman matron's dignity is not the stoic resistance to the expression of pain or pleasure but the Epicurean principle of human dignity which Wordsworth enunciates in the Preface of 1802, "the grand elementary principle of pleasure, by which he [man or woman] knows, and feels, and lives, and moves" (*LB*, p. 258). "The ancient Spirit" which lives in her reveals itself as the enduring power of this natural principle, a power which breathes in her pleasure in the bird and in the narrator's pleasure both in his vision of her and in her revelation of herself. He is not disillusioned, as Coleridge is, by the shift from vision to reality because the vision of her has prepared him, prepossessed him, as Wordsworth says in the *Prelude*, to look for an insight in the real woman, to expect a figure impressive as she is to teach him something, as indeed she does (see *Prelude*, VII, 254–339). Even his present pride and his pleasure need not abate after what she tells him, for he has discovered that the strength and dignity which impressed him are rooted more deeply than in a cultural moment which has given a typical image of those characteristics. The sailor's mother replaces the Roman matron as the embodiment of those qualities the narrator admires, because her natural and enduring source of strength and dignity underlies the other's historically and culturally bound one.

"Alice Fell" suggests parallels with several of the poems we have examined. Like "Simon Lee" it begins with overtones of an adventurous tale but modulates into an anecdote of the narrator's encounter with a person whom he helps to extricate a commonplace object.[30] Like "The Last of the Flock," it deals with an impoverished figure, one whom the narrator in this poem aids in the way in which Dr. Burney wished he had aided the poor man of the other poem; if he suffered the shepherd to part with the last of his flock, he at least bought Alice Fell a new cloak. A strange dissonance emerges from these parallels, however, for in "Simon Lee" the point of the poem seems to be that there are depths of human misery discoverable to the thoughtful mind in the gratitude of men, but in "Alice Fell" the narrator finds satisfaction in his vision of the "Proud Creature" his generosity has clothed, and he distinctly does not find cause for mourning in the gratitude he imagines. Curtis aptly describes the incongruous effect of the narrator's gesture—"The new cloak, provided generously but somewhat pompously by the narrator on the next day, seems anticlimactic, the child's pride slightly tainted" (*Experiments*, p. 105)—but he does not recognize that the taint he senses in the "child's pride" is felt in part because the narrator attributes to the child an attitude that says more about his feelings than about hers. The narrator, after all, has not seen the "Proud Creature," for he has left money with the landlord to buy the child a cloak, while he has gone on with his journey or his business. His vision of the "Proud Creature" into which his gift has transformed the inconsolable child is the concluding attitude of his tale, not of his experience, and, like the concluding gesture of "Anecdote for Fathers" or the opening of "We Are Seven," it suggests the point of view from which the narrator can think well of himself, not the point of view which reveals the full meaning of his anecdote.

The narrator in this anecdote, like the narrator in "We Are Seven" emphasizes the irrational fixation of a child. This time, instead of refusing to grieve over the death of two siblings, the child in question will not stop grieving over the loss of a ragged cloak. The narrator four times dwells on the intensity of her grief, and three times interprets it in connection with her cloak. Of his first finding her on the back of the carriage, he says,

> "My Cloak!" the word was last and first,
> And loud and bitterly she wept,
> As if her very heart would burst.

He describes her, after they released the cloak and he invited her into the chaise, thus:

> She sate like one past all relief;
> Sob after sob she forth did send
> In wretchedness, as if her grief
> Could never, never, have an end.

After he tells of asking her whether she dwells in Durham and of her reply, he goes on,

> And then, as if the thought would choke
> Her very heart, her grief grew strong;
> And all was for her tatter'd Cloak.

And finally he describes her on the remaining journey toward Durham as

>   sitting by my side,
> As if she'd lost her only friend
> She wept, nor would be pacified.

His interpretation of this continuing grief is manifest in his orders to the landlord upon their arrival in Durham to purchase the child a new cloak and a good one, too:

> 'And let it be of duffil grey,
> As warm a cloak as man can sell!'

The narrator's purchase order, if it seems anticlimactic and pompous, is at least carefully prepared for in the poem. From his first effort to interpret the moan which he hears above the wind and his first stopping of the carriage to ascertain its source, through his discovery of the child, his extrication of her cloak, his inviting her into the chaise, and his inquiry into her circumstances, to his final order to the landlord, he is trying to help or console the child. His final vision of what a "Proud Creature" she became after her cloak had been purchased is a vision of his having succeeded in his efforts, but the story he tells is a story of repeated failure. Each gesture of aid is met by unmitigated tears, just as each repetition of the narrator's question in "We Are Seven" was met by an unchanged answer. His insistence that he has found and finally taken care of the true cause of her grief appears as an effort to cover his discomfort at her inconsolability by covering her with a cloak. But his effort seems inadequate not because her grief has resisted his efforts so far but because his interpretations of its cause have been pitifully literal.

He has taken the child's first word and made it "last and first" the cause of her crying, but he has not entered into her situation imaginatively. A. C. Bradley, the poem's only defender, has applied his imagination to the child in "all the individuality [she] possesses in the poem" and has revealed a number of additional motives for her tears:

> A child crying for the loss of her cloak is one thing; quite another is a child who has an imagination, and who sees the tattered remnants of her cloak whirling in the wheel-spokes of a post-chaise fiercely driven by strangers on lonesome roads through a night of storm in which the moon is drowned. She was alone, and, having to reach the town she belonged to, she got up behind the chaise, and her cloak was caught in the wheel. And she is fatherless and motherless, and her poverty (the poem is called *Alice Fell, or Poverty*) is so extreme that for the loss of her weather-beaten rag she does not "cry"; she weeps loud and bitterly; weeps as if her innocent heart would break; sits by the stranger who has placed her by his side and is trying to console her, insensible to all relief; sends forth sob after sob as if her grief could never, never have an end; checks herself for a moment to answer a question, and then weeps on as if she had lost her only friend, and the thought would choke her very heart. It was *this* poverty and *this* grief that Wordsworth described with his reiterated hammering blows.[31]

Bradley has gotten caught up in the poem and in the cadences of his own defense of it (a forgiveable excess, I think, given the kinds of cruel criticism to which the poem had been subjected), but in doing so he has revealed several crucial aspects of the child's situation which the narrator has not noticed.

First of all, the child is frightened, not just of the lonesome roads, the wild night, and the whirling wheel, I would suggest, but of being discovered by the driver or the "stranger" in the coach. When the coach stops for the first time (a detail not given in the version of the story as Dorothy writes it down from Mr. Graham) there is no sound, despite the child's having presumably already lost her cloak:

> But neither cry, nor voice, nor shout,
> Nor aught else like it could be heard.

She is capable of turning off her moan (she is not yet wailing in grief) when some other passion than that associated with the loss of her cloak predominates (Bradley significantly notes that she "checks herself" later in the scene). It is when she is caught, the second time the coach stops, that she directs attention toward her cloak and begins her loud and bitter weeping. The narrator never thinks to raise the question "What are you doing here?" not only because he has a more sympathetic temper than many might have had but because the child, who has no reason to think he is as kind as he is, has successfully distracted him.

Instead, his first question—" 'What ails you, Child?' "—addresses her tearful condition and her answer leads him to help her release her cloak from the wheel. His second question—" 'And whither are you going, Child, / To night along these lonesome ways?' " elicits a wild reply that leads him to invite her to come with him into the chaise, where she continues to sob inconsolably. It is in the chaise, sitting next to her, that he asks the third question, which checks her grief momentarily and elicits her strange reply:

> "My Child, in Durham do you dwell?"
> She check'd herself in her distress,
> And said, "My name is Alice Fell;
> I'm fatherless and motherless.
>
> And I to Durham, Sir, belong."

Curtis, without saying why, has identified this passage as the poem's " 'imaginative core' " (p. 104). Its strangeness is not only in the sudden cessation of tears but also in the form in which the girl answers the narrator's question. He has asked, "Do you live in Durham?" and she replies that she "belongs" to Durham. It is almost as if she is responding, not to the question but to the implication of possession in the narrator's first and only address to her as "My Child." There is a formality about her whole reply—a name, rank, and serial-number enumeration—as if she felt herself a prisoner and were asserting her independence of her captor's desire to intrude on her identity and participate in her life and grief. She states her name, gives her orphan status, and addressing the narrator as "Sir" for the only time in the poem, says she belongs, in effect, not to him but to Durham. She does not confess that she belongs nowhere or specify in what sense she belongs to Durham, but she does parry the gesture which she reads in the narrator's question and puts an end to his inquiries.

In interpreting the tears to which the child immediately returns, the narrator himself returns to his literal view that "all was for her tatter'd Cloak," but he goes on to describe the manner of her crying with a simile of complex import:

> and, sitting by my side,
> As if she'd lost her only friend
> She wept, nor would be pacified.

The narrator's use of this comparison seems odd, because the child *has* lost her only friend, not in her immediate loss of the cloak but in her absolute condition. She has just revealed that there is no person to whom she "belongs"; she is as "alone" as she appeared to be when the narrator found her on the back of the chaise. In fact she is even more alone, for her refusal of the narrator's gesture of friendship has identified her ultimate loss as one for which there is no compensation, one which another person no matter how generous cannot ameliorate. It is against the revelation of this "loss of friends and kindred" that the narrator's purchase of the cloak seems not only pompous but pathetically inadequate. He has offered himself, as the narrator did in "The Fountain," as a substitute for the lost loved one of another person, and, having, in effect, gotten the same reply which Matthew there gave—"Alas! that cannot be"—he denies the absoluteness of her loss and of his inability to restore it by reducing it to the loss of a cloak which he can replace with the best one available. To the indecency of exposed suffering he responds by providing a cover.

He also responds to the suffering he has seen and denied by telling this anecdote, however, and in doing so he reveals both the weakness of his own gesture and the strength of the child. If he saves himself from confronting the recalcitrance of her misery by purchasing a cloak, she saves herself from rebuke, arrest, or something worse and gets a new cloak into the bargain by using the one power at her disposal—the power to cry or not as she will. Though she reveals her absolute condition in her reply, she is preoccupied with her immediate condition, which has less to do with a cloak than with the narrator himself and what he might do to her. Her hysterics, and her strategic break in them, disarm him, though he is too wrapped up in his good intentions to see himself as a threat. The child so resourceful at surviving under such potentially dangerous circumstances might well be a "Proud Creature" the next day in the cloak which her quick wit had helped to provide for her. From this point of view it appears that, though the narrator cannot help her in the full depth of misery she has revealed, she can help herself even in the drastically reduced circumstances of her life. If his gesture seems insufficient against the image of the utterly lonely child, his pride in helping seems comic against the image of the self-sufficient gamin.[32] Both have had the encounter their way in the end, for he has turned his frustrated efforts to comfort the child into an undeniable act of kindness, and she has turned her captor into her benefactor. We have seen both a tragedy too keep for the kindhearted narrator to face and a comedy too ordinary for him to suspect, but we have also escaped from the sentimental and cynical responses that either reading of the event would by itself have warranted. The narrator's blindness is again the vehicle not only of his self-satisfaction but of our pleasurable discoveries.

"Beggars," last written of the personal anecdotes of 1802, combines the two kinds of anecdotes we have distinguished into a composite form, narrating two related encounters as one. The first part resembles those poems in which the narrator has told of his meeting an impressive adult figure in the high road, his envisioning that figure, and his hearing the figure's story. The second part resembles the other anecdotes in which the narrator and a child have talked at cross purposes and persisted in their unresolved differences.[33] In an early version of the poem the two parts were separately numbered, but in the first published version and all subsequent ones it is presented as a continuous narrative of what, in effect, is a single story for the narrator. What holds the episodes together for him must eventually concern us, but first let us examine them separately in the context of the poems they resemble.

The narrator's vision of the majestic beggar woman most immediately calls to mind the narrator's vision in "The Sailor's Mother." In both poems the narrator moves from describing the appearance of the woman he has met to comparing her or identifying her with familiar stereotypical figures. Both figures are tall and majestic, as Curtis recognizes, but the sailor's mother is in motion when he first presents her, the other beggar woman is stationary. If the dignified movement of the one suggests to him the bearing and moral character of the Roman matron, the height of the other ("a tall Man's height, or more") suggests powerful, dangerous, and exotic female figures, the Amazonian Queen, the "ruling Bandit's Wife, among the Grecian Isles." Her dark complexion adds to the impression of the exotic and the unlawful, its "Egyptian brown" linking her with the gypsies and their ways.

This vision, however, does not give rise, as did those of "The Sailor's Mother," "Old Man Travelling" and "The Last of the Flock," to a question. The woman tells her tale of woes unasked, and the narrator responds to the deluge of woes which she pours over him ("Before me begging did she stand, / Pouring out sorrows like a sea; / Grief after grief") not by discovering in it a correction or fulfillment of his vision but by doubting it. He tells his listener not what the woman said but what he thought and did:

> —on English Land
> Such woes I knew could never be;
> And yet a boon I gave her; for the Creature
> Was beautiful to see; a Weed of glorious feature!

He maintains his interest in her appearance and discounts her tale instead of presenting it as deepening the impression her appearance has made. Rather than extending his notion of what is probable on "English Land," he applies the notion he already has and judges her story incredible. By the standards of the other anecdotes it may appear that he is resisting an extension of his human sympathies and conserving a questionable esthetic perspective on another's sorrows, but at this point it is premature to enter such a judgment.

In the second part of the poem, the narrator tells of his continuing on his way to see two boys merrily chasing a butterfly, their hats wreathed and garlanded, one with laurel, the other with yellow flowers. They appear to him to be brothers to one another and sons of the woman he has already seen ("And like that Woman's face as gold is like to gold"). They too begin a tale of woe before he has a chance to ask them anything, but instead of believing the tale and giving alms as the narrator of "Alice Fell" believed her story and helped her, the narrator first says that he has already helped their mother, and when they say that she is dead, gives them the lie and insists that it was indeed their mother he has already served. When he contradicts them, they do not stand their ground and insist but fly off to other play. A lie is again in question here as it was in "Anecdote for Fathers," but this time the narrator has no trouble naming it. The death of a child's loved one is again at issue as it was in "We Are Seven," but here it is the adult who insists that the loved one is alive while the child matter-of-factly states that she is dead. The conversation, instead of repeating the contrary insistences of adult and child, as it does in the latter poem, is broken off by the children's flight. The narrator here, as in the first part of the poem, does not change his mind as a result of the story he has heard, this time persisting not in his idea of what is possible "on English Land" but holding to his discovery of the resemblance between the woman he first saw and the boys he saw subsequently. Again the appearance of the figures is more important than their accounts of themselves.

What then is the point of this anecdote for its narrator? Is he rather shallowly showing us how he has not been taken in by two devious attempts at winning his sympathy, the first because of his general awareness of what is likely and the second because of his shrewd linking of it to the first? Is his pleasure in the power he has had over the formidable woman, whom he has chosen to aid for his own reasons and not for hers, or in his foiling of the boys and causing their rapid retreat at his exposure of them? Perhaps it is both in part, but it is also connected with the tenacity with which he holds to the vision he has created of the woman and to the resemblance he has perceived between her and the boys. He will not give up the one in light of the story the woman tells or the other in the light of the child's assertion to the contrary. His enjoyment is not in the reinforcement or correction of his perceptions by the speeches but in the persistence of his perceptions in spite of them. His mind here has remained the master of outward forms more fully than in any of the other personal anecdotes we have examined, and it is not surprising that, while Wordsworth classifies the other poems in his edition of 1815 as poems referring to the periods of childhood or old age or as poems founded on the affections, he classifies "Beggars" as a poem of imagination. For there is, as he says in his Preface to that edition, a pleasure proper to imaginative modifications of external objects, a pleasure which the mind takes in the activity through which it contemplates what it makes of things. The narrator in "Beggars" has felt this pleasure so strongly that he will not yield it even to the pleasures of discovering human nature and sharing human sympathies to which the other anecdotes have regularly led.

His pleasure in the appearances of the woman and children *as appearances* is nicely figured in a passage from Spenser's "Muiopotmos" to which Wordsworth alludes in calling the woman "a Weed of glorious feature":

What more felicitie can fall to creature,
Than to enjoy delight with libertie,
And to be Lord of all the workes of Nature,
To raine in th'aire from earth to highest skie,
To feed on flowres, and weeds of glorious feature,
To take what euer thing doth please the eie?
Who rests not pleased with such happines,
Well worthie he to taste of wretchednes.[34]

The narrator of "Beggars" has taken the attitude of the butterfly Spenser is here describing; he has assumed the position of lord of nature and fed on the weed of glorious feature which has pleased his eye, without allowing the moral and emotional bonds through which he is related to her and to all men to spoil his happiness. If as Spenser goes on to say in the next stanza, such bliss cannot last on earth, he has already said in this one that whoever cannot rest pleased with the happiness which he can find in the appearances of things, deserves his misery. This is the defense of the esthetic perspective which the narrator here takes, though we can add that, when Wordsworth's narrators' perceptions have allowed them to discover human sympathies in other poems, their pleasure even then was their guide. We have here not a new principle but a new source of pleasure, for whether the narrator is led to sympathize with pain or to refuse sympathy with it, we have found the principle of pleasure leading him.

But what in this poem has it led him to? Where is the peculiar source of delight in these perceptions which led him to cling to them? What is it in the image of the stationary formidable woman and in the sense of her likeness to, even her identity with (how after all is gold like to gold?) the two wild bedecked brothers that provides the narrator's delight? What is he contemplating in the image he has made? We may suspect that what Wordsworth called in 1815 the "human and dramatic Imagination" (*Prose*, 3:34), the faculty which has guided us into all the anecdotes we have considered so far, may not carry us further into this poem. We are for the first time distinctly in the presence of a poetic mind—a mind as he tell us in 1802, "pleased with [its] own passions and volitions . . . delighting to contemplate similar volitions and passions as manifested in the goings-on of the Universe, and habitually impelled to create them where [it] does not find them." It is the poetical imagination which must be our guide here, the imagination Wordsworth characterizes in the 1815 Preface and takes credit for there and in the Essay Supplementary of the same date. The exercise of this kind of imagination links the poet to poets as the exercise of the other links him to men. Wordsworth's exercise of it links him, for example, to Spenser, whom Wordsworth contrasts with Milton and the Hebrew poets and their exercise of the poetic imagination, in the following way:

> Spenser, of a gentler nature, maintained his freedom by aid of his allegorical spirit, at one time inciting him to create persons out of abstractions; and, at another, by a superior effort of genius, to give the universality and permanence of abstractions to his human beings, by means of attributes and emblems that belong to the highest moral truths and the purest sensations.
>
> (*Prose*, 3:35)

If the narrator in "Beggars" has worked such a transformation of the persons he has encountered into figures carrying the significance of universal and permanent abstractions, what attributes and emblems has he ascribed to them and what truths do they figure forth? To answer these questions we must turn not to the common human insights which have helped us to grasp the other personal anecdotes but to poems or prose statements beyond this poem which may help us to interpret the attributes and emblems of its figures and grasp the truth which their relation here exemplifies.

What, then, may it mean to insist that the tall, stationary, domineering, dangerous female figure is the mother of, and as such is virtually identical with, the two garlanded, merry, rapidly appearing and disappearing, playful brothers? The attributes here listed are not unfamiliar in Wordsworth, resembling as they do the attributes of the imagination and fancy as he describes them in the 1815 Preface. The woman's unspecified but great height ("a tall Man's height, or more"), her associations with dominion and majesty, the profusion and permanence of her outpourings link her with attributes of imagination, while the boys' rapidity of movement, evanescence, transitory decoration, and playfulness link them with the fancy. To see the figures for these powers as identical in substance, to see the fancy as the child of imagination is to unite the great oppositions of the eternal to the temporal, duty to delight, and fearful impotence to fecund love. In perceiving the relation he does between the figures he meets on the road, the narrator has envisioned a union profoundly pleasant to contemplate, a union in which a power beautiful and dangerous which confronts one with an overwhelming flood of sorrows is recognized as the mother of joy, liberty, and luxuriant play, while those ephemeral delights are recognized as of one substance with her enduring presence.

The narrator's relation to these figures, however, may be more compelling to him than his vision of their relation to each other. He is not overwhelmed by the majestic woman and the flood of sorrows she pours out nor is he taken in by the boys' independent claim on him. Though she halts him in his progress like the apparition of Imagination in Book VI of the *Prelude*, he is not lost but self-possessed, capable of judging her claims and appreciating her as a distinct and beautiful figure. Though the boys press their claim on him as if they required special sustenance from him, he holds that his care for their mother is also care for them, that he need take no separate trouble to nurture them because he knows them for what they are. Applying here what Wordsworth says of Spenser, we can say that the narrator here has "maintained his freedom by the aid of his allegorical spirit," for he has freed himself of the claims which the woman and children have made on him by giving them the "universality and permanence of abstractions." If he has not made himself master of the powers he has envisioned—capable of summoning them at will, he has at least not let them master him. At this he must be pleased.

By linking the dialogic personal anecdotes of 1802 with "Resolution and Independence," Jared R. Curtis has opened a suggestive line of inquiry which we must now pursue (*Experiments,* pp. 97–113). But though he draws parallels between the poems, Curtis insists upon the distinction between the latter poem and the anecdotes on two counts, the difference in their stanza forms and the difference in their relative emphasis on the persona of the poems and the figures they present. The persona of "Resolution and Independence," he claims, has "moved to center stage, no longer merely relating and commenting on the doings and undoing of the figures he observes." What he has brought to center stage in place of literal attention to what the character he meets does and says is a depiction of what his own mind has done with the character; what, through "the special power of figurative language," he has made of the old man. It is striking to note, as Curtis does, that the earliest known version of "Resolution and Independence" contained an extended version of the old man's speech which made the poem more closely resemble "Old Man Travelling," or "The Last of the Flock," or "The Sailor's Mother," but it is over-hasty to draw a distinction in kind between the early " 'ballad' " version that "describes another's character" and the later " 'lyrical' " version that presents a personal vision. At the very least, this distinction underestimates the "lyrical" aspect of the lyrical ballads we have so far explicated, which present the characters' literal speeches from imaginative points of view; it may also obscure the narrative complexities of "Resolution and Independence" by reducing problems of narrative diction to problems of lyric "voice" and language. The critical history of this poem, like that of the other dialogic personal anecdotes, has been drawn away from narrative diction to lyrical language both by Wordsworth's 1800 pronouncements and by Coleridge's comment on its "disharmony in style," and Curtis, like many other commentators, attempts to answer Coleridge's judgment without questioning his emphasis on lyric diction or his preference for harmony.[35] Curtis accordingly points out that the poem reveals a breakthrough from "the language of men" to "the language of vision," while he asserts that "the two languages harmonize" in the poem. He does not consider the relations among what the narrator heard and experienced at the time of the episode he narrates, what he is trying to accomplish in narrating it, and what his speech reveals about him.

But to focus on narrative diction, as I wish to do, is to encounter a serious difficulty at the very beginning of the poem. The first two stanzas evoke a scene in impersonal present and present progressive tenses, a scene which only in the third stanza becomes the past location of the narrator's travels. We have noted before in "Old Man Travelling" a shift which might appear similar, a lyrical present-tense description abruptly shifted to a narration of a past encounter, but the point of view there seemed to be interpretable as the result of the present narrator's desire to recreate for his reader the immediacy of his previous vision, while the scene here seems distinctly more comprehensive and orderly than what the narrator saw and heard when he "was a Traveller then upon the moor." Though we are told that he then "saw the Hare that rac'd about with joy" and "heard the woods, and distant waters, roar; / Or heard them not," we are presented with a representation of the sights and sounds of the scene which reveals more than this, and something different as well.

In the scene as presented in the first two stanzas, the "roaring in the wind" of the night before has modulated into the "pleasant noise of waters" and the heavy rain reappears as the bright drops upon the grass and the mist raised by the feet of the hare. In place of the overwhelming sound and downpour, a world of distinct but related sounds and sights, incorporating the aural and visual evidences of the storm, emerges in response to the "calm and bright" rising of the sun. The birds, each with his own metaphorically characterized voice, sing as if in conversation with themselves or with one another (cf. Conran, p. 69), against a continuo of the "pleasant noise of waters." Visual things, unified, again metaphorically, as "All things that love the sun," appear joyously beautified and animated by the presence of their beloved and his reflections in the rain-drops that bejewel them and the mists that they stir up. The "animation and vitality" which Alan Grob finds in the scene is undoubtedly there (p. 218), but I find those qualities ordered in a way which makes Wordsworth's terms from the Preface of 1802, "relationship and love," seem more apposite. A community is roused by the rising sun, whose light glorifies the world as the world returns its tribute of love. Wherever the hare runs "in her mirth," raising her mist about her, the light of the beloved sun catches the mist and surrounds her with light. No *as if* or *seems* interferes with the metaphorical transformation of the scene into a joyful cosmos and community, brought into being from the chaos of the previous night by the rising of the bright and beneficent sun.

In the third stanza the "now" of the first two stanzas becomes the "then" of the newly emerged narrator's past travels; the world he has so lovingly represented becomes "the moor" across which he traveled; and the scene as he then experienced it is recapitulated in the lines:

I saw the Hare that rac'd about with joy;
I heard the woods, and distant waters, roar;
Or heard them not, as happy as a Boy.

Though we may be tempted to read this as a shorthand meant to place the whole of the first two stanzas in the consciousness of the narrator at the time he crossed the moor, several things prevent us. The hare is the most striking detail of the previous stanza, but her joyous motion is there the occasion for her raising of the mist which the sun illuminates, "wherever she doth run." In stanza three, she has been taken out of the loving relationship in which she was first presented and seen simply racing about in isolated joy. The sounds which focus the first stanza are the songs of the birds and the "pleasant noise of waters," but what the narrator heard, or perhaps did not hear, in his boyish bliss as he crossed the moor was a "roar" of "woods" and "distant waters," sounds which suggest the chaotic storm out of which the morning scene emerged but not the sounds of that scene itself. A joyous motion seen and a threatening sound perhaps heard but perhaps not heard are all the narrator, whose present awareness includes the opening scene he has just described, tells us he was aware of as he traveled then upon the moor. His absorption then in the "pleasant season" was not an attention to the pleasant scene, whose structure and quality reflect the imagination of the narrator who has been through the experience he is beginning to narrate, not the partial vision and uncertain attention of the person he was when he experienced it (cf. Eggenschwiler, p. 79; Heath, p. 127). The scene then, as we have it, should help us to clarify not the frame of mind in which the narrator began his experience but that in which he returns to it (cf. Robson, p. 120), and the difference between what he envisions now and what he tells us he was aware of then should clarify the judgment he now makes on what he was then and the lesson he learned which has brought him to that judgment.

The usual places to search for that lesson have been the last two stanzas of the poem, where the narrator reports his vision of the old man's perpetually pacing about the moors "alone and silently" and his resolution with God's help to " 'think of the Leech-gatherer on the lonely moor.' " But though the attitude he reports in the concluding lines comes across as a kind of moral to the story, its particular point and force has been a matter of dispute. For one thing, he is telling of the way he envisioned the old man at the time, of his feeling then that he "could have laugh'd [himself] to scorn, to find / In that decrepit Man so firm a mind" and of his determination for the future to " 'think of the Leech-gatherer.' " He does not say on what occasions he will think of him or, more significantly, what thoughts the recollection of the leech-gatherer will bring to mind or what form those thoughts will take. Though efforts have been made to find the memorable core of the poem in the narrator's final vision of the leech-gatherer pacing about the moors or in some sententious reminder to himself in adversity of the old man's independence or of the old man's dependence on divine Providence, only David Eggenschwiler has suggested that the form in which he might "think" of the leech-gatherer would be the "form of the entire poem" (p. 89), a narration in which he would try both to conserve the lesson which had been given him and to interpret its source and meaning. We have seen in each of the dialogic personal anecdotes we have examined that the form which the story takes itself reflects the narrator's self-pleasing interpretation of the encounter he narrates, and "Resolution and Independence," though more complex in form than any of the poems we have examined so far, is no exception. The final lines direct our attention not just to the vision at which the narrator then arrived or to the scornful laughter with which he then ridiculed himself but to the subsequent reconstruction of the experience which the whole poem presents.

What, then, is the narrator thinking of the leech-gatherer and what shape does his thought take in the poem? It begins, as we have seen, with an imagined vision of the scene through which the narrator walked on the day of his encounter with the leech-gatherer and shifts to an extended development of what was and was not on his mind at the time. Only in "Anecdote for Fathers" among the poems we have considered does the narrator take such pains to describe what his earlier mood was, but if in that poem the narrator emphasized how the pleasures of the present scene were great enough to allow him to entertain nostalgic reminiscences of another lovely scene he had left behind, the narrator here emphasizes how his involvement in the present scene took away all remembrances of other times and places until, having reached the peak of his forgetful joy, fears and fancies crowded in upon him. The narrator of the earlier poem says that he became strong and careless from excess of joy, but the narrator of this poem tells us that, recollecting himself, he suddenly became aware of his carelessness and vulnerability in his joy and plunged from it to the depth of despondency. Each emphasizes the mood from which his encounter issued, for the father imposed his feelings on his son from the overflowing strength of those feelings, while the poet of this poem exposed his feelings to the leech-gatherer from the vulnerability of which he had become aware. Because of their moods, the one carelessly forgot the vulnerability of the child to whom he spoke, while the other sympathetically projected his own loneliness onto the old man he had met.

The "fears and fancies" with which the narrator of "Resolution and Independence" tells us he became preoccupied have several aspects. As he thought of the skylark (a solitary bird who sings from the sky above the aviary community in the wood of the opening stanza) and the "playful Hare" (again isolated from the sunlit mist which follows her in the second stanza), he saw himself as at the moment, like them, "a happy Child of earth" and a blissful creature, but he recognized that "there may come another day to me, / Solitude, pain of heart, distress, and poverty." He went on to reflect on how his present bliss fit the pattern of his whole life lived

> in pleasant thought,
> As if life's business were a summer mood;
> As if all needful things would come unsought
> To genial faith, still rich in genial good;

but the fearful recognition of other possibilities to which his recovery from joyful self-forgetfulness brought him led him to ask his first question:

> But how can He expect that others should
> Build for him, sow for him, and at his call
> Love him, who for himself will take no heed at all?

The heedlessness from which he had just been taken came to stand not for the aberration of a moment but for the pattern of his whole life, and the question he asked himself clearly implies that the despondency into which he had fallen led him to fear that one cannot reasonably expect others to care for one who takes so little care of himself. This pattern which he has found in his own life suggested to him a comparison with the lives of other men like him, poets who have begun their lives "in gladness" but "thereof," almost as a necessary consequence, come to "despondency and madness." Such men might be "deified" by their youthful poetic spirits and led to live as if they were gods in the faith that accompanies their genius, but the change of mood he had undergone prefigured a depression of those spirits from which a permanent loss can be anticipated. His thoughts moved, he tells us, from contemplating the possibility of an unhappy change to discovering a reason for its probability to identifying a pattern in which it seemed necessary. His imagination worked superstitiously to turn a momentary mood shift into a tragic vision attributed not to the workings of his mind but to the real structure of the poetic career. He recognized the idyll he had been living as a hypothetical construct ("As if life's business were a summer mood; / As if all needful things would come unsought") but he took literally the tragedy he discovered in the lives of poets. There is no "As if" about "we Poets in our youth begin in gladness; / But thereof comes in the end despondency and madness."

It was in this frame of mind, the narrator tells us, that he "saw a Man" before him, and it is at this point in his telling that he begins interpreting what he saw, hypothetically describing the man he met and repeatedly offering alternative explanations for his presence and his characteristics. He introduces the encounter with uncertainty concerning its source—"Now, whether it were by peculiar grace, / A leading from above, a something given, / Yet it befel"—and he initially characterizes the age of the figure he encountered with the first of many verbs of seeming: "The oldest Man he seem'd that ever wore grey hairs." He goes on to describe the oddity of his presence and the peculiar state of his animation ("not all alive nor dead, / Nor all asleep") with the famous simile of the stone and the sea-beast, his doubly bent body with a hypothetical account of the pain and sickness he might have suffered long ago, his motionlessness, integrity, and obliviousness with the simile of the cloud, and his concentration on the muddy water which he stirred with a hypothetical comparison to "reading in a book." All of these comparisons and hypotheses belong to the narrator's effort to describe the man who appeared to him, not, as the next two visions do, to his mind at the time of the encounter. They do not cohere into a unified metaphor which would fix the mode in which the narrator understands the figure he encountered nor do they develop as a psychologically plausible series of transformations. They represent the narrator's efforts to find an equivalent for each of the old man's striking qualities and the narrator's inability or unwillingness to see him, as it were, steadily and whole (cf. Meyers, p. 447). Far from presenting a single vision of the apparition which he might be tempted to take literally, he seems deliberately to multiply possibilities of interpreting and ways of seeing the old man, to indulge in elaborate comparisons which call attention to themselves as comparisons and to him as their maker. Wordsworth's citation of the stone/sea-beast and the cloud similes in his 1815 Preface seems to verify their status as almost detachable evidences of his mind's work, themselves of considerable interest apart from their narrative context.

But though the similes and hypotheses do not cohere with, modify, or grow out of one another, they do connect with both the present and past concerns of the narrator. The two similes indirectly link the old man to the scene which the narrator presented in the first two stanzas, for the first one, through the comparison with the "Sea-beast crawl'd forth, which on a shelf / Of rock or sand reposeth, there to sun itself," grotesquely includes the old man among "All things that love the sun" (cf. Gérard, p. 16), while the second one, through comparison with the cloud "That heareth not the loud winds when they call," makes him independent of the "roaring in the wind" out of which the initial scene emerged. The emphasis on his "extreme old age" links him to "the end" which the narrator at the time was imagining, while the emphasis on his previous sufferings attributes to him experience of the sort which the younger man fearfully anticipated. The old man is at once made an incongruous part of the happy scene the narrator now imagines and a final stage in the process he then anticipated.

In addition, the consciousness and concentration attributed to him in the description of his staring into the muddy water "As if he had been reading in a book" make his relation to the pond an emblem of the narrator's present and past situations. Trying to interpret the murky waters he has himself stirred up, the old man is like the youth trying to interpret the course of his life amid the conflicting visions his passions have raised and like the narrator trying to interpret his encounter with the old man again amid his own competing visions. The old man's laborious stirring and fixed scrutiny of the "moorish flood" "about his feet" recalls the hare who in her joyous motion "with her feet . . . from the plashy earth / Raises a mist; which glittering in the sun, / Runs with her all the way, wherever she doth run." Her effortless raising of what Coleridge in "Dejection" calls a "fair luminous mist" is replaced by the old man's deliberate stirring of the same waters, and her thoughtless participation in the glittering cloud of her own raising is replaced by his interpretive concentration on the murky water he has beclouded. The narrator now can be imagined to see himself no longer as "a happy Child of earth" like the hare but as a struggling interpreter of waters like the old man.

It is striking that the narrator's interpretation of the old man as himself an interpreter is the narrator's last attempt to interpret, at the time of retelling, the old man's presence. From here on he narrates what he said and what he thought at the time he met the old man in relation to what and how the old man replied. The disjunction between the language of his interpretive efforts and the language of his narration has seemed incongruous to some critics who take the poem as a lyric utterance, but it need cause us no more difficulties than any other narrator's return from reflecting on what happened to telling what was said and done. The narrator's present efforts to interpret are more developed in this poem than in any of the other personal anecdotes—a fact that accounts for critics' emphasis on a new language or a new voice here, but when he turns to narrate his encounter with the old man, the problems of reading the words and gestures he recounts are the same ones we have met in all the personal anecdotes we have examined.

What then are we to read in the peculiar way the young poet opened his conversation with the old man, the deference with which he tells us he approached him and the commonplace remark with which he addressed him—" 'This moment gives us promise of a glorious day' "—a remark which seems so out of keeping with his own mood at the time of the old man's appearance, and with the elaborate interpretations he just engaged in? The deference has no precedent in any of the personal anecdotes we have examined, for the narrators in those poems have either directly questioned the persons they have met, with no polite preliminaries or, in "Beggars," "The Sailor's Mother," and "Expostulation and Reply," responded after an appeal from the other which breaks the ice. The relation established in all cases but "Expostulation" is one in which the narrator assumes a kind of superiority to his interlocutor, whether it be that of adult to child, begged to beggar, or person in control of his emotions to one out of control. We are not directly given the tone in which the narrator inquired about the old man's destination and purposes in "Old Man Travelling," the poem in which the relation of narrator to interlocutor most resembles that in "Resolution and Independence," but in most of the other poems the narrator presents himself as one in possession of himself and his resources, who approached another who lacked those resources and so lacked a claim to equal respect. Here the roles have reversed, and the narrator tells us he approached the old man, in effect, as a child to an adult, as one out of control of his emotions to one who appears in control, as one in need to one who appears to have resources. The commonplace with which he opened expresses at once the indirection with which he felt he must approach the old man and the hope which he wished the old man to confirm. He spoke not of the lovely morning it already was but of the "glorious day" promised by such a morning, revealing indirectly his need both for conversation and for confirmation of a hope he has been tempted to deny.

The young man's indirection was such that the old man did not yet recognize the nature of his appeal, but the old man's "gentle" and "courteous" answer encouraged him to ask a question—something the narrators of the other poems have done without encouragement—in a form which seemed to reveal his predicament to his interlocutor. He asked, " 'What kind of work is that which you pursue? / This is a lonesome place for one like you,' " and the old man is described in the 1807 version as answering "with pleasure and surprize; / And there was, while he spake, a fire about his eyes," while in later versions the narrator says that "a flash of mild surprise / Broke from the sable orbs of his yet-vivid eyes." Both descriptions emphasize the animation of the old man's response and the surprise with which he responded to the narrator's question, the later version in language which is usually reserved for the recognitions undergone by poet-observers in Wordsworth's other poems.[36] It is almost as if the old man had heard the young man confess his own loneliness in his sympathetic acknowledgment of the old man's loneliness, or at least as if the narrator thinks he noticed a response which indicated recognition of his plight. The old man's reply seems to confirm his recognition of the youth's condition, for the terms in which he replied were so close to the terms in which the young poet had previously been worrying that the latter was thrown into a revery about the man and reminded of his "former thoughts." The man's voice, he says, became to him "a stream / Scarce heard" in which he could not divide "word from word" and his body "did seem / Like one whom I had met with in a dream; / Or like a Man from some far region sent; / To give me human strength, and strong admonishment." It appeared to the narrator as if the old man's words were so appropriate to his feelings that he must be a figment of his own consciousness or else a figure "sent" from some all-knowing source to address him. What he needed seemed so uncannily supplied, after he had doubted that he could rely on being provided for, that at first the intervention had to seem imaginary or supernatural. This man, who appeared in this lonely place not only to provide his own "honest maintenance" but also to provide the narrator's comfort, could not be real if one cannot "expect that others should / Build for him, sow for him, and at his call / Love him, who for himself will take no heed at all." But, since he did appear and seem to have comfort to offer, the narrator, "not knowing what the old Man had said" repeated his question in a form that made his need even clearer, " 'How is it that you live, and what is it you do?"

In presenting the old man's cheerful repetition of his answer, the narrator reports the man's exact words and his own image of the man wandering on the moors. Much has been made of this image, which many critics have taken to be the climactic vision of the poem, a triumph of the poet's imagination, after which the concluding lines of the poem seem anticlimactic (cf. Bloom, p. 170). I agree with Thomson, however, that the image, like the report of the old man's words, shows that the young man has recovered his capacity to see the old man as he presented himself, not that the young poet has transformed him into a visionary figure (pp. 195–96). For the old man, who is said to "pace / About the weary moors continually, / Wandering about alone and silently," has already described himself as roaming "From Pond to Pond . . . from moor to moor" and a second time as traveling "far and wide." The youth upon hearing the repetition of this description could see the old man in this way instead of in relation to his own need, just as he could hear and recall the old man's specific words instead of hearing a stream of undifferentiated words. What he heard and saw was a bracing example of perseverance in the face of scarcity and dignity in isolation and silence, qualities the lack of which had brought him to the weak state in which he met the old man and appealed to him for comfort. Identifying with the character he perceived, he felt scornful of his own weakness and, it seems, determined to emulate the old man's firmness of mind.

The form of his resolution, however, leaves its content ambiguous, for to " 'think of the Leech-gatherer on the lonely moor' " is not to think anything definite about him. Even the motive of emulation is uncertain in this formulation, for it does not say that he will be like or act like the leech-gatherer but only that he will "think" of him. The young poet might be just as impressed by the old man's seemingly providential appearance to him in time of need as by the old man's admirable strength of character, but he does not say that he will think with gratitude of the help he has received any more than that he will think with bracing emulation. His resolution is only to "think of the Leech-gatherer." But in the context of the poem that resolution itself takes on significance without further specification, for whatever the value of his encounter with the leech-gatherer, the young man is shown resolving to conserve it for future need, instead of assuming that other needful corrections will appear at other critical moments. Though this needful thing has "come unsought," he determines no longer to act "As if all needful things would come unsought / To genial faith, still rich in genial good" but to become his own providence to the extent of saving up those needful things which Providence has given. In this respect it is not the old man's strength or his providential appearance but his management of scarcity that touches the poet and makes him recall only the words that address this problem:

"Once I could meet with them on every side;
But they have dwindled long by slow decay;
Yet still I persevere, and find them where I may."

The significance of the poet's determination to think of the leech-gatherer becomes still clearer in the context of the other dialogic personal anecdotes which resemble this one, for none of them dramatizes the motive to conserve the experience it narrates as part of the experience itself. Each presents a narrator who seems entirely occupied with his discovery of an immediately significant experience, as if he had never had such an experience before and did not anticipate having or needing one again. Each narrator is represented as having been in the frame of mind which prepared him to have just the experience he recounts, but none of them attempts, as does the narrator of "Resolution and Independence" to generalize that frame of mind, to characterize himself and his life, and thereby to generalize the experience as one of recurrent applicability to himself. The other narrators discover significance in the relation of their encounters to a single mood, or a single idea or question which occupied their minds at a given time, but the narrator here discovers a significance in relation to *himself,* to the character of his "whole life" as he has recognized he lives it. Because he recognizes the mood shift he has undergone as part of a pattern characteristic of men like himself, he also recognizes the encounter which helps him this time as a resource of enduring value, and he determines accordingly to conserve it for future use. While the other narrators are defined as transitory consciousnesses absorbed by the present significance of an isolated experience, he is defined as an enduring self whose awareness of his past makes him find in his present experience "food / For future years" (*LB,* p. 115).

In recounting the anecdote which ended with his resolution to think of the leech-gatherer, the narrator may be seen at once to be feeding on his experience and preserving it in a lastingly nourishing form, like the one Wordsworth attributes in the *Prelude* to those "spots of time" which have much the same nourishing virtue. Their "efficacious spirit chiefly lurks / Among those passages of life in which / We have had deepest feeling that the mind / Is lord and master, and that outward sense / Is but the obedient servant of her will" (1805 *Prelude,* XI, 268–72). This spirit does not, however, lurk in moments which reveal the fitness of nature to the mind in the discovery of form clear and complete and satisfying in itself, but in those moments which evidence imaginative activity in excess of their object and in defiance of adequate formulation. Such is the first spot of time to which Wordsworth points in the *Prelude,* "in truth, / An ordinary sight" but one which would demand "colours and words that are unknown to man / To paint the visionary dreariness"; such too is the experience recounted in "Resolution and Independence." The garrulous old man who continues his cheerful discourse even as the young man envisions him in silent isolation is "in truth, / An ordinary sight," but the narrator has lavished his capacity of imaginative representation upon the sight without attaining to a consistent and complete image of his vision of the man. There is an excess of vision which rewards return to the encounter in memory instead of satisfying the mind in narration, as do the other personal anecdotes we have examined. This experience is represented as one from which there is some residuum worth saving and returning to, while the experiences of the other poems are presented as fulfilled and fulfilling. Readers who seek a satisfying resolution in this poem must be ultimately disappointed, for the narrator's interest in the poem as of future use to himself takes precedence over the motive to produce a clear and satisfying vision. He moves beyond the idyllic vision which deceived him and the tragic vision which frightened him at the time of his experience, but he does not replace them with a stoic or a providential vision which might close the experience and complete the poem. Instead he represents himself as a maker and preserver of visions (cf. Heath, p. 135), who, having been provoked in one instance to visionary activity, carries out a resolve to "enshrine the spirit of the past / For future restoration" rather than to narrate an encounter from the past for present pleasure.

Chapter Five

When I began to enquire,
To watch and question those I met, and speak
Without reserve to them, the lonely roads
Were open schools in which I daily read
With most delight the passions of mankind,
Whether by words, looks, sighs, or tears, revealed;
There saw into the depth of human souls,
Souls that appear to have no depth at all
To careless eyes.

Wordsworth, 1850 *Prelude*

From Anecdote to Episode
The Discharged Soldier in *The Prelude*

The tales and dialogic personal anecdotes we have examined in the last two chapters do not exhaust Wordsworth's narrative experiments in *Lyrical Ballads* or elsewhere. They do, however, include all of the poems upon which the claim of his experiment's failure has been based, and they illustrate his working with the two principal variables of a poetics of speech, the narrator's relations to his listener and to his hero. My intention in any case has not been to offer what Bacon would have called a "magistral" treatment of Wordsworth's narrative works but to initiate a way of reading his narrative experiments, especially those long treated with contempt, that would suggest the sorts of pleasure they can offer to active readers. I am convinced that this way of reading has fruitful implications for Wordsworth's other narrative works as well as for his lyric and dramatic poems, but I do not propose to pursue those implications here. Instead I shall take up one instance in which the interrelations of speaker, hero, and listener and the distinctions between a tale and a dialogic personal anecdote can help us to clarify what is going on in an important episode in an admittedly major poem. In examining the episode in *The Prelude* most like the dialogic personal anecdotes, the encounter with the discharged soldier, we can bring to bear the same concern for the emphases with which it is presented that has guided our inquiry into the separate poems. Our task, however, is interestingly complicated by the point of view of the narrator of the long poem, who tries to subordinate the dialogic personal anecdote to his tale, the story of his life, and by the different emphases in the several versions in which the anecdote exists.

The narration of the encounter with the discharged soldier first existed independently in the form of a personal anecdote before it was modified and incorporated into *The Prelude*. Before finding its place at the end of Book IV, this narrative stood alone as a first-person past-tense account in blank verse of a meeting between the speaker and an ailing soldier whom he had queried and aided. We may first attempt to read this

separate poem in itself and in its relations to the other personal anecdotes, especially "Resolution and Independence," with whose central
figure the figure of the discharged soldier is most often compared, before
going on to estimate the changes in its form and function that its placement in *The Prelude* entails.

The version of this anecdote that Beth Darlington has identified as
the "fullest manuscript extant of the poem conceived as an independent
work" is the longest and most detailed version of the encounter and,
consequently, perhaps the most pregnant with the "rich, varied, and
often uncanny symbolic implications" that Paul Sheats has noted in such
poems.[1] These implications emerge from a simple narrative format parallel to that of "Resolution and Independence" except for its lacking the
initial present-tense evocation of the scene of the encounter. In both
poems the narrator's state of mind at the time of the meeting is first
developed; then his perceptions of the figure he meets are elaborated;
and finally his interaction with the man is presented. Within this format,
however, the specific determinations of each poem are strikingly different.

While the narrator at the opening of "Resolution and Independence"
presents himself as having fallen from a state of thoughtless absorption
in enjoying the present season to one of worried dejection in contemplating his life, the narrator of "The Discharged Soldier" presents himself
as having attained to a "happy state" of "self-possession" in rhythmic
movement and reverie. Though he judges this state subsequently in
contrast to one in which he would have been worthy "of the deeper
joy / Which waits on distant prospect, cliff or sea, / The dark blue vault,
and universe of stars," he presents it as a positive condition deliberately
sought and achieved in the face of tempting distractions. If the narrator
of "Resolution" tells that he had been brought to the point of worrying
about his recognition that his whole life has been "liv'd in pleasant
thought," the narrator of the "Discharged Soldier" speaks of having
successfully found refreshment in present enjoyment of pleasant thought.
If the one was frightened by his own improvident inattention to exter-
nals, the other was restored by his very success in shutting out the world
and communing with his body and with the beauteous pictures of his
own mind. The narrator of "Resolution" was in doubt and in need when
he first saw the leech-gatherer, and even in retelling he is not sure
whether the encounter should be attributed to "peculiar grace, / A leading from above, a something given." The narrator of the other poem,
however, was self-possessed and without felt need or worry when the
soldier was presented to his view, and in the retelling he describes
himself confidently as "step by step led on" to the encounter with that
"uncouth shape."

That the soldier first struck him as an "uncouth shape," whose human identity he only gradually "confirm'd" through a part by part inventory of his figure, countenance, and dress, distinguishes his initial apprehension from that of the narrator of "Resolution," who immediately "saw a Man" before him. Both figures are out of the ordinary, the one "tall, / A foot above man's common measure tall, / And lank, and upright," the other "the oldest Man . . . that ever wore grey hairs" with his body "bent double, feet and head / Coming together in their pilgrimage; / As if some dire constraint of pain, or rage / Of sickness felt by him in times long past, / A more than human weight upon his frame had cast." Both figures are motionless and suggest an ambiguous condition neither certainly living nor certainly dead; both seem at one point in the encounter to be part of the poet's inner world, dream figures or visionary apparitions. The narrator of "Resolution" attempts to resolve these ambiguities in the telling by comparing the appearance of the leech-gatherer to that of natural forms, to the motionlessness of a cloud, integral and insensible, and to the incongruous appearance of a "Sea-beast crawl'd forth, which on a shelf / Of rock or sand reposeth there to sun itself." The narrator of the other poem takes no such imaginative liberties in retelling, emphasizing instead his uncertainty about the figure's status at the time of their meeting.[2]

The appearance of the two figures raises problems not only about their ontological statuses but about their moral conditions as well. The leech-gatherer is described as self-sustaining ("Himself he propp['] d, his body, limbs, and face, / Upon a long grey Staff of shaven wood"), self-moving ("At length, himself unsettling, he the pond / Stirred with his Staff'), and intently interested in his environment ("and fixedly did look / Upon the muddy water, which he conn'd, / As if he had been reading in a book"). The soldier is passively supported from without ("From behind / A mile-stone propp'd him"), stirred only by the narrator's greeting, and apparently indifferent ("His face was turn'd / Towards the road, yet not as if he sought / For any living thing"); his staff, at first unseen by the narrator, lies "neglected in the grass, / But not forgotten" until the narrator takes charge to lead him to food and shelter. While the leech-gatherer responds immediately to the narrator's question about his livelihood with "pleasure and surprise" and even with "a fire about his eyes," the soldier persists under questioning in a "strange half-absence & tone / Of weakness & indifference" until at the very end, after the narrator's charitable acts and concerned questioning, he seems "To speak with a reviving interest / Till then unfelt." The leech-gatherer is described as speaking in a style "solemn" and "above the reach / Of ordinary men" while the soldier's speech might have seemed "solemn & sublime" *except* for his air of indifference and weakness,[3] which transforms the superficial signs of dignity and sublimity into a pathetic but impressive otherworldliness.

Though the ontological questions initially occupy both narrators, it is the moral attributes of the figures they meet that seem to bear the burden of their narratives. The leech-gatherer's strength and capacity, "with God's good help," to help himself interests the narrator, who has recognized that he has taken no care for himself and fears he cannot do so. He quotes those words of the man's speech that emphasize his perseverance in the face of scarcity and tells of how he laughed himself "to scorn, to find / In that decrepit Man so firm a mind." The self-scorn suggests his reaction against the weakness that has led him to approach this apparently weak man in search of help and his discovery not only of the man's sufficient resources but of his own unexpectedly abundant ones. He has received the help he sought, but its effect is to move him not to gratitude but to the recovery of his lost self-respect. The narrator of the "Discharged Soldier" emerges from his "shade / Of a thick hawthorn" in the character of benefactor rather than of supplicant, but the object of his good offices is notable, until the end, for his seeming indifference to them and to the life, health, and comfort which the narrator takes it upon himself to save.

The soldier's two quoted speeches are made in response, first, to the narrator's asking him why he had waited by the roadside "nor had demanded rest / At inn or cottage" and then to the narrator's admonishing him not to "linger in the public ways / But at the door of cottage or of inn / Demand the succour which his state required." In the first speech, present only in this independent version of the poem, the soldier explains that

> My weakness made me loth to move, and here
> I felt myself at ease & much relieved,
> But that the village mastiff fretted me,
> And every second moment rang a peal
> Felt at my very heart. There was no noise.
> Nor any foot abroad—I do not know
> What ail'd him, but it seemd as if the dog
> Were howling to the murmur of the stream.

Here his indifference to the condition which moves the poet to aid him is evident in his concern not to find food or shelter but to find relief from the incessant howling of the dog, and his detachment from his own needs is revealed in his curiosity about what ailed the dog to make him howl so.[4] His response to the narrator's admonition to seek help for himself, however, reveals beneath his indifference a radical faith in God and his fellow man which implicitly transforms the situation:

> At this reproof
> With the same ghastly mildness in his look
> He said, "My trust is in the God of heaven,
> And in the eye of him that passes me."

He reveals in this reply a confidence that includes the narrator's act of charity in an impersonal framework that calls neither for self-concern or personal gratitude on the part of the soldier nor for deliberate responsible charity or embarrassed discomfort at "the gratitude of men" on the part of the narrator. The soldier's reply interprets the narrator's act as part of a reliable providential order in which benefactor and beneficiary can participate without embarrassment at giving or receiving aid—an order which at once dissolves the benefactor's painful reflection at the end of "Simon Lee" and the embarrassed beneficiary's self-scorn at the end of "Resolution and Independence" by removing their givings and receivings from the realm of selves serving and being served by one another to that of agents impersonally serving a beneficent power. The soldier thanks the narrator "with a reviving interest" and the narrator returns "the blessing of the poor unhappy man," recognizing in their exchange not cause for the "mourning" occasioned by the aid of Simon Lee in the context of continuing human needs and failing human powers, but the occasion for reciprocal beneficence in the context of shared grace. The sense that the narrator has of being "step by step led on" to this encounter is clearly the issue of the encounter itself and its disclosure to him of his participation in the providential plan to which the soldier is so absolutely committed. Far from issuing in a resolution to take care for himself from now on, this encounter issues in a sense of being cared for and caring *without* the proviso that heaven helps those who help themselves.

Here a distinction in one of the common generalizations about the Wordsworthian "solitaries" is in order. John Jones has written, "all his solitaries of the next few years are in their different ways at peace with their environment; and although they live on the other side of tragedy, there is no attempt to derive their situation from tragic conflict—they have always been where Wordsworth finds them, and they remain there after he has gone."[5] Jones explicitly includes both the leech-gatherer and the discharged soldier under this generalization, but they exhibit differing relations to that peace which is on the other side of tragedy and the experience which *is* tragedy. Only the soldier has been through much but stands beyond what he has been through, "Remembering the importance of his theme, / But feeling it no longer." Although he has suffered, he retains from his suffering, not the interests and regrets intrinsic to it, but the recognition of a providential pattern implicit in it that makes the tale itself uninteresting to him. Of all the figures met in the personal anecdotes and related poems he is the only one indifferent to his own welfare and to familial bonds, the only one whose condition is almost uninterpretable in terms of "the general passions and thoughts and feelings of men" and the "grand elementary principle of pleasure" which Wordsworth in 1802 claims as the staple of his poetry. Were it not for his irritation at the howling of the dog and the narrator's sense that, in the end, he "seem'd / To speak with a reviving interest / Till then un-felt," his "ghastly mildness" would place him beyond the community of pleasure and pain which Wordsworth identifies as the human com-munity, for he is not concerned, it appears, with "storm and sun-shine, with the revolutions of the seasons, with cold and heat, with loss of friends and kindred, with injuries and resentments, gratitude and hope, with fear and sorrow."

Every other figure in the anecdotes, including the leech-gatherer, is involved with at least one of these human interests. The leech-gatherer is in fact a type of "gratitude and hope" who, in spite of "many hard-ships" and in spite of the narrator's self-indulgent wish to project his own tragic vision of himself upon him, remains hopefully persistent in his calling and cheerfully grateful for "God's good help" even in ad-versity. It is only the narrator who imagines from his bent figure that he has borne "A more than human weight"; the man himself shows no sign of self-pity or of traumatic suffering that has placed him beyond caring about his own maintenance and his converse with other human beings.[6] He is what he always has been and what the narrator comes to imagine he always will be, but the discharged soldier, as Jones else-where sensitively observes in commenting on the description of his dress as "though faded, yet entire," the discharged soldier is "changed" (*Ego-tistical Sublime*, p. 69). The details of his appearance that make him seem "a man cut off / From all his kind, and more than half detached / From his own nature" are confirmed in the revelation of his inner life, which barely retains signs of the susceptibilities we identify as our own. His lack of the inner and outer vital signs of motion and emotion accounts for his characterization as ghastly or ghostly. He seems as far on the "other side" of tragedy as the leech-gatherer seems from any vulnera-bility to tragic experience.

In the extreme case which the discharged soldier presents, the actions of the narrator in relation to him take on special significance, for his efforts to aid the soldier are not just sympathetic acts of charity from one man to another; they are efforts to reclaim a tragically transformed man for humanity, to arouse in him the interests characteristic of man and so return him to the community of men who share those interests and the joys and sorrows connected with them. The narrator finds this

"Stranger" on the edge of a village whose doors are silently closed to them both and leads him, "through shades gloomy & dark" to an open field and the cottage of a friend where succor may be found, and where, the narrator hopefully concludes, the signs of reviving interest may be seen in the man almost lost. What I have called the ontological and moral aspects of the poem come together here in a situation in which the moral issue is not merely to behave humanely to another man but first to affirm and then to revive the humanity of a seemingly inhuman figure. The soldier's faith "in the *eye* of him that passes me" (italics mine) instead of in his heart or conscience may perhaps hint at the importance of this act of human recognition to any subsequent act of charity.[7]

Viewed in the light of this formulation of its action, the anecdote of the discharged soldier would seem destined to take a place in *The Prelude*, a poem whose plot turns on the premise that humanity is in the eye of the beholder. Because its poet-hero is "furnished with that kind / Of prepossession" of human dignity which protects him from disillusionment at the sight of human degradation and wretchedness (1805, VIII, 459–60), he discovers, when confronted for the first time with the sight of woman abandoned to open shame, a barrier "that from humanity divorced / The human form, splitting the race of man / In twain, yet leaving the same outward shape" (1805, VII, 424–26). Here the problem of recognizing man as man receives explicit formulation and prepares for a crisis in which the distance between prepossession and experience becomes so great that the poet loses confidence in his idea of man and in himself and sinks into perplexity, apathy, and despair. Though brought to this condition not, like the discharged soldier, "through stroke / Of human suffering, such as justifies / Remissness and inaptitude of mind, / But through presumption" (1805, XI, 149–52), the poet too is reclaimed for humanity by the combined ministry of Nature, his sister, and his friend; his restoration, like that he imagines he sees in the soldier, is a recovery of ordinary human interests and the feelings associated with them.

The reflective reader may thus discover in the episode of the discharged soldier a foreshadowing of what the narrator will ultimately present as his own crisis and recovery, but it would exceed the warrant of the poem to think that the narrator himself is aware of this significance at the time he relates the anecdote or indeed at any subsequent time in his reconstruction of the story of his life. The context in which he introduces it is a different one, and its function for him there depends on other characteristics than those I have emphasized. *The Prelude* is not the utterance of a mind like those its narrator envisions at its conclusion, minds for whom "the consciousness / Of whom they are . . . [is] habitually infused / Through every image, and through every thought, / And all impressions" (1805, XIII, 108–11) but of a mind that struggles toward self-knowledge, frequently confessing its failures and limitations along the way, and graced in the end not with a comprehensive vision of itself but with a vision of what such a vision would be like.

Only the poet who has set up the sequence and shape of his narrator's apparently ongoing utterance may enjoy something like this total consciousness infused through an image like that of the discharged soldier, and the attentive reader may try to share his awareness. We may see the importance of this distinction nowhere more clearly than in the changes which the narrator's words undergo at the poet's hand from the version of the story in 1798 to that in *The Prelude* of 1805 and finally that in *The Prelude* of 1850. While the narrator continues to tell of what we can see is the same encounter, he is given different emphases that shift his and his story's meaning, but he is never given awareness of the compositional changes his words undergo. Though he may be halted in his progress or allowed to retreat over old ground and may be given consciousness of his own movements as he is at the beginning of Book IX, he is never shown wondering whether he should place the episode of the drowned man in Book I or Book V or deciding whether to open Book IV with the words "A pleasant sight it was when, having clomb" or with "Bright was the summer's noon when quickening steps." The modern habit of printing the 1805 and 1850 versions in parallel text editions should long since have made us aware that the narrator says nothing the poet does not make him say and that nothing that befalls the poet in the actual process of composition becomes part of the narrator's utterance and experience unless the poet chooses to have it do so. Even imagination cannot rise up from the mind's abyss for the narrator unless the poet gives it leave.

In the 1805 version, the narrator is made to give the anecdote of the discharged soldier a prominent place, even if he does not take it as a proleptic epitome of his whole story. He introduces it, singled out from among "many wanderings that have left behind / Remembrances not lifeless" (1805, IV, 361–62) to conclude his treatment of the theme which has occupied him in Book IV, "Summer Vacation." The theme which it brings to a close, however, is not merely the doings and undergoings of that summer but the "deep vacation" (1805, III, 542) which began during his year in Cambridge when he "slowly and insensibly" abandoned the solitary life of "deep quiet and majestic thoughts" (1805, III, 210–11) to indulge in a life of empty noise and superficial pastime on a "populous plain" (1805, III, 195). The important vacation here is not the absence from the labors of school time, for he had spent "the labouring time of autumn, winter, spring— / Nine months" (1805, III, 669–71) in "submissive idleness," but the absence from the visionary experience and high purpose, from the solitary self-communion and "community with highest truth" (1805, III, 120), that had been his in the "glory" of his youth when he early returned into himself and away from "the first glitter of the show" at Cambridge (1805, III, 94–97). The summer vacation itself does not increase this absence but permits the narrator to measure the change between the youth who had left his native hills for Cambridge and the one who returned to warm welcomes from the world which had nurtured him. While the youth himself greeted old friends with no sense of irony, though with occasional embarrassment for his altered dress, the narrator sees changes in himself then which provoke him repeatedly to involuntary expression of regret and even to ironic criticism of his youthful thoughtlessness.

The changes are of special concern to the narrator and disturb him in reconsidering them because they have an important relation to the problem from which his inquiry into his past began. The repeated failures "To brace myself to some determined aim" (1805, I, 124), to select and carry out a high poetic purpose in regular daily labors, which moved him to make the deep inventory of his preparation for such a task in *The Prelude*, find their first possible explanation in the attitudes which he exhibited at this time in his life. Up to this time, he has traced the unbroken development of his powers and of his recognition of them up to "an eminence" of power and self-possession, to the achievement of what he calls in Book I "The calm existence that is mine when I / Am worthy of myself" (1805, I, 360–61). But on the "populous plain" to which he descends, the calm disappears, even as an adjunct of other activities, let alone as a condition sought and enjoyed for its own sake, nor does he find in his new environment anything "to put to shame / My easy spirits, and discountenance / Their light composure—far less to instil / A calm resolve of mind, firmly addressed / To puissant efforts" (1805, III, 350–54). Although the narrator overtly accepts the blame for the condition into which he then fell, he explains his failure of effort in terms which raise a fundamental problem for him now:

For I, bred up in Nature's lap, was even
As a spoiled child; and, rambling like the wind,
As I had done in daily intercourse
With those delicious rivers, solemn heights,
And mountains, ranging like a fowl of the air,
I was ill-tutored for captivity—
To quit my pleasure, and from month to month

Take up a station calmly on the perch
Of sedentary peace.

(1805, III, 358–66)

It almost appears from the explanation offered here that it *was* "for this" failure of dedication to steady labor that Nature prepared him, that he is indebted to her for shaping a character that does not consort with the regular tasks to which, then and now, he has ineffectually attempted to bend himself.

If the narrator interprets his falling away at Cambridge in this way, he cannot but be plagued by regrets, but if he is to press his story forward to a satisfactory resolution, he cannot rest in this interpretation, and must combat his regrets. He can end his inquiry at once if he has truly found that his lack of discipline is just as "natural" as his moments of inspiration, for he will then have discovered his character and not a temporary departure from his true self, brought about by an accidental combination of circumstances. If this is what he is, he can give up his efforts to devote himself to high endeavors or he can appeal to a power outside himself, as Wordsworth does in "Ode to Duty," to bend him to the task he cannot consistently impose upon himself. He does not accept this interpretation, however, and repeatedly counters his temptations to regret with assertions and evidence that point to an underlying continuity with the "glory" of his youth, even in times when it seemed most completely forgotten. His declarations in Book III that "Imagination slept, / And yet not utterly" (1805, III, 260–61) or that "Yet was this deep vacation not given up / To utter waste" (1805, III, 542–43) or that "Yet something to the memory sticks at last / Whence profit may be drawn in times to come" (1805, III, 667–68) strike the note to which the narrator repeatedly returns from his regretful criticisms of himself and of the place in which he found himself.

He does not succeed, however, in bringing "peace to vain regrets" (1805, III, 491) in that book, and though the fourth book opens with an apparent recovery of "that sweet valley where I had been reared" and of a "throng of things . . . / And many of them seeming yet my own" (1805, IV, 11, 30–32) its effect upon the narrator is to intensify his self-criticism and regret and to call up stronger evidence to counter them.

I cannot agree with John R. Nabholtz's judgment that "a sense of unqualified recovery of a past experience on the part of the narrator-persona and the youthful self whose experience he is remembering is the crucial rhetorical stance" of the narration of Wordsworth's arrival from Cambridge or his view that "in its opening 190 lines, Book IV reaffirms the power of the early primitive connection between the youthful Wordsworth and the life-nourishing powers of nature which have stood

the test of separation by the year at Cambridge."[8] The differences between the narrator's present and past responses to the brook in the
garden are themselves evidence enough of the narrator's profound dissatisfaction with his youthful self's response and of his clear awareness
that the "sense of unqualified recovery" he then felt should even then
have been qualified:

And that unruly child of mountain birth,
The froward brook, which, soon as he was boxed
Within our garden, found himself at once,
As if by trick insidious and unkind,
Stripped of his voice, and left to dimple down
Without an effort and without a will
A channel paved by the hand of man.
I looked at him and smiled, and smiled again,
And in the press of twenty thousand thoughts,
'Ha', quoth I, 'pretty prisoner, are you there!'
—And now, reviewing soberly that hour,
I marvel that a fancy did not flash
Upon me, and a strong desire, straitway,
At sight of such an emblem that showed forth
So aptly my late course of even days
And all their smooth enthralment, to pen down
A satire on myself.[9]

The narrator here has penned down the satire of which he failed, at the
time of his return, to see the need, and that satire cannot be confined
in its application only to his days at Cambridge, as if the "smooth enthralment" were as magically dissipated by his return as it had been
magically precipitated at his departure. Rather the enthralment persisted
through the summer vacation as its predominant characteristic, and the
narrator, involuntarily and voluntarily, brings evidences of his occasional
contacts with the "early life-nourishing powers of nature" to counter
his insistent impression that the summer as a whole was a waste and
that he at the time was a passive, smiling, thoughtless, worthless fellow,
alienated from "the firm habitual quest / Of feeding pleasures, from that
eager zeal, / Those yearnings which had every day been mine, / A wild
unworldly-minded youth" (1805, IV, 278–81).

Nabholtz's division of Book IV into four journeys—the return from
Cambridge, the circuit of the lake, the morning return from the night
of revelries (usually called the "Dawn Dedication"), and the night walk
in which the discharged soldier is encountered—aptly represents the
primary divisions of the book (in both 1805 and 1850), but his interpretation of them as constituting two pairs, in each of which a physical and
a spiritual recovery is figured, attends too much to the circumstances

narrated and not enough to the motives of the narrator which occasion
their narration. The first "journey," as I have already suggested, represents the young man's joy at his return home to the greetings of his
familiars but at the same time expresses the narrator's critical judgment
of the young man who mistakenly felt himself unchanged and who, in
his thoughtlessness, could perhaps find more joy in returning to his
"accustomed bed . . . than if it had been more desired, / Or been more
often thought of with regret" (1805, IV, 73–74). The narration of the
second journey—the "circuit of our little lake"—is introduced to check
the narrator's impulse to regret his loss of the walks he enjoyed before
he left for Cambridge, walks "busy with the toil of verse" (1805, IV, 102):

> Those walks, well worthy to be prized and loved—
> Regretted, that word too was on my tongue,
> But they were richly laden with all good,
> And cannot be remembered but with thanks
> And gratitude and perfect joy of heart—
> Those walks did now like a returning spring
> Come back on me again.
>
> (1805, IV, 121–28)

The quality of the occasion which he goes on to narrate may perhaps
best be gauged by setting the narrator's description of it against the
outburst at his liberation from London, which he set down at the beginning of *The Prelude*. On both occasions he experienced a transformation, felt as the removal of an alien weight or covering. Thus in the
opening outburst: "It is shaken off, / As by miraculous gift 'tis shaken
off, / That burthen of my own unnatural self, / The heavy weight of
many a weary day / Not mine, and such as were not made for me"
(1805, I, 21–25), and in the circuit of the lake: "Gently did my soul /
Put off her veil, and, self-transmuted, stood / Naked as in the presence of
her God" (1805, IV, 140–42). On both occasions he "conversed with
promises" (1805, IV, 154) of peace and pleasure combined with high
endeavor. On both occasions the poet experienced a "breath" in nature
connected with the animated state of his own mind. The differences in
his attitudes towards these breathings on the two occasions, however,
point to the differences in his ways of experiencing them, for to the
mature poet, returning from London, the power of the "vital breeze . . .
does not come unrecognized" (1805, I, 48) while to the boy years earlier
the "breath-like sound" (1805, IV, 175) is repeatedly mistaken for the
panting of his dog. The maturer man takes the whole moment as filled
with promise for *his* life now that his wish to escape the alien city has
been fulfilled, while the boy receives the restoration of his return to the
lake without awareness that he has needed restoration and he muses

on "life . . . the immortal soul . . . [and] Man" (1805, IV, 155–61) almost impersonally, without the color of conscious wishes for his own life and career. His narration of the circuit of the lake confirms his intention to remember such walks "with thanks / And gratitude," for it emphasizes, as so many of his earlier accounts of childhood experiences had emphasized, his receiving gifts for which he had not even known to ask and his accepting those gifts in a spirit of "consummate happiness," (1805, IV, 130) finding even in promises of future endeavor not vexing signs and provocations demanding fulfilment but "perfect joy of heart."

But though the young Wordsworth might find such musings pleasing in themselves, the older narrator takes them as the first of several freshnesses which he found at that time of his life and goes on to enumerate the other ones—his new interest in the human life around him, its changes and its characters, and his new sense of "human-heartedness" (1805, IV, 225) in his love of natural objects. But even this compound enumeration of reasons not to regret the life he then led does not satisfy the narrator, who persists in dwelling on what was lost from the earlier glory of his youth. As he says, "Yet in spite / Of all these new employments of the mind / There was an inner falling off" (1805, IV, 268–70). That "falling off" is the familiar one, present since the early descent at Cambridge, to noisy revelry in thoughtless company from "the firm habitual quest / Of feeding pleasures, from that eager zeal, / Those yearnings which had every day been mine" (1805, IV, 278–80). Though he demurs from giving a full account of the effect of the "vanities" that preoccupied him, the description he gives is a suggestive one:

> Something there was about me that perplexed
> Th' authentic sight of reason, pressed too closely
> On that religious dignity of mind
> That is the very faculty of truth,
> Which wanting—either, from the very first
> A function never lighted up, or else
> Extinguished—man, a creature great and good,
> Seems but a pageant plaything with vile claws,
> And this great frame of breathing elements
> A senseless idol.
>
> (1805, IV, 296–304)

The loss which the narrator sees in his younger self is a serious one, because it involves the whole imaginative mode in which he apprehended man, nature, and himself. In his grateful celebrations in Book I, he had thanked the "Wisdom and spirit of the universe" (1805, I, 427) for providing him with just that "religious dignity of mind" that here he finds "perplexed" and "pressed too closely." In that early passage, he had seen that

> not in vain
> By day or star-light, thus from my first dawn
> Of childhood didst thou intertwine for me
> The passions that build up our human soul,
> Not with the mean and vulgar works of man,
> But with high objects, with enduring things,
> With life and Nature, purifying thus
> The elements of feeling and of thought,
> And sanctifying by such discipline
> Both pain and fear, until we recognize
> A grandeur in the beatings of the heart.
>
> (1805, I, 431–41)

His predicament during his "deep vacation" seems to counteract this "sanctifying" discipline because of its absorption in transitory things and in "the mean and vulgar works of man." It threatens to replace his sense of "grandeur in the beatings of the heart" with the melancholy vision of one for whom all the world is a stage, his sense of the vital presence of nature with the sterile image of a scene upon which vain actions are played. The narrator sees at stake in his early "falling off"—to use the language with which he corrects his account of Cambridge in Book III—whether human life in nature will seem to be a "mimic show" or "Itself a living part of a live whole" (1805, III, 625–26).

As he goes on to condemn his attitudes at that time and to enumerate how he might better have occupied himself, "the memory of one particular hour" rises up "in chastisement of these regrets" (1805, IV, 314–16). The sunrise scene that recalls itself to him is

> a memorable pomp,
> More glorious than I ever had beheld.
> The sea was laughing at a distance; all
> The solid mountains were as bright as clouds,
> Grain-tinctured, drenched in empyrean light;
> And in the meadows and the lower grounds
> Was all the sweetness of a common dawn—
> Dews, vapours, and the melody of birds,
> And labourers going forth into the fields.
>
> (1805, IV, 331–39)

It is not immediately clear what feature of this scene triggers the reaction which the narrator assures his auditor took place at that time, for it seems at first to have more to do with his present regrets than with anything in that glorious sunrise. He writes,

Ah, need I say, dear friend, that to the brim
My heart was full? I made no vows, but vows
Were then made for me; bond unknown to me
Was given, that I should be—else sinning greatly—
A dedicated spirit.

(1805, IV, 340–46)

What is recovered here, I think, is a vision consonant with that "religious dignity of mind" feared lost or diminished. The scene is a "memorable pomp" not a "senseless idol" and man is not "a pageant plaything with vile claws" but a figure dignified by his function in the scene of which he is a vital part, a laborer "going forth into the fields." The young poet, as his older self imagines him, finds his place in the scene as of one also about to embark upon labors, and so is received and consecrated into the life of nature. This is not the first time in *The Prelude,* as Nabholtz has suggested, but the first time since the outburst that opened Book I, where man appears in the natural scene not as a child or youth bent on play but as a laborer with a task to perform ("Journeys Homeward," p. 90). The narrator sees a new relation to nature here dawning with the sun, a relation which restores the "blessedness" which the vanities of that time had threatened.

Recalling this scene does not, however, completely put to rest the narrator's misgivings about himself at that period in his life, for he goes on to summarize his condition then in balanced terms which still do not assert the predominant power of those benign influences which so dominated his earlier years:

Strange rendezvous my mind was at that time,
A parti-coloured shew of grave and gay,
Solid and light, short-sighted and profound,
Of inconsiderate habits and sedate,
Consorting in one mansion unreproved.
I knew the worth of that which I possessed,
Though slighted and misused.

(1805, IV, 346–52)

But he makes one more effort to assert that predominance before he concludes his treatment of the theme of his "falling off" by turning to narrate his encounter with the discharged soldier and so illustrate his concluding claim that

                              in truth
That summer, swarming as it did with thoughts
Transient and loose, yet wanted not a store
Of primitive hours, when—by these hindrances
Unthwarted—I experienced in myself

Conformity as just as that of old
To the end and written spirit of God's works,
Whether held forth in Nature or in man.

(1805, IV, 352–61)

This is a large weight for any episode to bear, a weight which could not be carried for example by the circuit of the lake, in which the poet experiences restoration and hope, or by the Dawn Dedication, in which he experiences a kind of grace. To experience "Conformity . . . / To the end and written spirit of God's works" is not to experience the promise of future worthiness, or the gift of a blessing without reference to one's present worthiness, but to experience conscious righteousness in the awareness of one's worthy action and worthy orientation to an explicit Divine purpose. In recalling such an experience, the narrator frames the problem with which he has been grappling in a more fundamental way than he has previously done, for he allows, in effect, that the regrets he has felt over this time of "transient and loose" thoughts have not been regrets only at his departure from his former "glory" or from his incipient vocation or even from Nature alone but from a Divine plan which manifests itself in Nature and in man. He is not merely despondent, he is guilty, and he thus reminds himself of an occasion in which he experienced "conformity" to the Divine plan to put to rest an uneasiness which remembrances of restoration or dedication or even undeserved blessedness could not touch.

The pressing question at this point, of course, is how the narration of the meeting with the discharged soldier carries this weight and resolves that uneasiness. After all, it is not impossible for the narrator of this poem to introduce anecdotes to serve purposes which they in fact fail to serve, as, perhaps most glaringly, he later introduces the narration of his crossing of the Alps to illustrate a moment of "deep and genuine sadness" (1805, IV, 492) only to have it reveal to him cause for one of his most exultant outbursts in the poem. There is, however, no such evidence following the narration of the discharged soldier to hint that it has failed to serve its purpose for the narrator, and our task here must be first to discover how it might bring him to share in the "quiet heart" with which, after his encounter with the soldier in both *Prelude* versions of the episode, the young poet is said to have sought his "distant home" (1805, IV, 504). We may, then, consider how well the episode is confined to serving this purpose only.

Directed to look at the anecdote for evidence of the young poet's "Conformity . . . / To the end and written spirit of God's works," we will, I think, notice his act of charity and his impression of the soldier's faith in Providence. He is drawn at his encounter with the "uncouth shape" of the man out of self-absorbed reverie, however pleasurable and restorative, and into a situation in which the acknowledgment and execution of a charitable duty is called for. The question of whether this "shape" is "a man" is put to rest thirteen lines earlier than in the separate version of the anecdote, making the ground of the duty less ambiguous. His hesitation to undertake it and his "self-blame" in that hesitation become here important indices of what was at stake in the meeting. Further, his admonition to the man not to "linger in the public ways, / But ask for timely furtherance, and help / Such as his state required" involves a misunderstanding of the context of the charity and a displacement of the responsibility for obtaining help onto the one in need and away from the one who perceives the need and owes aid without its being requested. There is almost a note of resentment at the interruption of his self-enclosed reverie in this admonition—a wish to disburden himself of the responsibility he has momentarily assumed and to return to his carefully cultivated solitude. The soldier's reply, " 'My trust is in the God of Heaven, / And in the eye of him that passes me' " chastens this impulse by revealing the providential frame within which the act of charity should be interpreted and disclosing to the young man how the older man's faith in God entails his corresponding faith in *him*, the chance passerby who will see and provide succor. His act understood in this frame is more radically in conformity to "the end and written spirit of God's works" than might at first have appeared, for it involves not simply obedience to the duty of charity but also fulfilment of a plan in which that obedience is a necessary part. This discovery, consecrated in the exchange of blessings between man and youth, may help to explain something in the attitude with which the narrator relates his initial state of mind, for he seems critical of it, as he describes himself as "all unworthy of the deeper joy / Which waits on distant prospect— cliff or sea, / The dark blue vault and universe of stars" and as "stealing" along the road, as if in an effort to hide from something, even before he literally goes into hiding at the sight of the soldier. That he now recognizes himself as "step by step led on" to that sight is further evidence that he has been persuaded by the providential perspective he discovered in the episode.[10]

This reading of the anecdote identifies a ground on which it may be imagined to restore the narrator to a calm recognition of the providential context of his whole story and thereby to provide a more lasting "peace to vain regrets" than he has found in his other recollections of this period of his life. His discovery may then be seen as analogous to Hamlet's recognition of a "Providence in the fall of a sparrow" which puts an end to his vain urgings of himself to his task and leaves him in "readiness" for whatever comes. Certainly the narrator opens the next book of his poem in a calmer mood, in which, though he grieves, his grief is addressed not to the immediate circumstances of his own life as he recalls it but to a common human problem, evident only to more impersonal reflection. The pattern of repeated regret and chastisement of regret is broken by this narrative, and the reading to which we have pointed seems a sufficient explanation of how.

That reading does not, however, seem a sufficient account of the suggestiveness of the anecdote as it appears in the modified version of the 1805 *Prelude*. Though certain details from the original version of the poem which would have diverted us from this reading have been cut from this version—the emphasis on recognition of the "shape" as human has been diminished and the old man's answer to the question of why he lingers has been removed—still details remain which do not seem satisfactorily to serve the narrator's explicit purpose. The old man's murmuring and ghastliness, his apparent indifference and last-minute signs of reviving interest, his dismissal from his career and his return to his "native home," his motionlessness and solitude are all characteristics unnecessarily specific for one who functions as an object of charity and prophet of Providence. For these functions he need only suffer and speak. He need not raise questions about whether he is alive or dead, nor suggest that he is returning from the journey of life and vocation on which the young poet is just embarking. He need not stand for the solitude from which the young poet has strayed in the period this narrative closes nor need he seem almost to parody with his indifference the vital calm which had seemed a touchstone for the poet in his account of his early life. So many themes, even in the first four books of *The Prelude*, have resonance in this episode, and so many details have resonance of their own, that the anecdote will not stand still for the subordination in which the narrator places it but asks instead for consideration as the account of a happening pertinent beyond its declared limits as well as interesting in itself. As the poem progresses, the themes on which it bears continue to multiply as it comes to seem a stage in the development of the poet's love of mankind (Nabholtz emphasizes this) or to presage, as I suggested earlier, the poet's loss and recovery of human feeling. It seems, at first at least, to be one of those meetings in the public road in which the poet later discovers new faith in man and new themes for his poetry. It appears, or may tempt us to make it appear, as yet another "spot of time" on which the poet's mind feeds and in which its paradigmatic character may be discoverable.

The consciousness of which this episode is a function becomes so rich compared with the consciousnesses given in the individual personal anecdotes or even in "Resolution and Independence"—we know so much about its past experiences and present state of mind—that it cannot determine authoritatively for us the significance of its own experiences. In the larger context of *The Prelude*, there are innumerable connections between this episode and other narrative and reflective passages that the narrator does not have occasion to make, but nothing stops us from making them. He has simply told us too much to keep his control of us and has absorbed us so fully in the process in which he is engaged that we may carry it beyond the point where he has been made to stop. While the other poems that we have considered seem to function within a formal constraint that makes speculation about details not given or connections of episodes not connected seem impertinent, this poem positively requires an effort of reconstruction that, like the several versions of the poem itself, picks out episodes and tries them in various contexts, moving them from theme to theme, claim to claim, as our grasp of their possible relevancies grows.

We should not be surprised, however, that despite the impossibility of the task, the narrator should nevertheless attempt to control our readings. He introduces no episode, however significant in itself, for its own sake; he always turns recollections, even when he admits to fascination with them beyond the bounds of purpose, to some explicit point. Though they sometimes "rise up" without his soliciting them, he does not let them stand without the excuse of their pertinence to his theme. He cites episodes in evidence for the beneficence of Nature in Book I, and once, at the end of that book, he has deliberately chosen to prosecute the "story of my life" he cites them or fits them to that effort. He presents himself as a man carrying out a task of recollection and interpretation, not merely a man provoked by need or pleasure to tell this or that story, and he has a stake in the *character* of the conscious laborer which demands that he account for including this and excluding that, that he appear to have a reason for what he does, even though his reasons sometimes seem insufficient and his episodes seem to do more than satisfy the reasons which justify them.

The effort to unify into an intelligible whole the significant moments of his life is the effort of the poem; the image of such a unity and the power to create it is the unachieved goal which is emblematized in the closing meditation on the scene from Snowdon. The mind imagined there exerts a "domination" on things which "So moulds them, and endues, abstracts, combines, / Or by abrupt and unhabitual influence / Doth make one object so impress itself / Upon all others, and pervades them so, / That even the grossest minds must see and hear, / And cannot chuse but feel" (1805, XIII, 77–84). The mind of the narrator aims at this domination of the things of its own life, and the impressions made by them, but by his own admission, and the manifest character of the poem, he fails to achieve it. Though criticism of the poem has developed around memorable episodes and "spots of time," no "one object" so impresses itself upon all others in the poem, no single episode or interest so dominates all others that it governs our interpretation of them to the exclusion of other possible interpretations. We follow through the windings of this poem not the single consciousness of the individual personal anecdotes, absorbed completely in one experience, or even the rudimentary double consciousness of "Resolution and Independence," which experiences and narrates in terms of a single generalized recognition of its own character in the context of a felt immediate urgency; rather we follow the labors of a developing consciousness, rich in particular experiences, discovering and modifying generalizations of its own character and the character of the world, pressed by an initiating urgency but, in the course of its lengthy effort, subject to other urgencies and sometimes reflectively above them all.

The 1850 text of the discharged soldier passage is notable for the narrator's greater reflective transcendence of the event he recounts. Though the episode still figures as an illustration of "Conformity as just as that of old / To the end and written spirit of God's works," it is introduced not as one of "a store / Of primitive hours, when . . . I experienced in myself" such conformity but as one of those "intervals / When Folly from the frown of fleeting Time / Shrunk, and the mind experienced in herself / Conformity . . ." (1850, IV, 347–49). In the same way, the episode is no longer singled out from among "many wanderings that have left behind / Remembrances not lifeless" but is presented as a personal confirmation of a general kind of experience also present in the images of hermit, votary, and watchman—the discharged soldier like these others is the "appropriate human centre" of an image of Solitude "impressed upon the mind" (1850, IV, 353–68). This more general formulation of the episode's meaning goes along with a reduction of the narrator's account of the state of mind in which he met the soldier from the twenty-four lines describing his self-absorbed reverie to a brief description of the stillness that preceded his encounter with the "uncouth shape." Instead of giving the careful account of the internal condition in which he was impressed by that shape, he presents himself as having left a scene of late-night revelries like those that preceded his experience in the Dawn Dedication, and he remarks upon the "strange back-ground" such "trappings of a gaudy world" made to the desolation and simplicity of the soldier's appearance (1850, IV, 402–3). This background is the only one allowed to stand, as the nearby village and the laborer to whose cottage the young poet takes "the traveller" (no longer "my comrade") disappear, and the soldier occupies the foreground almost exclusively without the tantalizing suggestion in the poet's remark that " 'we must measure back / The way which we have come' " (1805, IV, 454–55) to link the soldier's solitude with his own. The soldier himself is the human center of the image the narrator relates, and the young poet's role is confined to doing the act of charity which demonstrates his conformity "to the end and written spirit of God's works."

These changes can be justified in the overall development of the poem. Though the editors of the newest edition complain, as de Selincourt did, of the addition of the new background of late-night revels and the substitution of the lines "in his very dress appeared / A desolation, a simplicity / To which the trappings of a gaudy world / Make a strange background" (1850, IV, 400–403) for "A desolation, a simplicity / That seemed akin to solitude" (1805, IV, 418–19), these changes go along with the excision of the lengthy description of his state of mind prior to the encounter and make this anecdote parallel, as Nabholtz has observed, to the Dawn Dedication.[11] Both scenes offer exceptions to and corrections of the "heartless chase / Of trivial pleasures" with which the narrator has been preoccupied in his younger self; the one provides a harmonious vision of man going to work in nature, while the other, as the narrator of 1850 makes clear without needing to add that the desolation of the soldier's dress appeared "akin to solitude," offers an image of "Solitude" made impressive by its "appropriate human centre." The state of mind on which the 1850 narrator focuses is not a newly described one of self-absorbed reverie but the enervated and distracted condition that has concerned him since the "falling off" he began to notice in his year at Cambridge, and the return to himself he sees in the episode of the discharged soldier is a return to the "quiet and exalted thoughts of loneliness" which gave way at Cambridge "to empty noise and superficial pastimes" (1850, III, 210–12). He exploits the contrasting associations he has built up since Book III of solitude, quiet, and absorption in valuable thought as against society, noise, and vain activity to make the closing anecdote provide the complete answer to the difficulties he has recognized from the beginning of this period of his life, and he adds "Solitude" to the list of "powers" whose importance for his development he traces and celebrates.

The poet's reductions and revisions of this narrative in the 1850 text thus achieve a greater subordination of the anecdote to the story in which it appears and reduce the suggestions which might lead an impertinent reader to probe it for other relevancies, but the concluding lines of the final version as they appear in the latest edition of that text complicate considerably the effect of the streamlined passage. The narrator in these lines is made to say: "This passed, and he who deigns to mark with care / By what rules governed, with what end in view, / This Work proceeds, *he* will not wish for more."[12] It is unavoidable for us, accustomed to read this version next to the longer one of 1805, to read this remark as the poet's defensive comment on the cutting of that version and as a violation of the established limitations of the narrator who, as I have said, is not otherwise aware of the process of revision which gives him his lines. This violation of the givens of the poem is enough to explain the copyists' queries which kept the passage from appearing in its first edition. But if we try to read the lines within the 1850 text alone it has oddnesses of other kinds. Coming at the end of an anecdote which purported to demonstrate the young poet's conformity "To the end and written spirit of God's works," it oddly intrudes consideration for the end and laws that govern the mature poet-narrator's work, breaking the mood of quiet satisfaction with which the young poet is said to have sought his distant home with the narrator's self-righteous justification of how he has told the story. The reader has no reason in the account itself to expect more or to ask for more than the narrator gives him, and the narrator's imagining that he might feel otherwise only betrays the narrator's own discomfort with something that he has left out and his need to appeal to rules and purposes to justify himself. Unlike his anticipation of objections at the end of Book I where he imagines that his friend will not think that he has "lengthened out / With fond and feeble tongue a tedious tale" (1805, I, 646–47), he does not here refer to what he has already said but to what he had not said, and he imagines a reader who will agree with what he has done not from prompt and indulgent "sympathy" but from acknowledgment of the general principles under which he is operating. Even in an added appeal to his listener earlier in Book IV the narrator still imagines an "indulgent Friend" (1850, IV, 275), and in the concluding lines of the poem, after the principles under which it has been written have received their most explicit formulation, the narrator still appeals to his friend for the special indulgence that issues from their common memories to justify his work and does not stand on the lofty abstract ground on which this passage justifies itself to its exclusive, impersonal, ideal reader.

The narrator in effect is made to assert his conformity in narrating to what Wordsworth in the Preface called "a distinct purpose formally conceived" and to demand a reading which formally acknowledges that purpose, rather than to rely upon the process through which "[his] habits of meditation have so formed [his] feelings, as that [his] descriptions of such objects as strongly excite those feelings, will be found to carry along with them a *purpose*" (*LB*, p. 246). He claims the character of deliberate workman here to the exclusion of the character of one whose spontaneously recounted experiences can be trusted to reveal important relations, and accordingly transforms an account of an exciting encounter whose significance must be discovered into the illustration of an explicitly stated general truth. The narrator's urgent need to affirm his own self-discipline in the face of his younger self's repeated yieldings to vanities and distractions is not satisfied in the recollection of an early moment of "Conformity . . . / To the end and written spirit of God's works" but asserts itself in his imposition of conformity to the end and written spirit of his own work on the telling of the story itself.

But his claim to conscious control of his narration, expressed without external provocation and with a note of urgency, may be taken not as an abandonment of reliance on the grand elementary principle of pleasure but as one more expression of its workings. The speaker with a passionate stake in proving his own rationality and deliberateness is not unknown to us among those whose motives for telling we have traced. The narrator of "We Are Seven," in particular, tells of his attempt to bring an intransigent child into conformity with his rational principles, indeed into conformity with his notion of the Divine plan, appealing to his listener to acknowledge the validity of the laws in terms of which he views the world and the irrationality of the child's stubborn refusal to bend to them. We have also heard Wordsworth, in his own person and character, appeal in the 1800 Preface to "the primary laws of our nature" which it was his "principal object" to "illustrate," and present himself almost as if he were an outside observer of human nature, pointing out its characteristics in experimental demonstrations but not himself subject to them.

We have sufficiently recognized the irony that undermines such claims, but perhaps we have not given due regard to the need to make them and even to believe them. It is not only the need to establish a public character as a poet and a consequent "claim to the approbation of the public," though this need is foremost for the speaker of the 1800 Preface. It is not just the need to keep distinctions like that between the living and the dead clear and unpolluted—the need that makes the narrator of "We Are Seven" so insistent in his questions and protestations. The need that becomes manifest in the narrator of *The Prelude* is the need to make isolated moments of significant encounter add up to those higher syntheses of plot, character, and thought that are the starting points of narrative understood in the Aristotelian categories we set aside in Chapter 1. The problem of *The Prelude* is to establish the character of the narrator through the discovery of a plot, "the story of my life," and to give those striking encounters with nature and with man that he has repeatedly experienced a place in a larger structure of thought which can make him known to himself. What is crucial to the work of *The Prelude* is not just the internal workings of the memorable episodes and "spots of time" into which criticism sometimes dissolves the poem but the efforts at arranging and subordinating and interpreting them as the experiences of one character whose life has but one story.

If we presume too quickly the impossibility of this work and emphasize the sense in which its formulations seem inadequate and its subordinations fail, taking satisfaction in the confirmation of our expectation that they must fail, we will miss the pleasure that comes from identifying with the narrator's efforts to make his story and himself. We need not, once we have rightly named Wordsworth's poetry as a "poetry of experience," dwell exclusively upon what Langbaum calls the "process of formulating values" and the "expanding potentiality for formulating values" but never upon the values formulated through that process (*Experience*, p. 26). If our awareness of the effort that struggles toward such formulations and the motives of the character who seeks them always qualifies our appreciation of the results he arrives at, it may sometimes qualify it with a respect for the immense labor and an admiration for the intelligent and self-conscious laborer that win special attention for what he claims to have discovered. The poetry of *his* experience may give us occasion not for another easy irony at the merely human limitations of his claims but for inspiration at the experience and thought which stand behind his vision of

> how the mind of man becomes
> A thousand times more beautiful than the earth
> On which he dwells, above this frame of things
> (Which, 'mid all revolutions in the hopes
> And fears of men, doth still remain unchanged)
> In beauty exalted, as it is itself
> Of quality and fabric more divine.
>
> (1850, XIV, 450–56)

Among the impressive demonstrations of this beauty of the human mind are the several personal anecdotes we have examined, which repeatedly reveal to us not only one mind's capacity to sense "whether by words, looks, sighs, or tears" (1850, XIII, 164) the significance of another mind for itself but also our own capacities, from words alone, to recover another mind's discoveries of meaning and to discover further significance for ourselves. However we may approach the world of nature, a question I have not raised in this study, we may take our discoveries of meaning in these poems as confirmation of the hypothesis that, in poetic works and words, "there was pleasure there."

Notes

Introduction

1. Hartman, *Wordsworth's Poetry, 1787–1814* (New Haven: Yale University Press, 1964), pp. 141–52; I am referring to Danby, *The Simple Wordsworth* (London: Routledge and Kegan Paul, 1960), pp. 35–72; Langbaum, *The Poetry of Experience* (1957; rpt. New York: Norton, 1963, pp. 38–74, 182–209); Parrish, " 'The Thorn': Wordsworth's Dramatic Monologue," *ELH* 24 (1957): 153–63; and "Dramatic Technique in *Lyrical Ballads*," *PMLA* 74 (1959): 85–97; both of these articles were incorporated into Parrish's *The Art of the "Lyrical Ballads"* (Cambridge, Mass.: Harvard University Press, 1973) to which all my subsequent references will be made. Though Hartman is not convinced of the experiment's success, he cites Danby and Parrish with admiration in his critical bibliography, pp. 371–75.

2. For an account of the changes in Wordsworth's attitudes parallel in some respects to the present one, see James A. W. Heffernan, *Wordsworth's Theory of Poetry* (Ithaca: Cornell University Press, 1969), pp. 89–93. Though Heffernan underrates the 1800 and 1802 Prefaces, he sees the significance of the 1815 Essay. See also W. J. B. Owen, *Wordsworth as Critic* (Toronto: University of Toronto Press, 1969).

3. *Anatomy of Criticism* (Princeton: Princeton University Press, 1957), pp. 3–29.

4. Sheats, *The Making of Wordsworth's Poetry, 1785–1798* (Cambridge, Mass.: Harvard University Press, 1973), pp. 203–4; Danby, p. 38; Parrish, passim. Heffernan and Owen note Wordsworth's turn to the student of poetry as his ideal reader in the course of discussions of the Essay Supplementary, but they do not draw its implications for reading the poems; Heffernan, p. 91; Owen, pp. 193–94.

5. "Coleridge's Criticism of Wordsworth," *PMLA* 54 (1939): 497.

Chapter One

1. Kroeber, *Romantic Narrative Art* (Madison: University of Wisconsin Press, 1960), p. 43; Parrish, *The Art of the "Lyrical Ballads,"* p. 119; Danby, *Simple Wordsworth*, pp. 36–37; Langbaum, *The Poetry of Experience*, p. 54.

2. 3:27–28. Wordsworth introduces the three categories I have focused on as part of a series of six (or seven if the last-mentioned combination of the fourth, fifth, and sixth kinds is considered a separate kind) "moulds" by means of which

the materials of poetry, "collected and produced" by the powers he has already enumerated, may be cast into "divers forms." But immediately after presenting what appears to be a list of parallel "moulds," he summarizes what he has presented so far in terms of three main topics, not the two he has already named: "It is deducible from the above, that poems, apparently miscellaneous, may with propriety be arranged either with reference to the powers of mind *predominant* in the production of them; or to the mould in which they are cast; or, lastly, to the subjects to which they relate." The mention of "subjects" at this point compels a rereading of the previous series which makes the first three categories appear as an exhaustive set of molds, while the second three categories are all distinguished, not by how they are presented but by a relation to what they are about—their subjects. Thus the "idyllium" is "descriptive chiefly of the processes and appearances of external nature, . . . of characters, manners, and sentiments, . . . or of these in conjunction with the appearances of nature"; the "principal object" of the "Didactic" is instruction; the "Satire," the sixth category, may treat either a universal subject and so be "philosophical," or a "personal and occasional" subject, whose particularity makes it fall outside the domain of true poetry. Describing, teaching, or satirizing are different ways of relating a subject to a listener. Narrative, dramatic, and lyric are different dispositions of voices which might be used in any of these ways. It is proper, then, to treat narrative, dramatic, and lyric as a self-contained series within the longer list.

3. See, for example, Kroeber, pp. 12–47, and Albert Lord, "Narrative Poetry," *Princeton Encyclopedia of Poetry and Poetics,* 1974 ed. Lord begins, "a n[arrative] poem is one that tells a story. The two basic types are epic and ballad."

4. Gérard Genette, *Narrative Discourse,* trans. Jane E. Lewin (Ithaca: Cornell University Press, 1980), p. 25. This is the first of three meanings of "narrative" Genette distinguishes. The second is "the succession of events, real or fictitious, that are the subjects of this discourse," and the third is "the act of narrating taken in itself" (p. 26). Both of these additional definitions preserve the idea that "narrative" is concerned with events, for not all discoursing but only that which recounts a story satisfies the strict criteria for an "act of narrating."

5. See for example, Paul Shorey's notes in volume 10, part 1, of the Loeb Classical Library edition of the *Republic* on which I rely primarily. He repeatedly attempts to assimilate Plato's distinctions to Aristotelian categories, making the distinction between λόγων and λέξεως the practical equivalent of the distinction between matter and manner and insisting upon a common theory of art as imitation in both theories, despite his awareness of Plato's "sometimes using imitation in the narrower sense of dramatic dialogue as opposed to narration" (*Republic,* I, 224n). Similarly Gérard Genette, influenced by the Aristotelian emphasis on narrative as the representation of events, reads the Platonic distinction in Aristotelian terms, drops the lyric mode out of consideration (or mistakenly identifies it as pure diegetic narrative), and finds that the Platonic and Aristotelian classifications agree in essentials. See his "Frontières du Récit," in *Figures II* (Paris: Editions du Seuil, 1969), pp. 50–56. In recent literary criticism, Paul Hernadi has most clearly recognized the distinctiveness of the Platonic categories in question, though he uses the three-fold Platonic structure to answer questions posed by Aristotle's mimetic orientation, in his "Dual Perspective: Free Indirect Discourse and Related Techniques," *Comparative Literature* 24 (Winter 1972): 32–43; reprinted in Hernadi, *Beyond Genre* (Ithaca and London: Cornell University Press, 1972), pp. 187–205, esp. pp. 187–88, 201–2. I should perhaps add that throughout this argument my use of the adjectives "Platonic" and "Aristotelian"

refers to the specific contexts of poetic theory I am drawing from and not to the two great classes of intellectual dispositions into which all of us supposedly fall.

6. I rely primarily on Kenneth Telford's translation of the *Poetics* and his glossary of Greek terms (Chicago: Henry Regnery, 1970).

7. I have previously tried to characterize Wordsworth's interest in speaking situations as a rhetorical interest. Gene W. Ruoff has made a parallel effort in terms of speech-act theory and pragmatics. See my "Coleridge's Interpretation of Wordsworth's Preface to *Lyrical Ballads*," *PMLA* 93 (1978): 917, and Ruoff, "Wordsworth on Language: Toward a Radical Poetics for English Romanticism," *TWC* 3 (1972): 207–8. Though I think I have coined the phrase "poetics of speech," the position characteristic of this poetics has been worked out by a number of theorists. In America Barbara Herrnstein Smith has developed it most fully in *On the Margins of Discourse* (Chicago: University of Chicago Press, 1978). In this century, the work of Mikhail Bakhtin is the most comprehensive and fruitful elaboration known to me of a poetics of speech. See especially [V. N. Vološinov], "Discourse in Life and Discourse in Art (Concerning Sociological Poetics)," printed as an appendix to *Freudianism: A Marxist Critique*, trans. I. R. Titunik, ed. Neal H. Bruss (New York: Academic Press, 1976), p. 107. I follow Michael Holquist in attributing this essay and the other works printed in Vološinov's name to Bakhtin. See Holquist's bibliography of Bakhtin's works in M. M. Bakhtin, *The Dialogic Imagination*, trans. Caryl Emerson and Michael Holquist, ed. Michael Holquist (Austin: University of Texas Press, 1981), pp. xxxiii–xxxiv. Jerome McGann has recently called attention to the importance of this essay and of Bakhtin's other works for understanding romantic poetry and poetry in general. See his "Keats and the Historical Imagination," *MLN* 94 (1979): esp. 988–94 and 1027 n. 6. In subsequent quotations from Bakhtin's essay, all italics are from the original.

8. Stephen Parrish describes the difference between Wordsworth and Coleridge as that between Wordsworth's "dramatic" and Coleridge's "poetic" handling of language, in *The Art of the "Lyrical Ballads*," p. 79. His attempt to distinguish Wordsworth's and Coleridge's poetic assumptions in his second and third chapters on "The Ballad as Drama," the most comprehensive treatment of this topic to date, has been useful to me throughout this chapter.

9. I refer of course to M. H. Abrams, *The Mirror and the Lamp* (New York: Oxford University Press, 1953).

10. "The Contemporaneity of *Lyrical Ballads*," *PMLA* 69 (1954): 486–522.

11. For a refutation of Coleridge's interpretation of the Preface see my article cited in n. 7 above. The present chapter is, in part, an attempt to clarify the fundamental grounds of the differences between Wordsworth and Coleridge, a clarification I called for at the end of that essay. My argument there is restricted to discriminating what Wordsworth said from what Coleridge said he said, but here I am interested in comparing their fundamental terms and the distinct systems of poetics those terms entail. For criticisms of my earlier essay's argument by Robert Sternbach, W. J. B. Owen, and Nathaniel Teich, and for my replies, see the "Forum" sections of *PMLA* 94 (March 1979): 326–27, and 94 (May 1979): 479–82.

12. The most influential and careful attempt to establish this interpretation is M. H. Abrams, *The Mirror and the Lamp*, p. 21, and passim. Parrish traces the use of Wordsworth's Preface as a locus of ideas about the spontaneous, "natural" poet to Arnold's Preface to his "Golden Treasury" selection of Wordsworth's *Poems* (London, 1879). A more recent source of this emphasis (whose references to Arnold suggest that he helped shape its view) is Irving Babbitt's *Rousseau and*

Romanticism (Boston: Houghton Mifflin, 1919). Babbitt warns us that he is using Wordsworth for his own purposes and that he is not claiming to tell "the whole truth about Wordsworth" (p. 10), but this qualification is soon forgotten in his passionate defense of "reason" against the irresponsible emotionalism and irrationalism of which he makes Wordsworth the representative. Despite Walter Jackson Bate's efforts to counter these exaggerations in *From Classic to Romantic* (Cambridge: Harvard University Press, 1946), they remain the basis of current judgments, often expressed in far more reasonable tones, in such works as James Heffernan's *Wordsworth's Theory of Poetry* (Ithaca: Cornell University Press, 1969), chap. 2, and Abrams's *Mirror*. They also underly much of T. S. Eliot's early criticism of Wordsworth and romanticism and so connect with many "modernist" and new critical opinions on such topics as "emotion" and "personality" in poetry.

13. The passage in which Wordsworth develops this argument and articulates the "grand elementary principle of pleasure" at its heart has not generally been treated as important by the critics. Abrams omitted all but its final paragraph from his selection in the second edition of *The Norton Anthology of English Literature* but has reinstated it in the third edition. W. J. B. Owen calls it "a digression upon the element of pleasure in poetry," as if that element had a peripheral place in Wordsworth's theory of poetry, in his *Wordsworth as Critic* (Toronto: University of Toronto Press, 1969), p. 89. Lionel Trilling calls attention to Wordsworth's emphasis on "the grand elementary principle of pleasure" in this passage, but, despite his complaint against allowing certain "bold utterances" to stand for the argument of the Preface as a whole, he himself treats this remark as another "bold utterance" and goes on to discuss its cultural significance, not its significance in Wordsworth's argument ("The Fate of Pleasure: Wordsworth to Dostoevsky," in *Romanticism Reconsidered*, ed. Northrop Frye [New York: Columbia University Press, 1963], pp. 73–74). Parrish sees that pleasure is "at the heart of the 'sublime notion of poetry' " that Wordsworth is endeavoring to present, but he does not connect this observation, aimed at clarifying the place of pleasure in Wordsworth's account of meter, with his account of Wordsworth's dramatic experiments (*Art of the "Lyrical Ballads,"* pp. 20–21). The only critical essay I have seen which focuses on this passage and develops its significance is B. R. Breyer's "Wordsworth's Pleasure: An Approach to His Poetic Theory," *Southern Humanities Review*, 6 (Spring 1972): 123–31. Breyer contends that "the underlying purpose of the Preface as a whole is just to define the sort of pleasure which Wordsworth does consider solely proper to genuine poetry." He contrasts Wordsworth's view of the relation of poetic pleasure and truth with Coleridge's, interprets Wordsworth's view as implying that poetry is "essentially truth" but that pleasure is inseparable from truth, and suggests some consequences that his reading of Wordsworth's theory would have for the reading of his poetry. I have not seen this essay cited in any subsequent criticism.

14. I should perhaps note that I am here using "Aristotelian" and "Platonic" in different senses than I have used them earlier in the chapter. The usage here is more familiar.

15. For Bakhtin's account of this aspect of the problem of reported speech, see [V.N. Vološinov], *Marxism and the Philosophy of Language*, trans. Ladislav Matejka and I. R. Titunik (New York: Seminar Press, 1973), pp. 115ff. For my attribution of this work to Bakhtin see n. 7 above.

Chapter Two

1. For the first and third sense, see Harry Shaw, *A Concise Dictionary of Literary Terms* (New York: McGraw-Hill, 1972), pp. 273–74; I quote Richards's definition of tone from M. H. Abrams, "Persona, Tone, and Voice," in *A Glossary of Literary Terms,* 3d ed. (New York: Holt, Rinehart, and Winston, 1971), pp. 124–25; Kenner's from *The Art of Poetry* (New York: Holt, Rinehart, and Winston, 1959), p. 17; and Bakhtin's from "Discourse in Life and Discourse in Art," pp. 104–5.

2. I am here going through the poetic possibilities to which M. H. Abrams's well-known scheme of theoretical orientations calls attention, the objective, expressive, pragmatic, and mimetic respectively. None of those reductions of the relations among speaker, listener, and hero as they appear in a literary work permits the kind of interrelations of autonomous participants Bakhtin describes. Abrams's scheme has provided a convenient organizing device and an attractive debating ground to many critics, but it has unduly restricted our vision of the whole problem it anatomizes. See *The Mirror and the Lamp,* passim.

3. The first remark is from Andrew L. Griffin, "Wordsworth and the Problem of Imaginative Story: The Case of 'Simon Lee'," *PMLA* 92 (1977): 392; Danby, *Simple Wordsworth,* pp. 40–41.

4. Griffin himself scarcely attends to the metrical workings of the poem—his only notice is a tendentious comment on the fifth and sixth stanzas of the 1832 version that "the poem is on its way toward a dead stop, and even the verse slows down, limping through many pauses" ("Imaginative Story," p. 400).

5. The translation is from *The Republic,* in *Great Dialogues of Plato,* trans. W. H. D. Rouse (New York: New American Library), p. 322.

6. Parrish calls attention to the importance of the fluxes and refluxes but makes this substitution of "imagination" for "mind" in *Art,* p. 32.

7. I take the sonnet from *The Poetical Works of William Wordsworth* (Oxford: Clarendon Press, 1946), 3:18. The explication is in *The Letters of William and Dorothy Wordsworth: The Middle Years,* ed. E. de Selincourt, 2d ed. (Oxford: Clarendon Press, 1969), 1:145–51.

8. "Narrative Versions, Narrative Theories," *Critical Inquiry* 7 (1980): 232–33.

9. The most thorough treatment of the relation of speaker's and hero's diction is Bakhtin's account of the problem of reported speech in [V. N. Vološinov], *Marxism and the Philosophy of Language,* tran. L. Matejka and I. R. Titunik (New York and London: Seminar Press, 1973), 115–59.

Chapter Three

1. My thinking about these constraints has been informed by Jürgen Habermas, "Some Distinctions in Universal Pragmatics," *Theory and Society* 3 (1976): 155–67.

2. Sheats identifies Wordsworth's statement of intentions with the poem's narrator in *Making,* p. 188.

3. Darwin, *Zoönomia,* 2 vols. (London, 1794–96), 2:359, quoted in Jacobus, *Tradition and Experiment,* p. 235. All further references are to the passage as it appears there.

4. Neither personal suspicion nor repeated waiting appears in Darwin.

5. "The Narrator's Voice in 'Goody Blake and Harry Gill'," *English* 19 (1970): 15.

6. There is some violence already in Darwin, who says the farmer "springing from his concealment . . . seized his prey with violent threats."

7. Compare my account of what happens to Harry with the Hartleyan view of Sue Weaver Westerbrook, "A Note on Hartley's Theory of 'the Sensation of Chilliness' in Wordsworth's 'Goody Blake and Harry Gill'," WC 10 (1979): 124–26.

8. I have been helped in thinking about the various "voices" of the narrator of "Simon Lee" and about their "interruption" of each other by discussions of these concepts in David Silverman and Brian Torode, *The Material Word* (London: Routledge and Kegan Paul, 1980). Their project in ethnomethodology and sociolinguistics has interesting affinities with and relevance to inquiries into a poetics of speech.

9. The strong enjambments after "perceive," "expect," "mind," and "find" and the exclamations after "reader" in lines 74 and 76 are all marks of passion.

10. My emphasis on the narrator's contribution to what he describes could be taken as a development of the position Parrish and Owen advance following Wordsworth's Note to "The Thorn." See Parrish, *Art*, pp. 97–105, and W. J. B. Owen, " 'The Thorn' and the Poet's Intention," WC 8 (1977): 3–17. Mary Jacobus states this position in terms I find most congenial in *Tradition and Experiment*, pp. 247–48.

11. See my comments in Chapter 1 on the poet's "vantage ground." Jerome Christensen, whose essay reminds me that his phrase comes from BL, 2:32, claims that "the poet whom Wordsworth envisages enjoys no 'vantage ground' from which to nicely calculate and control the interaction of sympathy and judgment." Sympathy and judgment, however, are not the only matters for which a vantage ground is required nor is Wordsworth as confounded with his speaker as Christensen imagines. See "Wordsworth's Misery, Coleridge's Woe: Reading 'The Thorn'," PLL 16 (1980): 272–75.

12. Among recent commentators, Parrish examines the parallel between "the growth of the poem in the mind of its author" and "the growth of the story in the mind of its narrator" (*Art*, pp. 106–9); Hartman sees the narrator as "a caricature of Wordsworth's imagination in process" (*Wordsworth's Poetry*, p. 148); Sheats, who sees the narrator as part of Wordsworth's triumph over his earlier errors and fears, thinks this speaker "burlesques the division of sensibility he had himself suffered" (*Making*, p. 197); Owen takes the narrator as "an image of Wordsworth's own questioning imagination, which also pursues insoluble questions and receives only uncertain answers," though he replaces Hartman's term "caricature" with " 'partial model' " (" 'The Thorn' and the Poet's Intention," pp. 14–15); Christensen, who defends the analogy at length, goes as far as to argue that the narrator's utterance shares the tendency of Wordsworth's enterprise to excite the mind "without the application of gross and violent stimulants" and that the narrator "dramatizes a Wordsworthian scene with a Wordsworthian tact." Though he concedes that the analogy breaks down, it does not do so before the narrator and poet have strangely exchanged roles: Wordsworth "slips into the character slipping into nature," while his narrator emerges with "an amiable inventiveness that modifies identification toward pleasure" ("Wordsworth's Misery," 273–75). James H. Averill claims that " 'The Thorn' confronts poet and reader with grotesque images of themselves" and "undresses the artistry of *The Ruined Cottage*" and other poems concerned with human suffering. It seems to reveal the unpleasant reality which the other poems unsuccessfully attempt to cover up. For him, too, "Wordsworth's relation to the

real thorn approximates the relation of the narrator to the one in the poem" (*Wordsworth and the Poetry of Human Suffering* [Ithaca: Cornell University Press, 1980], pp. 166–80).

13. See especially Christensen's elaborate reading of this scene, "Wordsworth's Misery," pp. 283–84. See also Danby, pp. 70–71, and Hartman, *Wordsworth's Poetry*, p. 375.

14. Angus Easson calls attention to the irony in the relation between the tales the narrator wishes to tell and the tale he in fact tells in " 'The Idiot Boy': Wordsworth Serves Out His Poetic Indentures'," *CQ* 22, 3 (1980): 14. Mary Jacobus demonstrates the narrator's ability to communicate Betty's and Johnny's passions through his accounts of their words and gestures and his reflection in his own diction of Betty's accents. Her definitive appreciation of the poem in *Bicentennial Wordsworth Studies* (Ithaca: Cornell University Press, 1970), pp. 238–65, is not superseded by the shortened version subordinated to the argument of her *Tradition and Experiment*, pp. 250–61. Like the poem it helps us to read, her essay shares the joy of loving critical attention to human words and movements. Anyone who has cared enough to follow my argument this far should not read further without having read hers.

15. Geoffrey Hartman describes the poem as "a little progress of the Imagination, which leads from one type of animism to another: from the martial type of the Knight, to the pastoral type of the Shepherd, and finally to that of the Poet." He sees that Wordsworth allows "the characters of the knight and shepherd their own being," but his view of the first part of the poem as "an impersonally narrated ballad" shows he has missed the formal device through which the speaker takes the perspectives of the others into his own. See his "False Themes and Gentle Minds," *PQ* 47 (1968): 67, also printed in *Beyond Formalism*. In this essay Hartman has implicitly abandoned his claim in *Wordsworth's Poetry* (p. 372) that "the imagination of the foil character (the shepherd) and that of the poet are explicitly identified."

16. James Averill overlooks the presence of human signs in the natural scene when he claims that the poet forces forms with no necessary relation to man into that relationship out of a wilful craving for story. It is simply not true that "no reason exists why the configuration of four tree trunks in an approximate square should import anything at all. Only the imagination lends them ominous significance." Geometric arrangement of trees and stones is a good sign that " 'Here in old time the hand of man has been,' " and the speaker of the poem is reasonable to try to read them as such. The speaker's imagination in this poem is much closer to Collingwood's historical imagination (*The Idea of History* [New York: Oxford University Press, 1956]) than to Averill's "imperialistic, visionary imagination." See *Suffering*, pp. 216–18.

17. James Averill links these two poems through "the motif of 'driving the flying deer' " (*Suffering*, p. 213). His use of "Ruth" as "a cautionary tale against the temptation to take pleasure in improper and extravagant stories" allegorizes the poem to serve his theme more than it accounts for the poem (*Suffering*, pp. 204–7). "Ruth" seems to have been ignored or mentioned only in passing by other critics.

18. Averill asserts in passing that "Ruth" "is a parable of Nature's betrayal of the heart that loves her" (*Suffering*, p. 204).

19. The first phrase is Hartman's in *Wordsworth's Poetry*, p. 262. He treats the poem apart from both *Lyrical Ballads* and narrative categories in a chapter on "The Major Lyrics." The second phrase is Averill's in *Suffering*, pp. 231–34. He

considers it "the simplest of Wordsworth's extended tales of suffering" and tries
to explain away the success he concedes it achieves in representing its painful
subject. The last phrase is Kroeber's in *Narrative Art*, pp. 78–81. He sees the
poem as "the high point of Wordsworth's narratives" in which Wordsworth
dispenses with a "fictive narrator" and "introduces a story significant to *his* life."
The most recent and extensive treatment of "Michael" does not isolate it from
the other experimental narratives. See David B. Pirie, *William Wordsworth: The
Poetry of Grandeur and Tenderness* (London and New York: Methuen, 1982), pp.
89–125.

20. The phrase is from Roger Sharrock, "Wordsworth's Revolt against Literature," in *Wordsworth's Mind and Art*, ed. A. W. Thomson (Edinburgh: Oliver
and Boyd, 1969), p. 67. Sharrock goes on to cite other reasons for the superiority
of "Michael" to "the 'unsuccessful ballads.' "

21. The most extensive discussion of this analogy (which Hartman first mentions as "a strange identity" in *Wordsworth's Poetry*, p. 262) is Sydney Lea,
"Wordsworth and His 'Michael': The Pastor Passes," *ELH* 45 (1978), 55–88.

22. Peter Manning, in effect, constructs this excluded story of Luke in his
essay on "the unspoken emotional tension underlying the narrative, generated
in particular about the figure of Luke." See his " 'Michael,' Luke, and Wordsworth," *Criticism* 19 (1977): 195–211.

23. Jonathan Wordsworth, who treats "Michael" in its resemblance to *The
Ruined Cottage* more than in its difference from the other lyrical ballads, feels
that the narrator of "Michael" is still not reticent enough: "far more could have
been taken on trust than Wordsworth assumes." Even he holds, however, that
"with the beginning of the second half . . . this unselfconscious verbosity suddenly disappears." See *The Music of Humanity* (London and Edinburgh: Nelson,
1969), pp. 79–86.

24. John P. Bushnell calls attention to these lines (425–27) and claims, I think
excessively, that the "but" "convinces us undeniably of the inevitability of Luke's
failure." His essay, though exaggerated, reveals important difficulties in Michael's relation to Luke; " 'Where is the Lamb for a Burnt Offering?': Michael's
Covenant and Sacrifice," *WC* 12 (1981): 246–52.

Chapter Four

1. Barbara Herrnstein Smith distinguishes the personal anecdote from the tale
in the following terms: "The anecdote will be briefer, its approximation to the
conventions of direct speech will be closer, its significance will lie in its relation
to the speaker's own life and thought, and it will usually conclude with some
comment very much in the present." Though Smith introduces this discussion
in relation to a genre she calls the "narrative lyric" in *Poetic Closure* (Chicago:
University of Chicago Press, 1968), p. 123, I think her more recent account of
narrative in "Narrative Versions" would have no problem treating the personal
anecdote as a narrative genre, since in the later essay she treats not just lyric
but narrative also as represented utterance.

2. Coleridge lists "Anecdote for Fathers," "Simon Lee," "Alice Fell," "Beggars,"
and "The Sailor's Mother." All these poems except "Simon Lee" raise problems
of unevenness of style for him when their narrative diction shifts from the
"music" of the poet's thoughts to the speech of the characters.

3. "A Narrative Point of View in Wordsworth's *Lyrical Ballads*," *PLL* 6 (1970):
197–202.

4. Mayo's well-known article "The Contemporaneity of *Lyrical Ballads*," has shaped much of the subsequent discussion of Wordsworth's ballad experiments.

5. Carl Woodring asserts that "We Are Seven" and "Anecdote for Fathers" both "present pedagogical situations with the adult in the unexpected role of learner" (*Wordsworth* [Cambridge, Mass.: Harvard University Press, 1968], p. 38); Paul Sheats sees them as clear examples of the type of poem in which "the narrator himself becomes an object of criticism and a butt of irony, and the reader is invited to rise above him" (*The Making of Wordsworth's Poetry*, p. 196). Yet Danby himself sees "Anecdote for Fathers" among those *Lyrical Ballads* which "approximate to straight narrative with a neutral narrator" (*Simple Wordsworth*, p. 36).

6. Alan Grob, *The Philosophic Mind* (Columbus: Ohio State University Press, 1973), p. 249. Grob's remark is consistent with his criticism throughout of David Ferry's reading of Wordsworth. Ferry sees the girl in her ignorance as possessor of "a real wisdom, for she knows about eternal life in a way that we, being adults, cannot know about it" (*The Limits of Mortality* [Middletown, Conn.: Wesleyan University Press, 1959], p. 85). The argument between Grob and Ferry continues a debate growing out of Bradley's note on "We Are Seven" (*Oxford Lectures on Poetry* [1909; rpt. London: Macmillan, 1950], pp. 146–48), which Arthur Beatty challenged in *William Wordsworth: His Doctrine and Art in Their Historical Relations* (1922; rpt. Madison: University of Wisconsin Press, 1962), pp. 208–10.

7. Woodring calls the poems didactic anecdotes (*Wordsworth*, pp. 37–38), while Grob claims that they are "essentially mildly comic dialogues whose subjects are incidental to their form" (*Philosophic Mind*, p. 249).

8. I take the translation from the notes to Jack Stillinger's edition of Wordsworth, *Selected Poems and Prefaces* (Boston: Houghton Mifflin, 1965), p. 506.

9. Donald Davie, "Dionysus in *Lyrical Ballads*," in *Wordsworth's Mind and Art*, ed. A. W. Thomson (Edinburgh: Oliver and Boyd, 1969), p. 117. See also Sheats's remark: "Perceiving what he has done, the speaker then recovers his humility before the landscape and his own son" (*Making*, p. 196).

10. *A Philosophical Enquiry into the Origin of Our Ideas of the Sublime and Beautiful*, ed. James T. Boulton (Notre Dame and London: University of Notre Dame Press, 1968), pp. 67, 116, and passim.

11. It is also striking that in 1800 Wordsworth drops this description of the child and allows the speaker not just to describe his child's hanging his head but to interpret his feelings: "He blush'd for shame, nor made reply." It is an interesting question whether that insight puts the father closer to his son's feelings or reveals him as even more obtuse. After all, the child has not yet lied in the action of the anecdote, and he has more reason at this point for feeling hurt or resenting his father than for being ashamed of his defenselessness. His father, though, in the time of the telling may have other reasons for this anticipation.

12. I find independent confirmation of this reading in Susan J. Wolfson's article, "The Speaker as Questioner in *Lyrical Ballads*," p. 551. Wolfson writes, "Edward may also be recalling that 'at Kilve' there was no inquisition either, and it is not surprising that he prefers the former situation. His answer may express intuitively that at this moment he would 'rather be' where his father is not." Wolfson does not distinguish here, however, between the grounds of the boy's initial declaration of his preference before the inquisition sets in and his reason for desiring the absence of the "weather-cock" afterwards.

13. Wolfson again arrives at a similar interpretation, observing that "the adult, though he thinks he has learned a lesson, is still unaware of the basic limitations in his way of thinking" (p. 552). Her theme does not lead her to explore the motives which preserve those limitations.

14. The phrase, of course, is Kenneth Burke's, in *Permanence and Change* (New York: Bobbs-Merrill, 1965), 2d rev. ed., pp. 71ff. That our interpretation needs reopening should be evident from the extent to which five critical loci outside the poem have served to orient subsequent readings of it. Wordsworth's remark in the Preface of 1800 that the poem shows "the perplexity and obscurity which in childhood attend our notion of death, or rather our utter inability to admit that notion," his account in the Fenwick notes of how Coleridge contributed the opening stanza, his account also in those notes—this time in relation to the Immortality Ode—of how his early inability to admit the notion of death *differed* from that of the child in the poem, Max Beerbohm's satirical portrait of "Mr. Wordsworth at cross-purposes in the Lake District," and Wordsworth's account of his rejection of Godwinism have given us a poem whose chief issue is the attitudes toward immortality and childhood it takes, whose first stanza "does not help to introduce this idea," and whose narrator—often identified with Wordsworth—makes a fool of himself and of Godwin in his insistent rational questioning of the child (see Brett and Jones, p. 286 n). Among recent readings of the poem, only Frances Ferguson's goes beyond the common judgments on these topics to suggest that the child, far from not admitting the idea of death, "is able to imagine and also to accept the possibility of death far better than her adult interlocutor" (*Wordsworth: Language as Counterspirit* [New Haven: Yale University Press, 1977], p. 25). This reading offers a new perspective on what the poem reveals about the child, but it does not explore how the interlocutor's inquisition or his narrative of his tale is motivated. The child's wilfull persistence in loyalty to her dead siblings, like Antigone's similar persistence, wins the admiration of some critics, while her persecutor, who in this case is also the narrator of the story in which he appears the fool, remains a type of rejected Godwinian rationality.

15. *The Quest for Permanence* (Cambridge, Mass.: Harvard University Press, 1965), pp. 70–71. Geoffrey Hartman notes that the "first stanza does seem . . . to contradict the rest of the poem. Could one consider the narrative proper a refutation of the sentiment expressed in that first stanza?" (*Wordsworth's Poetry*, p. 374).

16. David Ferry combines these possibilities in his reading of the line, p. 84. His reading of "and feels its life in every limb" also is close to the one I develop.

17. *Antigone*, in *Greek Tragedies*, vol. 1, ed. David Grene and Richmond Lattimore (Chicago: University of Chicago Press, 1968), line 1342.

18. Wayne Booth has recognized and explained the need for this turn away from internal evidence in his discussion of the problems of reading an ironic monologue, *A Rhetoric of Irony* (Chicago: University of Chicago Press, 1974), p. 150.

19. Bakhtin's definition is worth quoting: "We shall use the terms *behavioral ideology* for the whole aggregate of life experiences and the outward expressions directly connected with it. Behavioral ideology is that atmosphere of unsystematized and unfixed inner and outer speech which endows our every instance of behavior and action and our every 'conscious' state with meaning" (*Marxism and the Philosophy of Language*, p. 91).

20. Parrish classifies "The Last of the Flock" among the "complaints" in *Lyrical Ballads* ("The Female Vagrant" and "The Complaint of a Forsaken Indian Woman"

are the other examples) and notes its close resemblance to "The Mad Mother." For him "the important thing about the poem is the character of the rustic speaker, as revealed in his dramatic address to the poet" (*The Art of the "Lyrical Ballads,"* pp. 124–25). Mary Jacobus links "The Complaint of a Forsaken Indian Woman," "The Last of the Flock," and "The Mad Mother" as instances of "the poetry of passion." She reads the narrator's introductory description solely for the image of the figure with which it confronts us, not for a development of the narrator's attitudes (*Tradition and Experiment in Wordsworth's "Lyrical Ballads"* [*1798*], pp. 196–205). Jacobus, following John Jones (*The Egotistical Sublime* [London: Chatto and Windus, 1954], p. 63), also makes the most persuasive recent case for the inappropriateness of the narrative section in "Old Man Travelling," pp. 179–81). I examine her position below. John Danby reads the last version of the poem with the narrative omitted (*Simple Wordsworth,* pp. 76–78).

21. Coleridge's "less *compact*" prose paraphrase of the narrator's opening statement removes the repetitions and metrical emphases that help to identify what interests the narrator in this figure (*BL,* 2:44).

22. The attempt to find the significance of the shepherd's speech in such contexts beyond the poem (see the familiar theoretical and practical contexts in the note in Brett and Jones, p. 291, and Dr. Burney's review reprinted in their edition, p. 322) results, I think, from the failure to read his speech through the narrator's focus of interest.

23. It is used at the openings of *The Prelude* and of "Resolution and Independence," for example.

24. W. J. B. Owen detects and complicates this motive: "Society, or 'the young' (l. 13) standing in for society, or the poet (who was twenty-eight at most when he wrote these lines) standing in for the young and hence for society—all or any of these envies, paradoxically, in the Old Man what the Old Man is unaware he possesses" ("A Shock of Mild Surprise," *The Wordsworth Circle* 8 [Autumn 1977]: 298). John Danby sees that in the opening stanza, "The old man, without effort and without consciousness, has what the young man can restlessly strive for, miss, and finally envy" (*Simple Wordsworth,* p. 77).

25. Cf. Danby, *Simple Wordsworth,* pp. 38–47; Sheats, *Making of Wordsworth's Poetry,* pp. 188–93; Griffin, "Wordsworth and the Problem of Imaginative Story," pp. 392–409. David Pirie's recent treatment of "Old Man Travelling" arrives at a position close to the one I develop here. See his *William Wordsworth,* pp. 163–75.

26. *Wordsworth's Experiments with Tradition* (Ithaca: Cornell University Press, 1971), p. 103. I am using neither the 1802 manuscript versions of these poems (and "Resolution and Independence") as Curtis prints them in the second part of this book nor the poems in Wordsworth's final version, influenced by Coleridge's attack on them in *Biographia Literaria,* but his first published versions from *Poems in Two Volumes,* ed. Helen Darbishire (1807; rpt. Oxford: Clarendon Press, 1914). All subsequent references to these four poems are to this edition.

27. Curtis's reading of the relation of those parts is reminiscent of the readings we saw earlier of "The Last of the Flock" and "Old Man Travelling," which see no unifying vision to hold the two parts of the poems together. He writes of the second part of the poem: "Here the poet has not provided his own response, but in the manner of 'The Forsaken Indian Maiden' [sic] or 'The Female Vagrant' he has let the speaker's voice do its own work. As he says of the latter, 'The woman thus her artless story told' " (*Experiments,* p. 104). Gene W. Ruoff recognizes that "the expressive qualities of the woman's story depend largely upon the situation in which she tells it and the predispositions of the poet to whom

she tells it, which are the joint subjects of the poem's first three stanzas" ("Words-worth on Language," p. 207).

28. The "Roman matron" was already a proverbial type of self-possession and nobility for Plutarch, as Judith B. Herman has noticed ("The Roman Matron with the Bird-cage: A Note on 'The Sailor's Mother,' " *WC*, 6 [1975]: 302). An interesting contemporary use of the figure that by 1802 Wordsworth would have known and perhaps ambivalently admired (see James K. Chandler, "Wordsworth and Burke," *ELH* 47 [1980]: 741–71, esp. 752–58) appears in Edmund Burke's description of Marie Antoinette in captivity, a context which may help to clarify Wordsworth's narrator's odd combination of conservative values and revolu-tionary perceptions. The passage follows:

> I hear, and I rejoice to hear, that the great lady, the other object of the triumph, has borne that day (one is interested that beings made for suffering should suffer well), and that she bears . . . the imprisonment of her husband, and her own captivity, and the exile of her friends, and the insulting adulation of addresses, and the whole weight of her accumulated wrongs with a serene patience, in a manner suited to her rank and race, and becoming the offspring of a sovereign distinguished for her piety and her courage; that, like her, she has lofty sentiments; that she feels with the dignity of a Roman matron; that in the last extremity she will save herself from the last disgrace; and that if she must fall, she will fall by no ignoble hand.

See *Reflections on the Revolution in France*, ed. Thomas H. D. Mahoney (India-napolis and New York: Bobbs-Merrill, 1955), p. 85.

29. Judith Herman suggests that the caged bird has analogies with "an ancient religious symbol of the soul in the body" and that "on some level of belief . . . [the] bird in the bird-cage embodies her dead son." Certainly the singing bird in the cage is both the form in which she carries the burden of her son's death and his legacy to her. Her confusion over her reason for delight may be seen as her simple response to a powerful archetype, a response utterly unlike the self-possession to be expected from a Roman matron.

30. Carl Woodring sees "Alice Fell" as a near duplication of the theme of "Simon Lee" (*Wordsworth*, p. 53).

31. Bradley, "Wordsworth," *Oxford Lectures on Poetry* (1909), in *Wordsworth: A Collection of Critical Essays*, ed. M. H. Abrams (Englewood Cliffs: Prentice-Hall, 1972), p. 16.

32. An intimation of this reading may underlie Curtis's sense of this counter-figure's self-sufficiency. His specific comments on the poem are brief (*Experi-ments*, pp. 104–5).

33. Curtis notes this combination of features not in terms of form but only in terms of the sorts of figures represented. " 'Beggars,' " he says, "combines the garrulous adult and the almost silent but entirely expressive child in one poem" (*Experiments*, p. 105).

34. Darbishire notes this use of Spenser, *Poems in Two Volumes*, 2:377. The passage is quoted from *The Poetical Works of Edmund Spenser*, ed. J. C. Smith and E. de Selincourt (London: Oxford University Press, 1924), p. 518.

35. The modern critical history of "Resolution and Independence" epitomizes the developing interests of Anglo-American criticism over the last thirty years, though it reveals a number of sidelines, fugitive insights, and unsystematic contributions as well. The first "reading" of the poem in the New Critical sense, W. W. Robson's "*Resolution and Independence*" (in *Interpretations*, ed. John Wain

[London: Routledge and Kegan Paul, 1955], pp. 117–28) attempts to answer Coleridge's charge of unevenness. It shows the characteristic New Critical emphasis on medium, on *Resolution and Independence* as "a poem, self-sufficient and existing in its own right," and on the poem's achievement of "maturity" of attitude, but it also takes exception to I. A. Richards's theory "that great poetry must in some way immunize itself to irony, by 'containing' or neutralizing unsympathetic reactions, or by anticipating them." Its conclusion points in the direction of the dialogic perspective we have been working out: "Properly viewed, the incongruities disappear, or seem to be functional; the artlessness and clumsiness serve to high-light, to dramatize a contrast which the poem intends to bring out (the 'Two Voices' in the same poem); they are intentionally set against a formal deliberateness of manner so noticeable that it suggests a stylization." Albert Gérard elaborates Robson's reading within the same critical framework, dwelling more than his predecessor on the "formal design" of the poem, but sharing his view of its theme of "maturity." Gérard, too, hears the "Two Voices" but hears them harmonized in "perfect conjunction," not functioning in the dramatic contrast Robson describes ("*Resolution and Independence*: Wordsworth's Coming of Age," *English Studies in Africa* 3 [1960]: 8–20).

In the same year Anthony E. M. Conran made a fresh attempt to answer Coleridge in the promising contexts of Wordsworth's other narrative poems and of Chaucerian and Spenserian narratives, but his analysis was hampered by his reliance on New Critical terminology, which led him to look for "dialectical" tensions in both the larger and smaller "structures" of the poem. His specific analogs are often illuminating, but his essay adds little to Robson's and Gérard's readings of the poem, which Conran did not take into account (*PMLA* 75 [1960]: 66–74).

Stanley Edgar Hyman also enters the discussion without connection to Robson, bringing to bear what might have proved a fruitful "sociological" perspective from Kenneth Burke, but Hyman's interpretation of the "symbolic action" of the poem as "a serious and complicated strategy for pulling oneself out of neurotic depression" is more psychological than sociological, and his elaboration of the old man's relation to the leeches he gathers—"stirring the leeches about his feet, literally feeding them on his own blood"—bears fruit only in a later "vampire" reading of the poem (Hyman, "A Poem of Resolution," *Centennial Review* 5 [1961]: 195–205). The "vampire" reading is by James B. Twitchell, "The Character of Wordsworth's Leech Gatherer," *Research Studies* 43 (1975): 253–59.

Alan Grob, Harold Bloom, and Geoffrey Hartman all treat the poem in the context of thematic interests, and all appear to presume in their readings what Hartman makes explicit in his, that the poem is a lyric to be read primarily as the present movement of the speaker's mind and voice. Grob is interested in the philosophical and religious opinions that voice attains to and so dwells on the concluding lines ("Process and Permanence in *Resolution and Independence*," *ELH* 18 [1961]: 89–100, incorporated into Grob's *The Philosophic Mind*, pp. 217–31). Bloom is interested in the speaker's renovating imaginative visions and so dwells on the next to the last stanza (*The Visionary Company* [1961; rev. and rpt. Ithaca: Cornell University Press, 1971], pp. 164–70). Hartman, concerned with the way in which "Wordsworth's greatest lyrics are acts of a living mind open to the terror of discontinuity," offers a helpful formulation of the connection between past event and present telling: "The past event is not so totally in the past, not so determinate, that it cannot confront the poet in a new way. This new and further confrontation must then be honored in addition to the old.

There is the question of the poet's original recognition, and then of his insight as he tells, so to say, his story back to himself. The two do not coincide in all respects." Hartman, however, taking literally the commonplace of Wordsworth's spontaneous overflow, treats the poem as a record of its spontaneous utterance, not as a composed work of the poet. For him the present tense of the first two stanzas signifies a crossing over from past to present that "happens during composition, and shows that time itself can still dissolve at the touch and even the mere memory of nature" (*Wordsworth's Poetry* [1964], pp. 266–73). Hartman thus distinguishes the lyric speaker from himself as character in the experience he recalls but not from the poet as composer of the poem; Grob and Bloom identify all of these figures.

Curtis, who makes reference to Robson, Gérard, Conran, Hyman, Hartman, and others, comes closest to Hartman's view of "Resolution and Independence" as a lyric in his claim that the action of the poem "*is* the turning of his own [the poet's] mind at the time of composition, and turns the reader's mind, as a spoken tale could not, by demanding recognition as an emblem of experience rather than as experience itself" (*Experiments*, p. 108). His attempt to demonstrate the ultimate harmony of the languages of the poem continues to apply the New Critical (and Coleridgean) criterion.

The last four relevant essays on "Resolution and Independence," published from 1968 to 1970, exhibit a full range of answers to the question of the poem's diction. In one, A. W. Thomson offers a "reading" squarely in line with Robson's New Critical suppositions. Attentive to the poem's language line by line, he follows it as a lyric unfolding of a present mental process that may be modified by but is not governed by an unspecified "mode of the poem" ("*Resolution and Independence*," in *Wordsworth's Mind and Art*, pp. 181–99).

Two of the other readings, both of which allude or refer to Langbaum's *Poetry of Experience*, take different approaches to the poem as a dramatic composition. Jeffrey Meyers counters the common identification of poet and speaker by introducing a distinction among a dramatic persona who speaks the words of the poem, Wordsworth, and the reader, each with a different point of view and "independent values," but nowhere does he distinguish between the speaker of the poem and himself as the character whose experience he relates. Further, he complains that "the leech gatherer has no independent existence in the poem. He speaks only indirectly and through the persona, and in the poem is evaluated only by the persona"—a criticism which betrays the desire for the unmediated and reliable presentation of all speakers in dramatic diction ("A Revaluation of Wordsworth's 'Resolution and Independence,' " *Discourse* 9 [1978]: 441–49). More subtle and complete is David Eggenschwiler's "Wordsworth's *Discordia Discors*," *SIR* 7 (1969): 78–94. Though he speaks of the "dramatic process," "dramatic conflict," and "dramatic complexity" of the poem, he sees its narrative character—"it presents, rather than describes, the movements of the speaker's mind; even his analyses of his own mind are progressive gestures that reveal him in two senses, as subject and object"—clearly distinguishes "the present speaker's reflecting on his past experience" from the "speaker's feelings while he was confronted by the Leech-gatherer," and nicely formulates a criterion of value to replace imaginative reconciliation of opposites and harmony of diction. He writes,

> By recognizing that change and contradiction are inevitable, the speaker could achieve a measure of stability; and, by renouncing the pride of self-deification,

he could achieve "human strength" to prevent the misery of mighty poets. These achievements, however, were not merely the products of his experience, but a summation and a comprehension of them. He had learned what the form of the entire poem had demonstrated, what Coleridge criticized as "incongruity." In a sense, he had learned to mitigate the push toward unity represented by his imaginative *discordia concors*.

Only Eggenschwiler clearly sees the difficulties created by the tendency of critics "to stress the synthetic qualities of Wordsworth's poems at the expense of antithetic ones."

Finally, William Heath, without explicit reference to any previous readings, treats the speaker of the poem as a "narrator" and makes some important distinctions in attributing images and figures to the narrator now and himself at the time of his meeting with the leech-gatherer, but when he comes to name what he calls the "mode" of the poem, he is reluctant to classify it as a narrative. Though he shows a sharp awareness of "how much difference mode makes," he can only say that, though *The Prelude* is "organized somewhat as a narrative" the mode of "Resolution and Independence" is "more difficult to name" (*Wordsworth and Coleridge: A Study of Their Literary Relations in 1801–1802* [Oxford: Clarendon Press, 1970], pp. 121–41). I believe that "narrative," as I defined it in Chapter 1, and "dialogic personal anecdote," as I have used it here, are names that define the features Heath and Eggenschwiler notice.

I am indebted to many of these essays for specific observations and emphases, which I have tried to acknowledge in parenthetical citations in the text.

The latest contribution to the understanding of "Resolution," which came to my attention after this argument was completed, appears to move outside the terms in which I have worked here. Samuel E. Schulman, who treats the poem primarily in relation to its dense Spenserian allusions, argues that the problem with the poem is "not simply a matter of reconciling what Coleridge judged a 'disharmony of styles'. . . . The poet must become an allegorist within his poem, rather than simply introduce the leech-gatherer and let him speak for himself." Again he appears to go outside my terms when he claims that the poet has moved "from a lyrical to an exegetical mode." Still, in his emphasis on what the poet makes of the leech-gatherer as against what he finds in the leech-gatherer's own words and being, he allies himself most closely with those who have preferred the poet's lyric diction not just to predominate but to prevail ("The Spenserian Enchantments of Wordsworth's 'Resolution and Independence,' " *MP* 79 [1981]: 24–44).

36. See W. J. B. Owen, "A Shock of Mild Surprise," *WC* 8 (1977): 292–94.

Chapter Five

1. I rely throughout on Darlington's text printed in "Two Early Texts: *A Night Piece* and *The Discharged Soldier*," in *Bicentenary Wordsworth Studies in Memory of John Alban Finch*, pp. 425–48. Sheats's remark is from *Making*, p. 172.

2. C. F. Stone III, who argues that the independent version of this anecdote is aimed at an "objective vein of narrative subtlety," claims that both this description of the soldier and the narrator's description of the leech-gatherer "represent the narrating poet's present effort to describe adequately the enduring qualities of a past experience," not in "conveying his own first impressions" ("Narrative Technique in Wordsworth's Versions of 'The Discharged Soldier,' "

JNT 4 [1974]: 32–44). I believe he is right about "Resolution" but fails to see how the narrator's emphases in the other poem recreate his earlier difficulties in recognizing the soldier as a man. Stone's essay, which has been useful to me throughout this chapter, focuses on narrative technique as story-telling and tends to exaggerate the "dramatic possibilities" of the telling and criticize the "bending away from an original narrative thrust" to "the analysis of subjective relationships." He is mistaken, I believe, to hold that the narrator of this version of the anecdote "is in the process of constructing a narration independent of immediate significance to himself." The narrator here, like the others we have discussed, has his own interest in what he tells and is not just trying to inspire a "dramatic interest" in his hearer.

3. Herbert Lindenberger identifies the solemnity and sublimity of these figures, where Wordsworth makes a distinction between them. See his *On Wordsworth's Prelude* (Princeton: Princeton University Press, 1963), p. 219.

4. Stone's reading of this passage, in "Narrative Technique," p. 38, was especially helpful to me.

5. *Egotistical Sublime*, pp. 61–62. David Pirie, whose essay on the discharged-soldier passage appeared after mine was completed, presents a discriminating elaboration of Jones's topic of the "solitaries" and confirms a number of this chapter's emphases. See his *William Wordsworth*, pp. 185–97.

6. Wordsworth has removed from his earlier version and from the episode that was the source of the poem references to the leech-gatherer's loss of wife and ten children and to his physical suffering. See *Journals of Dorothy Wordsworth*, ed. Mary Moorman (New York: Oxford University Press, 1971), p. 42, and *The Poetical Works of William Wordsworth*, 2d ed., E. de Selincourt, ed. (Oxford: Clarendon Press, 1952), p. 541. Parrish discusses the revisions in *Art*, pp. 213–21.

7. For a useful commentary on "in the eye of," see A. D. Nuttall, *A Common Sky* (London: Chatto and Windus, 1974), p. 135.

8. "The Journeys Homeward: Drama and Rhetoric in Book IV of *The Prelude*," *SIR* 10 (1971): 83–84. Nabholtz's attention to the overall structure of Book IV has been helpful to me throughout. His focus on "drama and rhetoric" follows the line of Aristotelian narrative theory that treats story as drama and narration as a rhetorical presentation of story. He clearly distinguishes "the youth of 1788" from "the true central character of *The Prelude*, the narrator-persona, who reviews and re-lives the past events in the hope of recovering the creative union with nature experienced in the 'correspondent breeze' preamble" (p. 83). Though he relies on the 1850 text and I am here discussing the 1805, the structural issues are not substantially affected by the differences between the two texts. Where differences are significant, I have tried to note them.

9. 1805, IV, 39–55. This point is sharpened in the 1850 text.

10. Sheats, reading the poem in its independent version in the context of Wordsworth's earlier poems, comes closest to this reading. He writes that Wordsworth's "attempt to initiate a human relationship issues in an act of charity that recalls the parable of the Samaritan; in terms of the symbolic life-cycle of earlier poems, he ushers the exiled wanderer to a cottage-home, and in so doing exorcises his own guilt and isolation" (*Making*, p. 171).

11. See *The Prelude 1799, 1805, 1850*, p. 145 n. 1 and p. 147 n. 6. Nabholtz sees how this parallel is set up and the subordination of the incident strengthened in "Journeys Homeward," p. 84 n. 14. The editors of the new *Prelude* text have not made use of either Nabholtz's or Stone's helpful essays.

12. 1850, IV, 469–71. See *The Prelude 1799, 1805, 1850*, p. 151 n. 4.

Index

Abrams, M. H., 187 n.9, 187 n.12; on poet's feelings, 20, 27; on pleasure principle in Wordsworth, 188 n.13; scheme of orientations in, 44, 189 n.2

Anecdote, dialogic: defined, 107

Anecdote, didactic, 193 n.7

Anecdote(s), personal: "Alice Fell" as, 106; "Anecdote for Fathers" as, 106, 108–14; "Beggars" as, 106, 143–48; contrasted with tale, 105; critical estimate of Wordsworth's, 105; defined, 65; distinguished from anecdote of experience in nature, 106; distinguished from epitaphic anecdote, 106; "Expostulation and Reply" as, 106, 129–34; Haswell, Richard Henry, on formal features of, 105–7; in "Simon Lee," 106; in "The Thorn," 106; of 1802 and *Lyrical Ballads* project, 134–35; "Old Man Travelling" as, 106, 125–29; "Resolution and Independence" as, 106, 148–59; "The Discharged Soldier" as, 162–67; "The Last of the Flock" as, 106, 121–25; "The Sailor's Mother" as, 106, 136–38; "We Are Seven" as, 106, 114–18

Aristotelian criticism: and Wordsworth's poetry, 20; in John R. Nabholtz, 200 n.8

Aristotle, *Poetics*: and aims of *The Prelude*, 183; and *Oedipus Rex*, 113; and translation of *Republic* III, 13; lyric, narrative, and drama in, 13–

14; on diction as seen by poetics of speech, 17; theory of diction in, compared to Plato's and Coleridge's, 15–18

Arnold, Matthew, 187 n.12

Averill, James H.: on "Hart-Leap Well", 91, 191 n.16; on "Michael," 191 n.19; on poet and narrator in "The Thorn," 190 n.12; on "Ruth," 191 nn.17, 18; on "Simon Lee," 77, 80

Babbitt, Irving, 187 n.12

Bacon, Francis, 161

Bakhtin, M. M.: behavioral ideology in, and Wordsworth's immediate knowledge, 119, 194 n.19; bibliography of, 187 n.7; conditions of enduring intelligibility in, 45; consciousness in, 61; distinction of poetic from natural utterance in, 44; elaboration of poetics of speech in, 39–65; evaluative rank and degrees of proximity in, 61–62; hero in, 63; reported speech in, 188 n.15; selection of words in, 46; speaker's and hero's diction in, 189 n.9; tone in, 42–43

Ballad: as lyric form, 12; as narrative form, 12

Bate, Walter Jackson, 188 n.12

Beatty, Arthur, 193 n.6

Bialostosky, Don H., 187 n.7, 187 n.11

Bloom, Harold, on "Resolution and Independence," 156, 197 n.35